HOW TO READ AND UNDERSTAND

FINANCIAL

STATEMENTS

When You Don't Know What You Are Looking At

By Brian Kline

HOW TO READ AND UNDERSTAND FINANCIAL STATEMENTS
WHEN YOU DON'T KNOW WHAT YOU ARE LOOKING AT

ISBN-13: 978-1-60138-012-8   ISBN-10: 1-60138-012-7

Library of Congress Cataloging-in-Publication Data

Kline, Brian.
  How to read and understand financial statements when you don't know what you are looking at / Brian Kline.
      p. cm.
  Includes bibliographical references and index.
  ISBN-13: 978-1-60138-012-8 (alk. paper)
  ISBN-10: 1-60138-012-7 (alk. paper)
  1. Financial statements. 2. Managerial accounting. 3. Business enterprises--Valuation. 4. Corporations--Valuation. I. Title. II. Title: How to read and understand financial statements when you don't know what you are looking at.

  HF5681.B2K555 2008
  658.15'11--dc22
                    2007025043

COVER & INTERIOR LAYOUT DESIGN: Vickie Taylor • vtaylor@atlantic-pub.com

Printed in the United States

Over the years, we have adopted a number of dogs from rescues and shelters. First there was Bear and after he passed, Ginger and Scout. Now, we have Kira, another rescue. They have brought immense joy and love not just into our lives, but into the lives of all who met them.

We want you to know a portion of the profits of this book will be donated in Bear, Ginger and Scout's memory to local animal shelters, parks, conservation organizations, and other individuals and nonprofit organizations in need of assistance.

– Douglas & Sherri Brown,
President & Vice-President of Atlantic Publishing

Table of Contents

Preface

Financials are at the heart of every business, whether it is a transaction with a customer at a cash register or a multibillion-dollar corporate merger. Both follow the same set of accounting rules and are registered in financial statements, which are nothing more than a summary of all the financial dealings that occurred within the business over a specific period of time. The U.S. Securities and Exchange Commission has oversight responsibility for the financial statements of publicly owned corporations. One clearly stated goal is that these statements be transparent and understandable by non-financial readers. The goal of this book is the same, making financial statements easy to read.

Understanding how transactions get onto financial statements and being able to understand what different sections mean is only the beginning. The four different statements have evolved over many decades and are closely interrelated. The numbers on one statement are not independent of those on another, but each separate statement tells its own story. Being able to do some relatively simple ratio analysis reveals much more about the operations of a company than simply knowing how much was taken in as revenue last year and what the profit margin is. The efficiency of the company can be discovered, and trends can predict future financial results. Without a crystal ball, financial statements are the next best way to see future performance.

When the future does not look as bright as it might, financial statements provide evidence of where business owners can make needed improvements. This book also provides answers to what those improvements might be, based on what the numbers explain. For the investor, the ability can confirm what on the surface appears to be a solid investment. Likewise, it can avoid a financial blunder into an ailing company.

For public companies, the statements go beyond just numbers. An important part of the reports is the accompanying Management Discussion and Analysis. Here, readers learn about the business risks senior management is aware of and how they believe the business will be affected. Often the future business strategy is divulged from this information. Certainly, a potential investor would want to know this, and a business owner can learn what the big guys in the industry are planning.

For investors, over the long term, corporate ownership through stocks can provide a substantially better return than savings accounts, treasury bonds, or CDs. The risk of investing in a business is choosing the wrong one. Chapter 9 describes how corporate scandals in the early 2000s were pulled off and how the U.S. Congress made stringent improvements to financial reporting to thwart criminal managers from repeating them.

Similarly, owning a business can provide a much more substantial income than working for others. Accomplishing this requires growing a prospering business. Often this requires either loans or outside investors, both of which will demand the review of financial statements before providing funding. Although an accountant can prepare the statements, the owner will need to explain them to the people with the money.

A short trip through this book prepares the investor and the business owner to better succeed at their chosen endeavor.

CHAPTER 1

Introduction

Financial statements are the only direct source for gauging a business's financial performance—they tell the story about profitability, financial health, and the ability to pay obligations, including returning earnings to stockholders. People who rely on financial statements include managers, analysts, attorneys, investors, lenders, customers, and suppliers.

Financial statements and concepts prove simple once you know what you are looking at and understand the lingo. The four different financial statements — (1) Balance Sheet, (2) Income Statement, (3) Statement of Cash Flow, and (4) Statement of Shareholders' Equity — require nothing more than adding, subtracting, multiplication, and division.

Each statement provides the reader with specific information about the company, but none of the financial statements tells the whole story all by itself. In fact, most of the useful information is obtained by comparing the numbers from one statement with those on another. A comparison by creating ratios from the numbers involved with the statements finds the real information needed by investors and managers alike.

For investors, the numbers tell the financial health of the company and can be a powerful tool for comparing financials among several companies. While past performance cannot predict future profits, it does show how one company has performed against competitors in the same industry, and current trends indicate a company's future direction. The universal nature of financial statements simplifies the comparison of companies in different industries.

Managers always need to know their business's current financial health, but the numbers reveal much more. A solid financial analysis divulges if the company is positioned to improve profitability and can forewarn of future financial troubles to be avoided by taking early action. All this and more comes from discovering the meanings behind the numbers.

Look at the Numbers

Managers responsible for the business's financial health should have a constant eye on the numbers. Today's accounting software can provide instantaneous, up-to-the-minute information at the push of a button.

Many managers review sales reports and see the results of business conducted daily. Two activities make a regular review of the financial numbers very important. First, when a policy change has been made with the intention of improving the company's financial performance, management needs to know if the change is having the desired effect. Second, when a company is experiencing financial troubles, keeping a close eye on changes to its finances often averts disaster. Astute managers know the critical numbers and how to change them.

ALPHABETICAL LISTING OF 40 COMPANIES FROM STANDARD AND POOR'S 100

Abbott Laboratories

AES-CP Inc.

Alcoa Inc.

Allegheny Tech New

Allstate CP

American Electric Power Co.

American Express

American Intl. Group Inc.

Amgen

Anheuser Busch

Avon Products Inc.

Baker Hughes Intl

Baxter Intl Inc.

Bank of America CP

Black Decker CP

Boeing Co.

Bristol Myers Squibb

Burlington N Sante Fe

Campbell Soup Co.

Capital One Fiancial

Caterpillar Inc.

CBS Corp. CL B

Chevron Corp.

Cigna CP

CISCO Sys. Inc.

CitiGroup Inc.

Clear Channel COM

Colgate Palmolive

ALPHABETICAL LISTING OF 40 COMPANIES FROM STANDARD AND POOR'S 100
Comcast CP A
Computer Sciences CP
Conoco Phillips
Dell Inc.
DOW Chemical
Du Pont E I DE NEM
E M C CP
Eastman Kodak Co.
El Paso Corporation
Entergy CP
Exelon Corporation
Walt Disney — Disney Co.

Investors rarely need to keep daily tabs on the business's financial situation. In fact, investors only see the financial statements once every three months. Certain companies are legally required to publish a full set of financial statements on a quarterly basis. Once a year the most detailed information comes out in the Annual Report, followed by the Annual Shareholders' meeting where the owners (shareholders) question management about the company's financial performance.

There are three times when investors need to dig deep into the financial performance of a company. First is when an investor is making the initial decision to invest. Prudent, wise investors conduct a thorough analysis and comparison with other companies. Second is when the quarterly and annual reports come out. Investors want to be reassured that the company is performing as anticipated. Third is when an extraordinary event occurs. Hopefully, this will be a major contract or better-than-expected financial performance, but it also can be fraud or major customer loss. New financial statements are not issued until the next scheduled date, but information about breaking news can be found in financial media and news releases issued on the company's Web site. Although new financial statements do not come out, certain companies are legally required by the Security Exchange Commission (SEC) to disclose information about extraordinary events.

Where to Find the Financial Statements

Current and past financial statements for publicly traded companies are available to investors anytime. Publicly traded companies have shares bought and sold to the public on stock exchanges like the New York Stock Exchange or the National Association of Security Dealers and Automated Quotations (NASDAQ). The SEC provides the online Electronic Data Gathering, Analysis, and Retrieval system (EDGAR) containing financial statements of all publicly traded companies as far back as 1996, the year statements were required to be submitted electronically.

Filings made by these publicly traded companies are available at **http:// www.sec.gov/edgar/searchedgar/companysearch.html**. Not the most user-friendly database, EDGAR retrieves too much information. The advanced search page (**http://searchwww.sec.gov/EDGARFSClient/ jsp/EDGAR_MainAccess.jsp**) is often more useful because the search can be limited to specific forms such as the 10-K and 10-Q. Another simpler search solution is finding key information by visiting the company's Web site. The company has discretion about what it provides on its own Web site. There may not be as many years of information, and often companies do not post information about changes in corporate officers' ownership of shares. However, there should be enough years of financial statements to perform thorough research. Just look for the annual reports and quarterly results on the investor relations page.

Quarterly Report Overview

The quarterly results are a full set of financial statements that companies must issue once every three months. These are known as 10-Q reports because quarterly reports are made on SEC Form 10-Q. The exact issue date varies depending on the company's fiscal year. Many companies maintain a fiscal year that corresponds with the calendar year, making it relatively simple to anticipate when financials will be released. However, some companies elect to operate on a fiscal year that does not correspond to the calendar year. For example, retailers who want to capture sales from after Christmas might elect a fiscal year that ends January 31.

Once established, it is difficult for a company to change its fiscal year.

In addition to the four financial statements, the quarterly reports contain notes explaining the numbers in the financial statements. The notes contain important information about long-term debt, purchase and sale of subsidiary businesses, retirement and pension information, changes in accounting practices, and other critical information. The quarterly report also includes the Managements Analysis and Discussion, in which management provides more details about the numbers, such as explanations for increases or decreases. Management is also obligated to provide information it believes will affect the future of the company. It is important to note that an independent third party does not audit quarterly reports. However, SEC regulations require that management accurately reflect the true condition of the company.

Annual Report Overview

The annual report is the primary report issued by publicly traded companies to communicate corporate information to shareholders. It is important to know the difference between annul reports and SEC Form 10-K. The annual report must be sent to shareholders before the annual shareholders' meeting that elects members to the board of directors and conducts other company business. Annual reports contain the financial statements filed with the SEC on Form 10-K.

The annual report usually contains a letter for the chief executive officer (CEO) and information about new products, marketing efforts, subsidiaries, and the company's future. Images are used frequently to communicate management's message to current and prospective investors. Skepticism is needed when reviewing this information because it is intended to portray the company in the best light possible.

Management has more latitude about information presented in the annual report than it does for the 10-Q and 10-K filings. It selects the subjects included as well as the numbers emphasized with charts and graphs. Ultimately, the annual report is an informative document and a marketing tool for reassuring current and attracting new investors.

The time between the end of the fiscal period and publication of financial statements depends on company size. Companies with more than $700 million in assets must file annual reports (10-K) within 60 days and quarterly reports within 40 days. Companies with $75 million have 75 days to file the 10-K and 40 days for the 10-Q. Those with less than $75 million have 90 days and 45 days, respectively.

PERIODIC REPORT FILING DEADLINES		
Category of Filer	Form 10-K Deadline	Form 10-Q Deadline
Large Accelerated Filer (over $700 million)	75 days for fiscal years ending before Dec. 15 and 60 days for fiscal years ending on or after Dec. 15	40 days
Accelerated Filer (over $75 million but less than $700 million)	75 days	40 days
Non-Accelerated Filer (less than $75 million)	90 days	45 days

Public Versus Private Companies

We must differentiate between the financial reporting requirements of publicly traded companies and those of privately held companies. Every corporation is registered with at least one state government office. However, few privately held companies come under the authority of the SEC. Private companies do not have their shares traded on a major stock exchange. These shares are traded in private transactions or through over-the-counter transactions known as "Pink Sheets" (see Glossary). An exception requires certain private companies — those with more than

500 shareholders and $10 million in assets — to comply with SEC regulations. SEC authority extends to companies that deregister from a stock exchange ("go private") and still have more than 300 shareholders.

State financial disclosure requirements vary but are far less robust than SEC requirements. Few if any states require financial statements of private companies. There is no requirement for an independent audit of private companies that choose to create financial statements. Private companies prefer keeping their financial information out of the public view.

States will not change these policies anytime soon. If they began requiring public disclosure by private companies, it would encourage relocation to states with more lenient requirements. Relocation can be as simple as filing a few papers without physically moving. This does not mean that private companies do not have financial statements or audits by a third party. The board of directors may deem it prudent to have an audit to ensure the accounting system is performing correctly or that audits are in shareholders' best interest. A bank loaning money to a private company often requires audited financial statements. These and many other reasons result in audits of private companies. However, deciding to produce statements along with who has access is up to each company, and it is likely to be less frequent than for public companies.

Balance Sheet Overview

The balance sheet is one of the four major financial statements. Publicly traded companies are required to file all four statements on a quarterly basis using Generally Accepted Accounting Principles (GAAP). The quarterly statements are not audited, but the annual statements are.

The balance sheet has two sections that must equal each other (hence the name). The first section, the Asset section, represents all the resources available to the company to conduct business, including cash and cash equivalents, inventory, land, buildings, and equipment. The opposing section is Liabilities and Shareholders' Equity. In total, this section represents how every asset was bought or acquired. Liabilities are outstanding loans and other financing obligations that must be repaid. These can be short-term obligations to repay cash loans or long-term commitments to pay off mortgages on buildings and equipment. Shareholders' Equity represents the portion of the assets owned outright by the company. This includes the profits made from sales along with the portion of buildings, equipment, and all other resources free from loans or any other obligations. It is everything the business owns.

THE BALANCE SHEET EQUATION
Assets = Liabilities + Shareholders' Equity
-Or-
Shareholders' Equity = Assets – Liabilities

The balance sheet equation illustrates the importance of balance between the two sections. At the bottom of each section is a total dollar value. The total value in the Asset section will always exactly match the total value of the Liabilities and Shareholders' Equity section.

The balance sheet is a snapshot in time. Near the top will be the exact date the company was in that particular financial position. Every transaction is represented on the balance sheet, although it does not show the details. Change over time is one of the most important ways to analyze the balance sheet (covered in detail in future chapters).

Balance sheet is the most common name for this important financial statement, but it has other names, including Statement of Financial Condition and Statement of Financial Position.

Income Statement Overview

The next financial statement likely encountered is the income statement.

Here is where investors and managers learn if the company made a profit over a specific period.

INCOME STATEMENT EQUATION
Total Revenues – Total Expenses = Profit

The first number found on an income statement is the revenue from sales before expenses are subtracted out. Expenses are subtracted in a specific sequence to reveal useful information. First, the cost of goods sold (COGS) is subtracted from revenue to determine "gross profit." Next, administrative and depreciation expenses are taken out to determine "operating profit." Finally, interest paid on loans and taxes is subtracted to reveal the actual profit remaining after all the expenses. It is hoped there is money remaining after all the expenses are paid; otherwise, you have a negative number representing a financial loss for the period.

Earnings per share is the only ratio you will find directly on the financial statements. This appears at or near the bottom of the income statement. Profit is divided by the number of outstanding stock shares. This tells how much of the profit (or loss) is attributed to each share. If a company made $1 per share and an investor owned 100 shares, the portion of the profit attributed to her ownership is $100. The company does not distribute the $100 to the investor, but the investor is considered $100 better off for owning the 100 shares. When the return on investment is good, the value of the shares increases.

Importantly, where the balance sheet is a snapshot in time of the company's financial position, the income statement describes what happened financially during that time. Income statements include a comment near the top such as "income statement for quarter ended June 30, 20XX." The revenues and expenses contained in the statement explain the change in financial position shown on the balance sheet.

Like the balance sheet, there are such other names for the income statement as Statement of Operations, Earnings Statement, and (the unofficial but frequently used) Profit and Loss Statement.

Statement of Cash Flow Overview

Making a profit is not the same as having cash in the bank. Although the two are closely related, GAAP accounting procedures create a disconnect (see accrual accounting in Chapter 3) between profit and cash that is resolved with the statement of cash flow.

In business, cash is king. Investors provide cash for the company to invest in resources, which in turn are used to produce products or services for customers in exchange for cash. The cash flow statement keeps track of the cash coming into and going out of the business. This statement is separated into three sections: Operating Activities (the basic company functions that usually get the most attention), Investing Activities, and Financing Activities. It includes cash used to purchase or produce the products and services that it sells. Payments received from customers create positive cash flow from operations while payments to employees and suppliers negatively affect cash flow.

OPERATING CASH FLOW
• Initial Investments (positive)
• Sales Receipts (positive)
• Employee Wages (negative)
• Paying Suppliers (negative)

Investing activities are not directly related to the basic function of the business. Companies invest cash not immediately needed. Investments may be simply a savings account. Companies certainly need to invest in equipment required to conduct business, and they often use the money to invest in opportunities they think will provide a higher return than a savings account, including other companies' stocks and bonds. These investments can be either long- or short-term. Having funds in a savings account is the same as having cash, and these funds are counted as cash on hand. Investments, such as in another company's stock shares, have to be sold to convert them back into cash. Therefore, cash flow is negative when purchasing stock of another company and positive when the stocks are sold and converted back into cash. Even if the stock of another company is sold at a loss, the cash flow is positive. This financial statement is only about cash flow. Profit and loss is found on the income statement.

INVESTING CASH FLOW

- Purchase of Equipment (negative)
- Selling a Building (positive)
- Buying Other's Stock (negative)
- Selling Other's Stock (positive)

Financing activities can be a little tricky to grasp the first time. Financing typically involves borrowing money. When a loan or a mortgage is taken out, cash flows into the business. Therefore, a new loan represents positive cash flow to the business receiving it. Negative cash flow results when the company makes loan or mortgage payments.

FINANCING CASH FLOW

- New Bank Loan (positive)
- Repaying Loan (negative)

One of the most important points about cash flow is its contribution to being able to pay dividends to investors and enable the growth of the business by reinvesting in itself. Several ways to enhance cash flow are brought to a manager's attention in Chapter 5.

Unlike the balance sheet and income statement, the statement of cash flows does not have other terms commonly associated with it.

HOW TO READ AND UNDERSTAND FINANCIAL STATEMENTS

Statement of Shareholders' Equity Overview

The fourth of the major financial statements, the statement of shareholders' equity, bridges a gap between the balance statement, which shows a snapshot of the major accounts, and the income statement, which summarizes the income and expenses for the period. Shareholders' equity or value increases when the company retains earnings for investments, including growth of the business. The statement of shareholders' equity presents changes in shareholder equity over the period being examined.

Besides retained earnings, the other primary method of increasing equity is to pay additional capital into the business. Owners of private companies increase their equity in the company by contributing more money or other resources to the business. Public companies can sell additional stock in the company. When this happens, only the investors who purchase the new stock realize an increase in owners' equity.

A decrease in equity occurs when the business loses money instead of making a profit. Private business owners also experience a decrease in equity when money or resources are withdrawn from the business. Similarly, a public company paying dividends to owners does not retain those earnings, and therefore owners' equity does not grow in an amount equal to the dividends paid. Many companies retain part of the earnings and pay dividends from a portion of the earnings. Here, investors enjoy both the cash dividend and growth of their equity in the business. It is important to note that the combined payment of dividends and retained earnings is equal to the total profit made by the company during the period. This simply divides the profit between two uses.

An important concept to understand is that retained earnings appear on the balance sheet and the statement of shareholders' equity. Although related to each other, these two numbers provide different information to the reader. Retained earnings on the balance sheet represent the total earnings the company has retained since business began, less any adjustments. The number to focus on in the statement of shareholders' equity is earnings retained from that specific period, although an accumulative or ending balance also may be shown. Once the terminology is understood, the statement of shareholders' equity is the least complicated and easiest of the statements to read.

This statement of shareholders' equity also is known as Statement in Changes in Owners' Equity, Statement of Retained Earnings, Statement of Changes in Net Worth, and Statement of Changes in Capital Stock.

Other Common Financial Documents

Prospectus

The SEC requires companies file a prospectus before selling stocks. This applies to companies selling stocks for the first time, as well as those that previously have sold stock on an exchange but have a new stock offering. Companies that previously have sold stocks and meet additional SEC requirements may substitute an "offering memorandum" or "offering circular" for the prospectus when new shares are offered for sale.

A prospectus contains a lot of information and can be easily more than 20 pages in length. The most important information it contains is:

- Risk factors about company operations, products, services, and the marketplace

- How the money will be used: "Working capital," the most frequent explanation, gives management the most latitude of how the money can be used. Investors may want more specific information, such as if the company plans growth or expansion into new product lines. A telephone call to the company's investor relations office may be helpful.

- The Principal Shareholder section identifies anyone who owns more than 5 percent of the company, along with directors and executive managers. Investors should look for shareholders who are decreasing their ownership because they may have negative information about the company.

- The Certain Transaction section identifies transactions between the business and officers of the company. Investors should be wary of loans or leasing transactions between these parties.

- The Financial Statements and Notes provide the information described earlier in this chapter about the four major financial statements. Investors can learn about the company's profitability and financial position before buying ownership into a company making an initial public offering.

The prospectus can be the most important information available about a company offering stock for sale to the public for the first time. On the other hand, companies that have been traded publicly for a while can be researched through previous financial statement filings with the SEC.

Consolidated Statements

Many companies grow by purchasing other companies that offer complementary services or products or to enter a promising industry where the other company is already established. While there are many reasons for one company to purchase another, the fact is it happens all the time. When this is accomplished through a merger, the financial statements of the two companies are combined into a single seamless report. Otherwise, the parent company chooses to keep operations fully separate between the companies involved. In this situation, the parent company owns the other companies as subsidiaries.

It is not necessary to purchase the entire company to gain full control. Owning any amount that exceeds 50 percent of the company's stock effectively obtains full control over the subsidiary company. This brings up the subject of majority and minority interest, which is directly related to consolidated statements. When the parent company obtains majority interest, it is required to consolidate the financial statements of the parent and the subsidiary. However, the subsidiary will continue to publish independent statements that apply only to it.

Transactions between parent and subsidiary companies occur for many reasons. The parent company might charge management fees to the subsidiary, or the subsidiary might supply products or services to the parent company. These and other potential transactions must be eliminated from the financial statements for a good reason: Failing to eliminate transactions between the companies would cause revenues and expenses to be counted twice. Buying products from a subsidiary is an expense to the parent company and revenue to the subsidiary. The parent company obtains revenue when it makes the final sale of the product to a customer. Revenue would be counted twice if the parent company counted revenue to the subsidiary and again when the product is sold to a customer. Therefore, the parent company must file consolidated statements that eliminate all transactions between separate businesses.

In some cases, the parent company has a minority interest of less than 50 percent in the subsidiary and does not have controlling interest. In this case, the parent company's interest in the subsidiary is represented in the liabilities and equity sections of the financial statements. Whenever the subsidiary has minority shareholders, it must continue to provide financial statements specific to its own operations and separate from the parent company. An investor who owns a minority stake in a subsidiary will want to examine its financials, as those of the parent company will provide no meaningful information about the subsidiary's financial condition.

Management's Role in the Financial Statements

It is the responsibility of the executive officers and board of directors to ensure the business finances are accurate and fairly presented to the shareholders. This is not the responsibility of accountants and auditors.

CEO and CFO Responsibilities

The Chief Executive Officer and Chief Financial Officer (CFO) have the primary responsibility of ensuring the financial statements are accurate and fairly represent the company's financial condition. Key among these responsibilities is maintaining internal control of the accounting system that ensures accurate reporting and ensuring the accounting system, and ultimately the financial statements, is in full compliance with GAAP.

These two senior managers must have a complete understanding of the financial statements and be able to recite key numbers and ratios from the most current period. Not only is it critical they know the historic numbers; they also must have a vision of how today's operations will affect changes in future statements. They should look for trouble on the horizon and take steps to reduce or eliminate it. If they see opportunity in the future, they should act to financially position the company to exploit it and improve the company's future financial position. In the end, the CEO and CFO must answer to the board of directors and the shareholders about the financial position of the company. They are directly answerable for any fraud that occurs. Even if they are not the perpetrators, they have responsibility to ensure that it cannot occur through rigorous internal controls. Likewise, when the company performs especially well, they are amply rewarded through the handsome salaries and stock options granted to today's executives.

Management's key financial responsibilities can be summarized as maintaining timely, accurate, and secure accounting systems; being fully informed of the historic, current, and likely future of the company's financial statements; understanding the relationships and key indicators within the financial statements most critical to the success of the business;

managing the flow of cash; using this information to best position the company for the future; and keeping investors, other managers, and all interested parties accurately informed of the company's current and future financial condition in a timely manner.

Board of Directors' Responsibilities

The board of directors is the highest level of management in the company, making the chairperson of the board the most powerful person. In the United States, the most important role of the board of directors is to protect the assets of the shareholders and ensure they obtain a reasonable return on their investment. This priority responsibility is not the same in all countries and cultures. Any investor considering companies in other countries is best served by understanding the expectations of the board of directors in that part of the world. In Europe, the board considers its responsibilities more in line with employees than shareholders.

Shareholders elect individual directors to the board with the intention that they will be responsible for the company's financial performance. The shareholders own the company and, while directors and executive officers may own shares, their level of ownership is proportionate only to the number of shares they actually own. The number of directors on the board for any given company varies considerably. Eight to 16 is a common range for the number sitting on the board of public companies. Frequently, executive officers are also members of the board. Known as inside directors, they have an inside role in the daily management of the company. Directors at private companies are often all insiders with an active role in day-to-day operations. The majority of board members for public companies are outsiders and do not participate in the daily management of the company. Rather, they participate in oversight committees and attend periodic board meetings to ensure independent reviews of executive managers' performance.

In performance of its financial responsibility to shareholders, the board of directors' most important activity is the audit committee, another layer of oversight to ensure the company's financial records are accurate and fair. The audit committee is responsible for selecting, hiring, and working with the independent firm that audits the accounting system and financial records. All these protective layers must be compromised for white-collar criminals to commit financial fraud on the shareholders. Although infrequent, fraud is intentional and requires great effort. Other board of director responsibilities important to shareholder interests include appointing the CEO, determining the CEO's compensation and bonuses, approving or disapproving the financial statements, approving or denying dividend payments to shareholders, approving or disallowing stock splits and stock repurchase programs, and approving or disapproving of mergers and acquisition of other companies.

Financial Audits

Audits of public companies can be performed only by independent Certified Public Accountants (CPAs). More than accountants with a college degree, CPAs must pass rigorous exams and abide by strenuous ethics codes to be certified. The independent nature of the audit severely restricts the CPA from other business relationships with the company being audited. These restrictions have become more severe, and other steps have been taken to ensure the reliability of the financial statements following the fraud that collapsed Enron and World Com.

Important activities conducted during audits include testing the accounting system to ensure that individual transactions can be traced back fully to the originator and that fraud is not detected. The audit also examines the accounting principles used by the company. Auditors use and look for compliance to GAAP.

The audit concludes with the CPA issuing an opinion if the financial statements are "fairly presented" and "materially represent" the financial position of the company. Every opinion clearly states that ultimately the financial statements are the responsibility of company management. Two types of opinions are issued. The unqualified opinion is a finding that the financial statements appear to be fairly presented without needing further explanation. The qualified opinion, rare for a public company, requires further explanation about disagreements between the auditor and company management. The points of disagreement are reported to company management and the SEC. A failure to pass an audit occurs when the CPA "withdraws" from the audit. The CPA will withdraw when he is not able to issue either an unqualified or a qualified opinion. The SEC is notified when an auditor withdraws.

SEC Oversight

While company management is responsible to ensure fair and accurate reporting of the financial statements, the SEC is another layer ensuring management complies with these requirements. The Great Stock Market Crash of 1929 brought to the attention of the U.S. Congress that better financial disclosure was needed in the investment sector of the economy. As a result, the SEC was established in 1934 by the U.S. Congress to protect investors; maintain fair, orderly, and efficient markets; and facilitate capital formation.

Investing in securities is complex and risky to the uninformed. Purchasing partial ownership in companies does not come with a government guarantee the way a checking or savings account deposit does. The SEC's role is to ensure that investors have accurate financial information to understand and overcome the risks involved with investing.

The SEC oversees the key participants in the securities world, including securities exchanges, securities brokers and dealers, investment advisers, and mutual funds. Here the SEC is concerned primarily with promoting the disclosure of important market-related information, maintaining fair dealings, and protecting against fraud.

Crucial to the SEC's effectiveness is its enforcement authority. Each year the SEC brings hundreds of civil enforcement actions against individuals and companies for violation of securities laws. Typical infractions include insider trading, accounting fraud, and providing false information about securities and the companies that issue them.

President Franklin D. Roosevelt appointed Joseph P. Kennedy, President John F. Kennedy's father, to serve as the first chairman of the SEC. Today, the SEC has five commissioners who are appointed by the President of the United States with the advice and consent of the Senate. Their terms last five years and are staggered so that one commissioner's term ends on June 5 of each year. To ensure that the commission remains non-partisan, no more than three commissioners may belong to the same political party. The president also designates one of the commissioners as chairman, the SEC's top executive.

The commissioners meet to discuss and resolve a variety of issues. At these meetings they interpret federal securities laws, amend existing rules, propose new rules to address changing market conditions, and enforce rules and laws. These meetings are open to the public and the news media unless the discussion pertains to confidential subjects.

The SEC relies on two private-sector entities that guide reporting requirements. GAAP are grounded in public-sector expectations for fair and complete information. The private-sector Financial Accounting Standards Board (FASB) establishes and interprets the GAAP standards.

GAAP

GAAP govern financial reporting by all U.S. publicly traded companies and many private companies. As a government authority, the SEC requires this of public companies. Many banks and other lenders to private companies require financial statements to comply with GAAP, although an audit to confirm compliance may not be necessary.

GAAP is a dynamic set of principles and standards that evolve with changes in the business world and the needs of those that rely on financial information. To be useful and helpful, financial statements must be:

- Relevant: Relevance helps users make predictions about events (it has predictive value). Relevant information helps users confirm or correct prior expectations (it has feedback value). It also must be available before decisions are made.

- Reliable: Reliable information is verifiable (when independent auditors using the same methods get similar results) and neutral (free from bias) and demonstrates representational faithfulness (what really happened or existed).

- Comparable: Information must be measured and reported in a similar manner for different enterprises (allows financial statements to be compared between different companies).

- Consistent: The same accounting methods should be applied from period to period, and all changes in methods should be well explained and justified.

Details about how the GAAP principles are included in financial statements fill accountants' computers. However, the most authoritative GAAP setting publications are issued as "Statements of Financial Accounting Standards." In February 2007, the FASB had issued 159 statements.

FASB

The FASB is an independent nonprofit organization that provides accounting standards that result in GAAP. The FASB does not have any authority to enforce the rules. That is the role of the SEC. Yet, the SEC has no authority over the FASB. The theory behind this type of relationship is the FASB is not subject to political pressure. Backgrounds of FASB board members include scholastics, accounting firms, corporations, and the investment community. Members serve full-time and are prohibited from maintaining any connection with previous employers.

The FASB seeks input from all users of the financial information subjected to the standards that it creates. Efforts to ensure robust standards that fully disclose financial information include open board meetings. Anyone can propose changes, but decisions are not made until all constituents are given an opportunity to comment. The intent is to establish objective and unbiased accounting and reporting standards.

The very open process can slow the speed at which important changes happen. The collapse of Enron may be an example of the FASB changing too slowly. While there were many accounting irregularities on the Enron books, a few of the most damaging were enabled while the FASB struggled to adopt standards, which Enron would have been clearly violating. This example does not imply the FASB was a cause of Enron's failure. Rather, it emphasizes that the FASB decisions and GAAP pronouncements often lag behind what is occurring in the corporate and investment communities.

Nonetheless, U.S. financial statements and accounting practices are considered among the most revealing in the world.

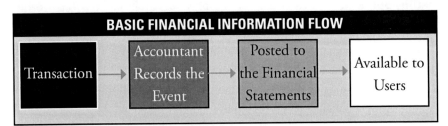

BASIC FINANCIAL INFORMATION FLOW

Transaction → Accountant Records the Event → Posted to the Financial Statements → Available to Users

CHAPTER 2

Important Basics

How are businesses structured, and how does accounting ease the transition into the details about financial statements? This book centers on financial statements for public and private corporations, but by no means should other business types be limited in the application of these tools, which are useful in managing all businesses.

Any businessperson should be able to set up basic financial statements regardless of business size. Most small businesses and some medium-sized businesses operate using cash-based accounting. Financial statements rely on an accounting system known as accrual accounting that needs understanding before reading financial statements becomes intuitive.

Business Structure and Financial Statements

Business structures in the United States are divided into sole proprietors, partnerships, and corporations, which have several substructures — most commonly C Corporations, Limited Liability Companies (LLCs), and S Corporations. As startup businesses achieve success, they begin transitioning incrementally from sole proprietorships toward complex corporate structures. Incorporating reduces owners' personal liability from business errors and enables growth. Whether reliable financial information leads to business growth or growing businesses need reliable financial information is debatable, but the two go hand in hand.

Sole Proprietorships

Sole proprietorships ("mom and pop" stores) are the most common US business structure. The financial reporting requirements are nonexistent in many states, and no financial reporting at all would occur if these individuals were not required to pay federal and state income taxes.

After deducting their businesses expenses, sole proprietors pay taxes on their business profits directly through their personal income tax return. Hundreds of individuals start up or shut down sole proprietorships every day. The successful ones soon learn the downside of being a sole proprietor: full liability for every business transaction that occurs, including anything employees do. Not only is the business financially liable for debts and legal judgments; the owner's personal property — cars, homes, etc. — can be used to settle business liabilities. Many thus decide to incorporate even modestly successful businesses.

In business, a corporation is afforded the same rights and privileges as a real person. The business pays taxes on profits before they can be passed onto owners as dividends when taxes are collected a second time. Double taxation is the downside of incorporating. The upside is that owners and investors enjoy limited liability. Bad business decisions, errors, and outright negligence result in a financial liability limited to the amount invested in the business. Even if a legal judgment financially wipes out a business, the owner's and investor's homes, cars, and other property cannot be used to settle the judgment. Incorporation separates the business from the owner and investors.

Partnerships

Unlimited personal liability is also true for partnerships. The only difference? All partners share the liability. When a partnership prospers, each partner wants to share proportionately in the financial rewards.

When the business flounders, each partner needs to know how bad the situation has become. Good decision-making requires accounting to determine if there is enough profit to pay the partners each month.

Keeping tabs on revenue and expenses reassures all partners that business is being conducted prudently or shows where changes need to be made. The sole proprietor and small partnerships may customize financial statements to their specific needs without meeting GAAP and other regulatory requirements. They also may use the least costly formal accounting process, compilation, or forego formal accounting.

Compiled and Reviewed Financial Statements

Less expensive than fully audited statements but still meeting many small businesses' needs are compiled and reviewed financial statements, which are prepared by an independent CPA not including examining or testing the business's accounting system. The CPA thus will not issue an opinion about adhering to GAAP and fair disclosure. Rather, the CPA relies completely on accounting figures provided by management, which, in a letter, acknowledges:

- The nature and limitations of services the CPA will provide.
- The financial statements are limited to information provided by management.
- The statements will not be reviewed or audited by the CPA.
- The CPA will not provide opinion or any form of assurance.
- Management knows the basic procedures and assumptions the CPA will apply in compiling the financial statements.
- The financial statements will not be relied on by third parties.
- The statements cannot be used to disclose errors, fraud, or illegal acts.

The letter from management also may include:

- Material departures from GAAP may exist and might not be fully disclosed.
- Substantial disclosures may be omitted.
- The statement of cash flow may be omitted.
- The CPA may not be fully independent of management.
- Other reference material may be included to supplement the financial statements.

In essence, financial statements compiled by a CPA are limited to use by management. Often, each page of the compiled statements will include a similar statement, such as "Restricted to management's use. Not intended to be used by third parties." Management uses of compiled financial statements include determining value of the company in preparation for selling part or all of it, building a business plan with the intention of borrowing money for growth, accurately determining proportional ownership when a new partner invests in an existing business or an existing partner exits the business, accurately determining the dollar amount owed to a deceased partner's estate, determining value of the company in preparation to merge with another business, early preparation for incorporation and offering shares for sale to the public, and preparing financial statements for review or audit.

There are certainly risks associated with compiled and management-produced financial statements. Setting aside fraud as a primary result of unaudited statements, the most probable cause of inaccuracy in the statements lies with either the business's accounting system or the input of data to the accounting system. Today's accounting systems are turnkey, and most anyone with basic accounting experience knows how to properly set up accounts that suit a particular business. That leaves data entry as the most likely cause of inaccuracy in unaudited reports. An example is entering a $25,000 cost for major remodeling of a retail showroom. This cost might be to ensure ongoing operations of the business, which would be classified as a maintenance and repair expense. The cost could be a remodeling improvement to the showroom with the primary intention of attracting new and more affluent customers. The second scenario should be classified as a leasehold upgrade, which is a long-term investment in the business. It actually would increase the value of the business on the balance sheet, whereas recording it as a maintenance expense decreases the earnings of the company. Accurate data entry is critical in creating accurate financial statements.

When a compiled report will be used by a third party, the CPA must attach a compilation report to the financial statements. Accounting standards that the CPA must meet include:

- A level of knowledge about the accounting principles and practice of the entire industry, which will enable compiling financial statements to meet the norms of the industry.

- An understanding of business conducted by the company having the statements compiled. This includes knowledge about major business transactions, the company's accounting records, and the accounting principles (GAAP or other) it uses, as well as qualifications of accounting personnel.

- The CPA will review the compiled statements for obvious omissions or material errors.

- The CPA is not required to ask management for information supporting the financial statements, but if the CPA does and receives questionable information or management refuses to provide the information, the CPA is required to discontinue the compilation and withdraw.

A review is the next level of assurance that financial statements are accurate. Still, a CPA will not issue an opinion about the statements. Rather, he or she will inform management about any changes needed to conform to GAAP, including how the changes would affect the financial statements. The financial needs of large companies cannot be met with only compiled or reviewed statements. Audited statements are a must.

Private Corporations, LLCs, and S Corporations

Any person or group can incorporate a business. In most states, incorporation is done by registering with the Secretary of State. The most common types of incorporation are C Corporations, LLCs, and S Corporations. The C Corporation, the most complex, must comply with government regulations on a continuous basis. In most states, the S Corporation can choose to comply with the same regulations or elect those most suitable to its purpose. LLCs, relatively new, lack standardization among states.

Private Corporations

Most people are familiar with C Corporations: Coca-Cola, General Motors, Boeing, Microsoft. These are all publicly traded companies, but thousands of private companies incorporate under the same state regulations. All 50 states structure their incorporation requirements based on the Federal Model Business Corporation Act (FMBCA). Although states' general requirements are similar, there are factors that drive management to select a particular state for registration. There is no requirement for management or the company to reside in the chosen state. Delaware is the most preferred state because of flexible corporation laws, lenient tax codes, and a business-friendly state government.

Incorporation requirements apply to public and private corporations: File articles of incorporation. Declare and record the number of shares of stock the company is authorized to issue. Declare and record the different classes (if more than one class) of stock the company is authorized to issue. Establish a board of directors. Board of directors members' and company officers' names are public information. Hold annual shareholder meetings. Create bylaws. Document and maintain records for board of directors meetings and decisions.

10 OF THE LARGEST PRIVATE CORPORATIONS			
Doing Business in the United States			
	Company	2006 Revenues	Employees
1	Cargill	$75.2 Billion	149,000
2	PricewaterhouseCoopers	$22.0 Billion	140,000
3	Publix Supermarkets	$21.7 Billion	142,000
4	Deloitte Touche Tohmatsu	$20.2 Billion	135,000
5	SemGroup	$20.1 Billion (2005)	Not disclosed
6	C&S Wholesale Grocers	$20.0 Billion	20,000
7	Earnest & Young	$18.4 Billion	114,000
8	Bechtel Corp.	$18.1 Billion (2005)	40,000
9	Mars	$18.0 Billion	Not disclosed
10	KPMG	$16.9 Billion	104,000

Private corporations range in size from a single independent owner to those with thousands of employees. The largest have billions of dollars in annual earnings. Those offering employee stock ownership programs can have thousands of investors. Stock shares of many of these companies may not be traded on stock exchanges but can be readily invested in.

Publix Supermarkets is a private company owned by the employees. Publix has over 58,000 stockholders and 85,000 participants in its employee stock ownership program. The board of directors periodically hires an independent auditor to conduct an appraisal of the company. The board uses the appraisal to help establish the price of the stock.

LLCs

Nothing similar to the FMBCA guides the 50 states in establishing requirements for registering an LLC. States began registering this business structure during the 1990s, and today it is available in every state to some degree. Owners of LLCs are referred to as members rather than shareholders. The LLC is a hybrid between a partnership and a corporation, a business entity that limits owners' personal liability to their investment in the business. However, the business entity does not create double taxation by first paying corporate taxes and then requiring owners to pay income tax on dividends. All profits pass through to the owners and are taxed only on the members' income tax return.

These companies file Articles of Organization similar to a corporation's Articles of Incorporation. However, legally complex bylaws are replaced with an operating agreement, and members decide on a suitable management structure that may or may not resemble a board of directors.

A major drawback preventing LLCs from being publicly traded companies is that LLCs are automatically dissolved upon the death of a member or if a member goes into bankruptcy. LLCs are generally best suited for small groups of people engaging in business. These people can include outside investors not actively engaged in running the business.

Because there is nothing similar to FMBCA guiding state regulations, it is important to understand the specific requirements in the state the LLC is registered. Lack of guidance can complicate LLCs' efforts to do business in multiple states. Liability and tax laws also vary among states.

LLCs and S Corporations are in a grey area between needing audited financial statements and meeting their needs with compiled or reviewed statements. Individual companies must determine specific requirements.

S Corporations

S Corporations are another popular hybrid of the traditional corporation. This structure can be suitable for small but growing businesses, as well as medium-sized businesses. Profits flow through the S Corporation direct to the owners' income tax without first paying a business tax. Still, the owners enjoy the limited liability of the corporation. States do not bestow S Corporation status; rather, that comes from the Internal Revenue Service (IRS). An S Corporation begins by first registering with the state as a C Corporation. Once the corporation is established, an application is made to the IRS for S Corporation status. The IRS grants the ability to pass taxes through to shareholders' federal income tax returns without paying a business income tax. The state incorporation limits personal liability. Most states allow S Corporations to do away with the C Corporation complexities once S Corporation status is established.

The S Corporation is limited to 75 owners but is not automatically dissolved upon the death or bankruptcy of an owner. With a formal agreement between the owners, it can conduct internal business without a board of directors, shareholder meetings, or formally documenting business decisions. This business structure is limited to a single class of stock, whereas LLCs and C Corporations can have several classes of stock, frequently a combination of preferred stock and common stock.

Many variables — number of shareholders, taxation, limited liability, complexity of corporate governance needed, ability to borrow growth funding or attract investors — go into the decision about which business structure best suits a private business. In turn, the decision about the business structure drives the decision about what financial information is needed and to whom it will be distributed.

Incentive Awards and Stock Options

IRS code section 409A requires private companies to accurately determine the company's value when using incentive awards such as stock options or other equity-based compensation. The most prevalent is the qualified stock option because it minimizes the income tax paid by the person receiving the option. A key qualifier for this option is that it be granted at its actual value on the day the option is issued. The person receiving a stock option has the right to purchase stock from the company at a future date for the price assigned on the day the option was granted. The underlying theory is the value of the stock will increase over time, and the holder of the grant will realize a profit by purchasing it for the lower option price and selling it at a higher future price.

Stock options often are granted to managers to encourage ownership in the company. It is an incentive to make decisions and take actions leading to higher profits and increasing the company's value. A vesting period often is associated with stock options. An example is a stock option grant to purchase 100 shares at a price of $25 per share with yearly vesting periods. After one year, the manager has the right to purchase 30 shares; after two years, she can purchase another 30 shares; and after three years, she can purchase the remaining 40 shares. The value of the stock will either increase or decrease over time. Without an open market determining stock values, these private companies must be revalued on a regular basis to determine the stock's value.

Changes in the value offer the manager several options. Obviously if the value declines, the manager will simply not exercise her option to purchase the shares for a higher cost than they are worth. If the stock's value rises from $25 to $30 after one year, the manager might elect to purchase the 30 shares at the options price of $25 and become a minority owner in the company. Ideally, this is what majority owners want to happen so managers are encouraged to act in the best interest of the business. The manager may decide not to exercise the options immediately but retain the right to acquire them for the same $25 price at a later date when the value has increased further.

Another option for the manager is to purchase the stocks and immediately sell them. The manager realizes an immediate profit equal to the difference between the current price minus the option price multiplied by the number of shares that have vested. In the example, the manager would earn $5 ($30 − $25) times the 30 shares vested at the end of one year for a profit of $150 ($5 x 30 shares). With prudent management and solid business practices, the share value could increase to $50 when the second vesting period ends. The manager would have the same options as before with each share now having increased in value by $25 per share ($50 − $25). The manager's profit on the 30 shares vesting at the end of year two would be $750 ($25 x 30 shares).

Often the majority owners, acting as the board of directors, will grant stock options to key managers on a regular basis for incentive reasons. Over time, the manager increases her ownership in the company or sells the shares as a bonus for the company's performance. Offering stock options on a regular basis leads to a requirement to determine the value of the company on a regular basis also. This can be one reason that a private company needs GAAP-conforming financial statements.

Note that there are many variations to stock option plans. Options can be provided to all employees as an incentive for the entire team to do well.

Lender Requirements

Lenders to businesses come in many forms and have many different financial reporting requirements that suit themselves or are particular to the business borrowing money.

Bankers generally want annually audited financial statements that comply with GAAP. Some banks also require GAAP-compliant quarterly statements that are not audited. This comes close to covering the SEC requirements for public companies, although the private company does not have to release the information to the public. Still, growing and midsize companies borrowing money generally have financial statement requirements similar to public companies.

Bankers usually ask for information that goes beyond financial statements. This often includes more detailed information about amounts the business owes others (payables), more detailed information about what others owe to the business (receivables), detailed information about money tied up with inventory (do the statements include obsolete inventory that cannot be sold?), and more detail about the company's cash flow than appears on the statement of cash flows.

Business loans include what are known as covenants: how much debt the business can take on in addition to what the bank has loaned. Often these ratios are similar to those used by investors to gauge a public company. Ratios comparing outstanding loans to company assets, cash on hand, or forecast cash flow are common. Bankers can have very specific ways these ratios are calculated that exceed the limits of what can be calculated from the numbers on the financial statements. This actually increases the financial reporting of private companies beyond that of pubic companies.

Investment bankers differ from traditional bankers in that they are interested in taking a private company public or helping other institutions and individuals purchase partial ownership of the company. They certainly want to see audited financial statements and more detail about assets the company owns. Appraisals also are used to determine the company's fair market value.

Besides the financial statements, private company investors typically want more information about operations — both historical and what is forecast in the future. Trends and year-over-year comparisons are important.

The bottom line is that people with a financial interest in a private company will require financial statements even if government authorities do not. Any company seeking money to fuel substantial growth must be prepared to provide statements and more.

Management Needs

There are a vast number of management uses for financial statement information. For management this depends on the company's objectives and goals. A startup needs to watch cash flow closely just to be sure there will be enough to keep the doors open each week. Early-growth companies closely watch how money is spent as they hire additional employees, open new locations, and purchase additional equipment. Management of early-growth companies calculates return-on-investment ratios to estimate how profitable each new investment will be.

It is not unusual for early-stage companies to be unprofitable, making it all the more important to keep close tabs on such specific sections of the statements as revenues, cash accounts, and accounts payable and receivable. These accounts control cash coming into the business as customers' payments and going out of the business for expenses. Senior and department managers must track these numbers to turn the unprofitable but promising company into a prosperous and growing company.

Production managers and material buyers keep tabs on the inventory and cost of goods sold. They watch for rising or decreasing inventory levels as indicators that adjustments in production rates and raw materials will be needed to meet demand. For the retailer this would be a change in quantities needing to be ordered.

Private companies may desire to stay relatively small and have no plans of attracting outside investors to fuel growth. Others seek outside investors to either grow the company rapidly or even take the company public in a short time period. During the dot-com heyday, it was common for venture funds to provide massive amounts of investment money based on nothing more than a good idea. That is no longer true today. Once a new business obtains growth from the original investment, management often begins positioning the company to appeal to outside investors. Today this means making a profit before professional financiers will take an interest. This puts additional focus on the income statement.

Ultimately, management cannot disregard any portion of the financial statement, although strategies and emphasis do change to meet the current needs of the business plan. Established companies review statements on a regular basis as a competent business practice. Ratios are an excellent way to understand how well or poorly the business is doing. This applies to early-stage, mid-stage, and mature businesses. The use of ratios is not limited to private companies or management. Investors, bankers, and anyone with a financial interest in the business needs to understand how to read, calculate, and understand ratios. An entire chapter is dedicated to this important task, and references to ratios are made throughout the book.

Examples of How Private Companies Use Financial Statements

Take for example a midsize manufacturer of high-tech equipment with an LLC business structure. Business is robust, and there is plenty of cash to operate the company and pay debts with some left over to pay profits to the owners. The company ha 2,500 employees but does not offer an employee stock ownership plan. Ownership is limited to seven managers and 12 outside investors. There are four operating divisions making up the company.

Internally, management has unaudited financial statements generated within one week after month end. The balance sheet, income statement, and statement of cash flows are all reviewed, but management is primarily concerned with strong cash flow to keep the business capable of meeting obligations.

The board of directors, which includes the outside investors, meets quarterly to thoroughly review all the statements and make major business decisions if necessary. The quarterly statements are compiled by an independent CPA but are not audited.

The company depends on one lender to periodically provide temporary infusions of cash and also has a multimillion-dollar loan outstanding for an equipment upgrade several years ago. The lender has determined the business is not a substantial loan risk and is satisfied to receive audited financial statements on an annual basis as a condition of providing an ongoing line of credit.

Another typical example of financial statement requirements for a private company is an employee-owned midsize health care provider with 3,500 employees. There are no outside investors, but the company is considering going public within two years and has been working hard to grow the business. There are substantial loans outstanding that the bank wants reassurance will be repaid. An investment banker also has been retained to advise about taking the company public. The board of directors is composed of 12 senior managers who are also department heads.

The monthly financial reports reviewed by management are not GAAP compliant. Typical of management, they are primarily concerned with cash flow. The reports are customized by the accounting department as department budgets supplemented with income information.

The management team meets quarterly in the role of the board of directors to review the full set of GAAP-conforming financial statements.

The same quarterly financial statements are sent to the investment banker and an appraiser. The appraiser assists in determining the company's value and ultimately the share price. The investment banker monitors for progress toward the initial pubic offering.

The lending bank receives copies of the unaudited quarterly statements and an audited annual report. In addition, the lending bank has several covenants in place that require detailed ratios be prepared. These include tangible net worth, debt-to-equity ratio, and cash-to-debt service. The bank is a little nervous the business is becoming overextended and can call the loan due if the ratios exceed limits set in the covenants.

Neither of these companies is required to produce financial statements by law, but neither would have obtained the level of success they enjoy without investors and loans. Banks and investors are not going to provide large amounts of money without understanding the financial condition of the company. Hence, many private companies have a real need for GAAP-conforming financial statements.

Investor Needs

Financial statements provide investors with a wealth of information to decide to buy or sell a company's stock. Investors should always be wary of financial statements because they can be a source of misinformation as well as a valuable source of information. The recent Enron, Tyco, World Com, and other public scandals make it clear that companies can manipulate financial statements fraudulently so the company appears in robust health while it is actually financially collapsing.

One way investors guard against this scenario is comparing multiple years of financial statements to see if radical and inadequately explained changes have occurred. A sudden reduction in discretionary expenses like research, advertising, maintenance, and training can provide a quick increase in profits but eventually destroy the company's capability to sustain business. The sudden need to reduce these necessary expenses also may be caused by a cash shortage. The fact that financial statements either cover a specific period or are a snapshot in time enables other short-term manipulation. Postponing the purchase of inventory until after the statement period will enhance the statements for that period. Delaying the payment of debt keeps cash on the statements for the period. These types of tactics are always short-term and must be accounted for in a future statement to pass an audit. The best defense against investing while the statements are being manipulated is to compare several years of ratios. Look for a steady pattern of increases in ratios like the current ratio, net profit margin, price to earnings, return on assets, and operating margins. A corresponding decrease in the liability-over–net worth ratio can be an indicator of good health, or increases should be explained by planned business growth. Gradual changes in these ratios, from quarter to quarter and year to year, indicate good business management. Sudden changes indicate management is not adequately controlling the business.

Studies have shown that individual investors and professionally managed institutional investors rate long-term capital gain as their first consideration when evaluating an investment opportunity. Steady and increasing dividend income is the next most closely monitored health indicator. Short-term capital gains are not considered a reliable indicator for the long-term investor, although those wanting to make a quick buck before selling the stock often look for exactly this.

The way investors use statements does not vary much whether they are investigating in private or public companies. While many private companies provide investors with GAAP-compliant and -audited financial statements, it is wise for investors to remain even more skeptical of private companies than public companies. Private companies are not subject to monitoring by the SEC and the stock exchanges where public companies trade.

Publicly Traded Companies

The public company is the most complicated of the business structures. Although public companies operate under the same state rules as private corporations, there are important differences in the management and financial structures intended to protect investors.

First, they do not have an option not to provide audited financial statements annually and unaudited statements quarterly. Lenders and investors can prompt this need for private companies, but it is a legal requirement for publicly traded companies. Likewise, it is not possible to restrict who sees the financial statements. In today's information age, almost every public company posts its financial statements on its Web site on an investor relations page.

Both management and outside board members are obligated to run the business in the best interest of the shareholder owners. A trend resulting from recent scandals is not having the CEO also serve as the chairman of the board. Rather, an outside director serves in this top management position. In contrast, private companies commonly have the majority shareholder act as chairman of the board and CEO. This can be a dangerous combination if a conflict of interest exists between the person with all the authority and minority shareholders.

The outside board members have an added responsibility to oversee that managers do not abuse their position of authority within the company. In addition to the audit committee, the compensation committee is another important role for outside directors. The compensation committee determines the salary and bonuses for senior management.

SIX KEY RATIOS FOR INVESTORS & MANAGERS OF THE BUSINESS
1. Current Ratio
2. P/E Ratio
3. Net Profit Margin
4. Liability Over Net Worth
5. Return on Assets
6. Operating Margin

Another important difference between private and public companies is the role played by financial analysts. Financial analysts work for banks, brokerages, and mutual funds, studying specific sectors of the economy and industries. They provide reports and buy, hold, or sell advice for specific stocks. Traders, institutional fund managers, mutual fund managers, and individual investors rely on this advice to make investment decisions. The ability of analysts to influence a public company's stock price can influence in turn how the board of directors and senior management conduct business.

The importance of understanding the differences between public or private companies should be clear. Public companies are open to considerable scrutiny of the financial statements that safeguard investors while private companies have limited, if any, scrutiny of financial statements. The wide-ranging review of public financials adds several layers of confidence for investors.

Summary

Financial statements provide substantial information to many different decision makers. Still, there are gaps in the information that often cannot be filled. Unknowns include future market demand, technology advances, government regulation of the industry, and availability of raw materials.

There is other valuable information that neither public nor private companies are required to disclose and frequently choose not to share. This may include union activities, the pending loss of an important contract or customer, potential legal liabilities, and an uncountable number of other scenarios that can affect the future of the business.

Since no one can predict the future with accuracy, multiple years of historical data provide management and investors the ability to see trends that repeat and performance under various economic conditions. Historical analysis also provides the investor with an insight as to how management has performed over time. Ratio analysis in particular enables management and investors the ability to determine if current performance is better or worse than previous performance. Ratios go a long way in making comparisons meaningful between the company today and the company under different conditions. Comparisons can be made before and after growth stages, when management changes occur, when new products are introduced, during economic downturns, and during other major influences to the business's financial performance.

FINANCIAL STATEMENT REQUIREMENTS AND DISCLOSURE AT A GLANCE BY BUSINESS STRUCTURE			
Business Type	Regulatory Requirement	Management Requirement	Investor and Lender Requirement
Sole Proprietors	None	Generally rely on common accounting software and reports. Financial statements are not relied on and audited statements are rare.	Lenders normally limit loan sizes and rely on owners' income tax returns and other personal information when making loan decisions. Loans are backed by the sole proprietor's personal property, in addition to business assets.
Partnerships	None	May rely on common accounting software. May have an accounting firm compile financial statements if a particular need arises.	Similar to the sole proprietor, except two or more partners provide personal resources to guarantee loans.

FINANCIAL STATEMENT REQUIREMENTS AND DISCLOSURE AT A GLANCE BY BUSINESS STRUCTURE

Business Type	Regulatory Requirement	Management Requirement	Investor and Lender Requirement
Private C Corp.	Generally none. Some states require annual disclosure of total assets and liabilities but not a full set of financial statements.	Typically the largest of the private business structures. Senior management uses financial statements to manage daily operations, to provide the board of directors with ability to oversee the entire company, to keep investors informed, as a requirement of bylaws, and to obtain loans. Stock option programs may make audited statements a requirement in the process of valuing the company and establishing a stock price.	Lenders frequently require GAAP-conforming audited financial statements and include covenants about the total amount a company can borrow from all sources against assets. Investors normally require unaudited quarterly statements and audited annual statements to track financial performance.
Private S Corp.	Generally none. Some states require annual disclosure of total assets and liabilities but not a full set of financial statements.	The need for financial statements is made at management discretion. Accounting software may or may not give adequate oversight of the business, and with up to 75 investors the corporate bylaws may mandate annually audited statements.	Similar to private C Corps. Lenders frequently require annual audited statements depending on loan sizes and associated risk. Investors who do not actively manage the business may require statements to verify management is competent.

FINANCIAL STATEMENT REQUIREMENTS AND DISCLOSURE AT A GLANCE BY BUSINESS STRUCTURE

Business Type	Regulatory Requirement	Management Requirement	Investor and Lender Requirement
Private LLC	Generally, none. Some states require annual disclosure of total assets and liabilities but not a full set of financial statements.	Generally, the same as private S Corps., but there can be more investors influencing the need.	Generally, the same as private S Corps., but there can be more investors influencing the need.
Public C Corp.	All financial statements publicly disclosed as defined by the SEC. Includes annual audited and quarterly unaudited reports along with other requirements.	Management regularly relies on financial statements to guide decision-making. Extensive public analysis requires that management thoroughly understand information behind the numbers and be able to explain significant changes. Board of directors determines the outside firm to conduct the annual audit.	Lender requirements are similar as those for private C Corps. Investors can obtain copies from the SEC EDGAR database and have an opportunity to ask questions of management at the annual shareholders' meeting.

CASE STUDY: PERSONAL FINANCIAL STATEMENT SOFTWARE

KISS Computer Company released Net Worth Express, an innovative personal financial statement software program, in 2003. Shortly after the release of the software, the Florida Institute of Certified Public Accountants recognized Net Worth Express as "2003 Rookie of the Year" at the Florida Accounting and Business Expo™. Also in 2003, it received a favorable review in *The CPA Software News*. Net Worth Express

CASE STUDY: PERSONAL FINANCIAL STATEMENT SOFTWARE

was awarded an honorable mention at the 2005 Tax and Accounting Technology Innovation Awards, sponsored by the CPA Technology Advisor.

Net Worth Express is a unique financial statement software program that allows users to create and maintain a Personal Financial Statement, also known as a Statement of Financial Condition. The software and its professional reporting capabilities are designed to make applying for or maintaining credit with a financial institution easier and more comprehensive. In addition, Net Worth Express gives users the tools they need to accurately calculate their net worth and gain a clearer understanding of their financial situation. The person can track his or her net worth over time to determine his or her progress financially. A Personal Financial Statement is the cornerstone report to use to begin a financial plan.

Net Worth Express PRO Edition — designed specifically for accounting and financial professionals — enables users to quickly compile a Statement of Financial Condition for individuals based on Generally Accepted Accounting Principles. In addition, with Net Worth Express PRO Edition, accounting professionals may include an accountant's compilation report, either using the report provided with the program (based on GAAP) or by creating a custom report. The compilation report may be printed on the company's letterhead. Notes may be inserted to explain the detailed supplementary information in the asset and liability schedules. Footers also may be added to the report.

Assets are items that an individual owns or that are owed to the individual.

Liabilities are items that an individual owes to other people or organizations.

Net worth is the difference between total assets and total liabilities. If the net worth figure is positive, the individual is solvent and has net worth. If this net worth figure is negative, the individual is insolvent and has no net worth.

Net Worth Express Home Edition provides a clear picture of a person's financial situation and simplifies the process of securing a loan or line of credit. While there are several ways to evaluate one's monetary situation, determining what is known as "net worth" is perhaps the clearest indicator of a person's financial condition at any given point. That is why many financial institutions require a Personal Financial Statement that includes a calculation of net worth when a person applies for a loan or maintains a line of credit.

With Net Worth Express HOME Edition, individuals may:

- Create a Statement of Financial Condition (also known as a Personal Financial Statement) to calculate and track their net worth
- List assets and liabilities using predefined schedules
- Specify personal contact and employment information

CASE STUDY: PERSONAL FINANCIAL STATEMENT SOFTWARE

- Provide information on an individual or joint basis — with a spouse, for example
- Identify important relatives, contacts, and documents
- Use the professional, customized printout when applying for a loan or maintaining credit with a financial institution

The Personal Financial Statement is the cornerstone report for understanding the financial condition of an individual. Everyone should have and understand his or her Personal Financial Statement. This is the best report to use to begin a financial plan for retirement or any other investment goal.

— Bay Gruber, President, KISS Computer Company

KISS Computer Company
Post Office Box 101341
Cape Coral, Florida 33910-1341
Telephone: 888-848-8105
info@networthexpress.com
http://www.networthexpress.com

CHAPTER 3

The Balance Sheet

Thoroughly understanding financial statements is enhanced by an understanding of frequently used accounting and financial statement terms. The most commonly used are explained here, and a full glossary in Appendix A provides definitions for other technical terms found on statements and used by financial professionals.

The Terminology of Financial Statements

Assets: Anything available to a business expected to produce a future benefit. Common examples include land, buildings, manufacturing equipment, office supplies, and vehicles. These are all examples of tangible assets that easily have a dollar value assigned. Businesses also have intangible assets that can be more difficult to assign a precise value to. Many companies claim employees are their most valuable resource, but actually assigning a value is not possible and is not done on financial statements. Patents, goodwill, and copyrights are intangible assets that often have a dollar value on the balance sheet. Patents can generate money by giving a business exclusive right to manufacture and sell a product. Patents also can be licensed or sold to other companies as a source of income. Many people misunderstand goodwill. It is not a value assigned to brand names or because customers prefer one company over another. Goodwill results when one business purchases another for more than the total value of its assets (book value). The purchase price includes the value of obtaining a company already doing business with an established customer base and an employee team in place. The price paid above the book value is known as goodwill. Copyrights are an intangible asset entitling companies to exclusively sell and license the rights of artistic and intellectual properties. Another asset that seldom has a dollar value is anything that reduces a business's future expenses. This might be a long-term contract with a supplier at a substantial discount.

Depreciation: An accounting method that reduces the value of equipment and property as it wears out. In this sense, property does not mean land. Property is anything tangible the business owns that has a value. Again, typical examples are office equipment, delivery trucks, and manufacturing equipment along with buildings. All lose value over time from wear and obsolesces. Depreciation records the reduced value of these items over time. There are two common types of depreciation: straight-line and accelerated. The internal revenue provides tables assigning percentages of depreciation for each year of ownership. The straight-line method is used most often on financial statements. Trucks have a five-year useful life. Using the straight-line method, the value of a truck is reduced slightly less than 20 percent each year until only a small salvage value remains at the end of five years. Depreciation is known as a non-cash or paper-only transaction on financial statements because values change but no money exchanges hands. The accelerated method is used for tax reporting. This allows property to be depreciated at higher percentages in the early years with less depreciation allowed in later years. Depreciation is a business expense for tax purposes. Accelerated depreciation rates allow this non-cash expense to reduce profits and thereby reduce taxes that the business must pay. In reality, profits actually increase because no cash changes hands but taxes are lowered. For this reason, it is common to find different depreciation values on a business's tax return than on the financial statements. Most but not everything owned by a business is depreciated. Land is not depreciated because it is assumed that land does not wear out. Supplies like printing paper, pencils, and cleaners are not depreciated because they are rapidly consumed. Instead, these supplies are accounted for as expenses. Raw materials and product inventory are not depreciated because the company sells these for a profit.

Expenses: The IRS defines business expenses as an ordinary and necessary expense common and accepted within a given industry. Expenses are typically divided into two categories. Variable costs change depending on the amount of product being manufactured or sold. Raw materials, labor costs, and electricity costs increase and decrease when production does the same. Rents, loan repayments, and property taxes are examples of fixed costs not easily changed in response to production rates. Businesses have a wide range of expenses that must be accounted for in financial statements. Exact expenses vary by industry but include travel, advertising, maintenance, office supplies, legal costs, and insurance. Total revenues – total expenses and taxes = profit (aka earnings).

Equity: Also called shareholders' equity, owners' equity, or net worth. Equity is the amount left when total liabilities are subtracted from total assets. The remainder is the net worth of the business to the owners.

Gross Income: Sales (also known as revenues) minus the cost of goods sold is gross income, which also is called gross profit. Cost of goods sold includes the cost of materials, labor, and direct overhead used to produce the finished product. Sales – cost of goods sold = gross income. Taxes and administrative costs are not subtracted out of gross income.

Liabilities: These are obligations the business has to other entities separate from the business. Money owed to suppliers and lenders are typical business liabilities. Liabilities are divided into short-term liabilities and long-term liabilities. Short-term liabilities are amounts owed within one year and known as current liabilities. Long-term liabilities are obligations not owed for at least a year. The five main subcategories of liabilities are accounts payable, accrued expenses, income tax payable, short-term notes payable, and long-term liabilities. The current ratio is one of the most important for determining a company's ability to repay debt. Current assets are divided by current liabilities to find this ratio. A company with $250,000 in current assets and $100,000 in current debt has a current ratio of 2.5, indicating that it has two and a half times the assets necessary to pay debts due the next year. Another important ratio using liabilities is liabilities over net worth. Total liabilities ÷ tangible net worth = leverage. This ratio indicates the amount of total debt the company is carrying compared to what the company owns.

Net Income: The bottom line, profit, or earnings. Several interchangeable terms are associated with this important number. This is the amount of money remaining when all expenses and taxes are subtracted from sales revenue. The all-important profit margin is found by dividing net income by sales revenue and multiplying by 100. A business with $750,000 of revenue and $100,000 of net income finds the profit margin with this equation: ($100,000 ÷ $750,000) x 100 = 13.33 percent profit margin.

Operations: The primary activities of the business. For a bicycle manufacturer, operations include purchasing raw materials and components from suppliers and converting them into finished bicycles for sale to distributors. A manufacturer's operations take place in a factory. A retailer's primary activity is purchasing inventory and providing a way for consumers to purchase the products. Retailers' operations occur in stores and warehouses. Both types of companies engage in other activities like investing profits, obtaining financing, and managing employee benefits, but these are not part of base operations.

Revenue: Everything that a company receives in exchange for the delivery of products or services to customers. Often referred to as the top line of the income statement, it is the total compensation received before deducting any expenses. Under accrual accounting, revenues are often recognized at the time of a sale but before the customer actually pays for the product or service. It is important not to confuse revenues with cash. Another word for revenue is *income.*

Accrual Accounting Versus Cash Accounting

Accrual-based accounting has significant differences from cash-based accounting, which most people are familiar with. Accrual accounting counts income or revenue when products or services are delivered even if the customer does not pay at that time. Businesses often provide services and products that are billed, and payment is not received for a month or more. With some types of credit, receiving payment can take even longer. Still, the revenue is counted when the service is provided, not when payment is received. In accrual accounting, the same system is used for expenses the business incurs but does not immediately pay. Suppliers often send products to businesses without receiving payment for several weeks or months. The business that received the product records the cost with its accounting system even if the bill will be paid in the future. These transactions make their way onto the financial statements when the accounting books are closed for any given period. The big advantage of accrual accounting is it keeps expenses and revenues in the same period. It provides a better picture of profit results.

On the other hand, cash accounting only makes changes when money actually is received or expenses actually are paid. Cash accounting dominates smaller businesses like sole proprietors and many partnerships. When the accounting books are closed for the period, they accurately reflect the amount of cash the business currently possesses.

A contractor accepting a home remodeling job for $8,000 near the end of the year that will not be paid until it is complete will have two different financial results for the year, depending on the accounting method used. If the job is completed on December 31 but payment is not received until January 15, the $8,000 would not be included for the previous year using cash accounting. Using accrual accounting, the income was earned fully on December 31 and would be included in the previous year, although not received until mid-January. The IRS recognizes the use of either method and requires taxes be paid for the year the revenue was recorded.

Large businesses use accrual accounting to match income with expenses in the same period. However, the result is that the financial statements do not accurately reflect the cash on hand. This is especially true of the income statement. The balance sheet shows the cash on hand but not the manner in which it was spent. These are the reasons that the cash flow statement is needed. The cash flow statement records the actual intake and disbursement of cash not visible on other statements.

Double-Entry Accounting

The balance sheet uses double-entry accounting where debits and credits equal each other. Math errors are detectable via double-entry accounting because two accounts must always balance. A failure to balance the accounts is a clear sign that a math error exists.

First, notice the balance sheet equation that appears at the top of the following example. The three sample transactions show cash either increasing or decreasing with a corresponding change in another account. The first transaction is a business owner investing $400,000 to begin a new business. In exchange for the $400,000, the company's accounts record an increase in shareholder equity. The business also takes out a $100,000 loan to finance the business and records a corresponding increase in the notes payable account. Transaction three shows two entries on the same side of the equation that balance each other out. $150,000 is subtracted from the cash account to purchase inventory, which results in an increase of $150,000 in the inventory account. Although both entries are on the asset side of the equation, it remains balanced.

DOUBLE ENTRY ACCOUNTING				
	Assets	=	Liabilities +	Shareholders' Equity
Transactions	Cash	Inventory	Note Payable	Paid in Capital
1. Initial investment by owner	+ $400,000			+$400,000
2. Loan from bank	+ $100,000		+ $100,000	
3. Acquire inventory for cash	− $150,000	+ $150,000		

Entries on opposite sides of the equation both will be either positive or negative entries. Both entries on the same side of the equation will always be opposite: one positive and the other negative.

Double-entry accounting is not limited to corporations. Most businesses use it, and financial statements could not be created without it.

The Balance Sheet

Like the balance sheet equation, the balance sheet is divided into three major sections: assets, liabilities, and shareholder equity. This Pretend Toys balance sheet takes a financial snapshot on June 30, 2007. The asset column is read first on the balance sheet. It begins with the most liquid asset of cash and progresses down to increasingly less liquid assets. Land and buildings are found at the bottom because selling them to pay liabilities is the last resort a business will take. The liabilities column follows the same format with the most current liabilities listed first, followed by long-term liabilities. It is no accident that shareholders' equity appears last. Shareholders have the last claim to assets after all other liabilities are paid.

Assets

Several asset accounts are displayed on the balance sheet following the ease of liquidity format. The total value of current assets accounts are shown below a single underline after the last account. Long-term assets or those the company expects to keep longer than a year may be labeled as long-term or simply as property, plant, and equipment. All the long-term assets are totaled together following the last account. After that comes the total of short- and long-term assets with a double underline used to indicate a final totaling of all accounts.

Cash and Accounts Receivable

The cash account represents money the business has on hand to pay immediate obligations. These include paying suppliers, taxes, payroll, and anything else required to conduct business. A company with too much cash should make investments to earn a return. Those without enough cash risk not being able to meet financial obligations required to continue conducting business. There is no magic formula determining the amount of cash needed, but major changes in the cash account need a closer examination and management should explain the change.

Accounts receivable is money owed to the business for sales that have been completed but customers have not paid for on the day the snapshot was taken. The cash and accounts receivable accounts are the most liquid for providing immediate cash.

Less allowance for bad debt is an account that anticipates some outstanding bills never will be paid. Generally, outstanding debt over 90 days past due is considered bad debt. If the debt remains unpaid, the company must remove it from the balance sheet and reduce accounts receivable by the amount. Because accounts receivable is affected by allowances for bad debt, these accounts are shown first to the left of the totals column. The adjusted accounts receivable amount of $34,250 ($35,000 – $750) is shown to the right along with totals from the other accounts. Some companies choose to use the term "accounts receivable net" that indicates bad debt already has been subtracted. The net amount then would be shown directly below cash instead to the left. Using accounts receivable net prevents the reader from knowing how much bad debt the company may have to write off.

Inventory

Inventory is what is available for sale. There are differences in the inventory accounts for retailers and manufacturers. For retailers the inventory account contains what is in the show room, in the warehouse, and on order. For manufacturers this includes what is in the warehouse ready for sale and what currently is being processed through the factory. Materials in the factory are known as "work in progress." Raw materials waiting to enter the factory are included as well. Finished inventory, work in progress, and raw materials are all combined in the manufacturer's inventory account. Most large companies have computerized inventory systems capable of updating this account frequently. Smaller businesses only may update the account shortly before the financial statements are prepared.

Prepaid Expenses and Current Assets Total

Prepaid expenses are resources already paid for but not consumed. Rent and insurance are typical prepaid expenses. The value is removed from the accounts at the end of the month when the value has been consumed.

Prepaid expenses are the last line of the current assets account. Liquidating prepaid expenses is not something a company is likely to do, but it remains a current asset because the company will obtain value from these in the near future. The last account in current assets is underlined followed by a subtotal for all current assets. The total of current assets is used in several important ratios.

PRETEND TOYS
BALANCE SHEET AS OF JUNE 30, 2007

Assets			Liabilities	
Current Assets			Current Liabilities	
Cash		$120,000	Accounts payable, trade	$130,000
Accounts Receivable	35,000		Accounts payable, other accrued expenses	5,000
				12,000
Less allowance bad debt	750	34,250	Short-term debt	1,000
Inventory		240,000	Income tax payable	87,500
Prepaid expenses		11,000	Total Current Liabilities	235,500
Total Current Assets		405,250		
			Long-term debt	90,000
Property, plant, and equipment			Total Liabilities	325,500
Land, buildings and equipment, less accumulated	270,000		Stockholders' Equity	87,500
Prepaid expenses		11,000	Total Current Liabilities	235,500
Total Current Assets		405,250		
			Long-term debt	90,000
Property, plant, and equipment			Total Liabilities	325,500
Land, buildings, and equipment, less accumulated	270,000		Stockholders' Equity Capital stock Retained earnings	150,000 169,250
Depreciation Net land, buildings, and equipment	40,500	229,500	Total Stockholders' equity	319,250
		229,500		
Other Assets		10,000		
Total Assets		$644,750	Total Liabilities and Stockholder's equity	$644,750

Property, Plant, and Equipment

Long-term investments are captured in this section. These are the resources the company uses to conduct business. If the company owns the land and buildings, it is included here. If it rents facilities, this section would include leasehold improvements. Leasehold improvements are major remodeling or even constructing a new building on leased land. Often a business will lease land or a building for 30 years and make major changes to suit its needs.

The equipment account captures factory equipment, office furniture, vehicles, and all the other equipment used by the business. Generally, anything with a useful life of more than one year is included.

Buildings and equipment are shown at the price they were purchased. The purchase price is the basis for depreciation. Both the total purchase price and total depreciation are shown to the left of the total column with the remaining value shown in the right column after subtracting the depreciation out.

A piece of equipment is not necessarily sold when fully depreciated. Until it is sold, the original purchase price remains with all the depreciation subtracted out. When the equipment is finally sold, the original value and depreciation are removed from the account, and any money received for scrap value is added to cash or accounts receivable.

Depending on the company's needs and demands by interested parties, more detail often is included in the asset side of the financial statement. Separate building and equipment accounts are common for smaller companies. Some might break it down to include an account for vehicles if the fleet size is important or separate factory equipment from office fixtures. Even when not done on financial statements it is done often for internal management reporting. Each department manager should have a regular report on all the resources she controls.

Other Assets

Other assets can be shown in a couple different places on the asset side but below the current assets section if they are long-term. These would be investments that the company plans to hold beyond a year but eventually turn back into cash. An example would be purchasing a section of land larger than needed for operations. If the business needed only ten acres but purchased a 15-acre section, the excess five acres might be planned for sale at a future date. Another example would be stock in another company that it is in the process of acquiring. Until it has a majority stake in the other business, it will show as an investment. After it owns more than 50 percent of the business, the financial statements of both will be consolidated.

Intangibles also are included below current assets and categorized as long-term. Goodwill, patents, and other intangibles are amortized similar to the way tangible property is depreciated. A patent has a limited amount of time that it is exclusively available to the company. As the remaining useful life decreases, the remaining value decreases as well and is reduced on the balance sheet through amortization.

In the end, everything of value to the business is accounted for on the asset side of the balance sheet. With that said, the fact that financial statements cannot tell the full story needs to be reiterated. None of the resources will produce value without employees to operate equipment and managers to keep it organized and operating efficiently. Nowhere on the asset side of the equation is an accounting of the people that make it all happen. A devastating union strike might be about to bring everything to a grinding halt, or a very talented researcher might be in a lab discovering the next technical wonder to change everyone's lives. The financial statements do not tell this part of the story.

Liabilities

On the other side of the balance sheet and balance sheet equation are liabilities (some formats will show this below assets). Again, the sequence begins with current liabilities followed by long-term obligations.

Current Liabilities

Accounts payable may or may not be broken into separate accounts for trade and other. Trade accounts include the amounts due to suppliers, vendors, and others directly involved in keeping the company operating. Most of these costs are due within 60 days. The same as accounts receivable on the asset side extends credit to the company's customers, the accounts receivable is the extension of credit to the company by suppliers. A company with a cash flow problem will attempt to collect accounts payable faster, while taking longer to pay on accounts payable. Typically, credit on neither account is extended beyond two months.

The accounts payable other is a catch-all account but does not include short-term loans that are due. This might include fees owed to consultants or attorneys or for office supplies.

Accrued expenses are similar to accounts payable, but the business has not yet received a bill or it is an internal expense that does not generate a bill. Utilities are an ongoing expense that businesses estimate while expecting to receive a bill in the future. Employee wages and salaries are internal expenses that accrue for several weeks before being paid.

Short-term debt or short-term notes payable are loans that must be paid within the year. These can include 90-day promissory notes to banks, credit card payments, and the current portion of long-term debt.

Income tax payable is just what it sounds like. It represents taxes owed on earnings but not yet due to the government. This is similar to accrued expenses except it is specific to taxes. Businesses operating in states with sales tax also will have a sales tax payable account.

Current liabilities are subtotaled the same as current assets. This is important because current assets will be used to pay current liabilities. Businesses assume that inventories will be sold and converted into cash used to pay liabilities over the next year. Current ratios and quick ratios are used to understand the company's ability to meet near-term obligations based on current assets.

Long-term Liabilities

Remaining are the company's long-term liabilities. There can be many sources for a business's long-term debt. Mortgages on land and buildings and loans to purchase vehicles or factory equipment are common. A major loan may be taken out for a large modernization program or an expansion. Expansions can be into other geographical regions or may require building a new factory for a new product line. Financially struggling companies have been known to take out long-term lines of credit to keep the business solvent while management attempts to resuscitate it back into a profitable operation.

Publicly traded companies often finance expansions or fund growth by issuing bonds to the public. Typically, bonds are issued for ten years. Interest on the bonds is paid to investors periodically with interest due within the next year counted in short-term debt. This is known as the current portion of long-term debt. The loan principle becomes due at the end of ten years and can cause a significant increase in short-term debt the year it comes due. Well-managed public companies spread bond issues out over several years that effectively smooth the financial effect into multiple years.

Private companies that do not want to register with the SEC or publish financial statements cannot make public bond offerings. Here, expansion and growth are funded with bank loans and sometimes loans from wealthy owners or board members. Some people theorize that having owners and board members invest in growth is a good indicator of faith in the company's future. Others become concerned that these insiders have too much at risk in the business and may become inclined toward unhealthy risk taking.

Just as current liabilities are compared to current assets, several ratios are used to compare long-term liabilities with long-term assets and the company's ability to make a future profit to cover these liabilities. Several of these ratios are calculated before taxes because payment of loan interest is tax deductible for corporations, the effect being that repayment of the loans will lower the taxes due and enhance profits. In the chapter on ratios, look for the return on sales and interest coverage ratios to provide more insight into repaying long-term financing.

Stockholders' Equity

The last section of the balance sheet is stockholders' equity. It appears last because the shareholders' claim on company assets comes after liabilities are paid. The good news is they own everything left over after the obligations are paid.

Capital Stock and Retained Earnings

Capital stock can be labeled in different ways. Often a par value will be listed first. Par value is an arbitrary number many states require be assigned to stocks when a company incorporates but before the stock is sold. The number of shares issued times the par value is what the dollar value represents. In reality, much more than par is paid when the company sold the stock, either in an IPO on the open market or in a private offering. The price the stock sold for is the capital the company actually raised and is known as "additional paid in capital" or "capital in excess of par."

Additional paid in capital or stock capital has no relationship to the price that the stock currently is trading at on the open market or in private transactions. The company only receives money from the original sale, and that is what is shown here. These are known as common stocks.

Often there is a second class of stock called preferred stock. Preferred stock has different rights than common stock. The company has no obligation to repay the owners of either common stock or preferred stock for their initial investment. However, a promise to pay dividends is made to the owners of preferred stock. If profits are not sufficient to pay all the preferred stock dividends, the dividends accrue. The company still has an obligation to pay all the dividends sometime in the future. There is no obligation to pay dividends to common stockholders, and preferred stockholders will be paid before common stocks. If the company is liquidated, preferred stockholders are paid ahead of common stocks. However, common stockholders can vote at the annual meeting to influence how the company is run, but preferred stocks have no say at annual meetings.

Retained earnings are profits the company chose to keep rather than pay to stockholders. This is another important financial source for growth and expansion. Retained earnings show the company's accumulated profit since it was originally incorporated less any dividends paid out or other adjustments. Normally this amount grows each time a balance sheet is issued. However, if the company has a financial loss rather than a profit, the loss is subtracted from retained earnings. In that way, it shows the total profit made by the company less dividends paid to stockholders.

Other items commonly found under stockholders' equity are treasury stocks and payouts of stock as stock options or profit sharing to employees. Treasury stock is stock that the company owns. A company comes about owning its own stock three different ways. At incorporation, the number of shares that can be sold is established. During the IPO the company

CHAPTER 3: THE BALANCE SHEET

may withhold some of the shares in anticipation they can be sold for a higher value at a later date to raise additional capital. The company bylaws also establish a method by which shareholders can authorize the company to increase the number of shares above the number authorized in the original incorporation papers. This is unusual because it dilutes the value of existing shares and lowers the market value for existing shares. More common is the share repurchase program. The board of directors can authorize the company to purchase shares on the open market. This can be a benefit for investors. First, it indicates to the market that the directors believe the shares are undervalued and can cause the market price to rise in response. Second, it removes shares from the market, meaning that those remaining on the market are entitled to higher earnings because dividends are not paid to treasury shares.

Treasury shares can be resold on the open market at any time to raise money for the company. This would have the opposite effect as the repurchase program. The market would believe the company is hurting for money and respond by lowering the price paid for the stock. More likely, the shares will be redistributed as stock options or through employee profit sharing plans. These are viewed more positively by the market, although the shares are again collecting dividends once they are redistributed. There is more about these diluted shares in the income statement chapter.

Following the shareholders' equity section is where the balance sheet actually balances. By adding liabilities to shareholders' equity, the total is the same as the total on the asset side of the equation. In the Pretend Toys example, total assets equal $644,700, and liabilities plus shareholders' equity equals $644,700. If the equation "assets = liabilities + shareholder equity" is not proven here, the company needs either a new chief financial officer or a major upgrade to the accounting system.

What You Can Learn From the Balance Sheet

In addition to the ratios in Chapter 7, the best way to view a balance sheet is by comparing it to previous years:

- Growth in cash and cash equivalents is good.

- Too much growth in debt is likely bad.

- Growth in shareholder equity is good.

- Compare accounts receivable between years. A growing company will have growing receivables, but they should be in proportion to cash on hand.

- Look to see that current liabilities are not growing faster than current assets. This can be a sign of real trouble. It could mean loans are being used to keep the company operating.

Much of the learning from financial statements comes from comparisons between the different statements. Changes in inventory levels make a good example. Dramatic increases in inventory on the balance sheet from one period to another can mean that products are not selling well. Or does it? The reader needs to determine if sales decreased or went flat or if inventory is increasing to keep up with rising sales. Quite possibly the product is selling very well, and inventory must keep pace. The needed information will be found on the income statement.

The Income Statement

I t is called big business because the amount of money changing hands is enormous. This is most visible on the income statement. Proctor & Gamble manufactures and distributes common consumer items. Its annual report shows over $68.2 billion in sales for 2006, a 20 percent improvement over 2005 when sales were a mere $57.7 billion. Of the $68.2 billion, P&G reported 2006 earnings of $8.68 billion, equating to a 12.7 percent profit margin. Obtaining this information and more takes nothing more than a quick glance at the income statement.

Getting from sales revenue to the profit earned is not difficult. Simply start with sales and subtract all the expenses and taxes to arrive at net earnings, which is the profit. Finding the profit margin only requires dividing earnings by sales and multiplying by 100. Proctor & Gamble's profit margin is calculated as ($8.68 ÷ 68.2) x 100 = 12.7%.

Profits and Losses Over Time

The SEC requires the current year's income statement and those from the previous two years to be presented for analysis. A common technique for evaluating five years of a company's income statement is to use the current one and the statement from two years ago. Between the two statements, readers view a total of five years' worth of information.

The income statement is only an estimate of the profit or loss during the period because it relies on accrual accounting where cash transactions have not been completed. A company bordering between a profit and loss or experiencing a small profit one quarter and a loss the next must question its profitability. Sustained profitability is the only way to be sure the company is truly profitable when using accrual accounting. Companies on the edge of profitability are susceptible to pushing the GAAP envelope to appear profitable each reporting period. Comparing net earnings over time is the best way to detect if profitability is sustainable.

Disclosure Requirements

SEC disclosure or reporting requirements vary by industry. Different information is required from commercial industries, the investment industry, employee stock purchase plans, insurance companies, and banks. The primary operations of the investment, insurance, and banking industries include earning revenue from investments. Earnings from investments are specifically excluded from operations of commercial industries (hence the need for different reporting rules). The income statement information presented here primarily deals with the details of commercial industries (manufacturers, retailers, and service providers):

1. Net sales and gross sales — Net sales are gross sales less any discounts, returns, or allowances.

2. Costs and expenses that specifically apply to sales

3. Other material costs and expenses applicable to sales not included in item 2

4. Selling, general, and administrative expenses

5. A provision for doubtful accounts

6. Any general expenses not captured in items 4 and 5

7. Non-operating income including dividends and interest earned on securities, as well as profits net of losses on the sale of securities

8. Other interest earned and debt expenses

9. Non-operating expenses

10. Earnings or losses before accounting for income taxes

11. Income tax expense

12. Income from consolidated (majority or wholly owned) subsidiaries

13. Dividend or other income from minority (unconsolidated) ownership in subsidiaries

14. Earnings or losses from continuing operations

15. Earnings or losses from discontinued operations

16. Earnings or losses before extraordinary items and the cumulative effect of any accounting practice changes

17. Identify extraordinary items less applicable taxes

18. The accumulative affects of changes in accounting principles

19. Net earnings or losses

20. Earnings per share

Not all this information must appear directly on the income statement. The SEC allows some of the details in the notes section. This information also appears on GAAP-conforming income statements for private companies with the exception of earnings per share, which is not GAAP required.

Single- and Multiple-Step Formats

There is no absolute format for income statements as long as the required information is presented. However, two easily distinguishable formats are commonly used, the single-step and multiple-step formats.

The single-step format collects all the revenue at the top of the statement, followed by grouping the expenses separately. Total expenses are subtracted from total revenue to obtain net income. Key information that managers and investors need to see is not presented with the single-step format.

The multiple-step format groups earnings with related expenses. COGS immediately follows sales to reveal gross profit. All other expenses are

Single-Step Income Statement
Revenue:
Net sales
+ Rent revenue
+ Interest revenue
= Total revenue
Expenses:
COGS
+ Salaries
+ Depreciation
+ Rents
+ Interest
+ Income taxes
= Total expenses
Total revenue
- Total expenses
= Net income

subtracted out, except taxes, to arrive at operating profit or earnings before income tax (EBIT).

Readers of a single-step income statement have all the needed information but must convert it to the more useable multiple-step format.

How to Count Revenue

The first line is either gross or net sales. There is a difference. Gross sales include everything sent to the customer on an invoice. The equation is simple: Price x Quantity = Gross Sales. Discounts, warrantees, and returns are unknown at the time of sale. Net sales are adjusted for unknowns.

A retail customer may be entitled to return to the manufacturer any products not sold. This creates change in the original sale reported under accrual accounting. Any returns along with warrantee obligations must be subtracted from gross sales to determine net sales.

Allowances include volume and cash discounts. A buyer might be entitled to a volume discount when multiple orders reach a certain volume. Cash discounts are given for prompt payment of the bill. Each company sets its own cash discount policy. An example is original sales terms for the full invoice amount to be paid within 30 days. As an incentive to pay sooner, the customer may be offered a 3 percent discount if the bill is paid within five days or a 1 percent discount if the bill is paid within ten days. These billing policies can be changed anytime to entice customers to pay faster. Managers will increase the

Multiple-Step Income Statement Format
Net Sales
− COGS
= Gross Profit
− Selling & administrative
− Depreciation & amortization
− Other operating expenses
= Operating profit
− Income taxes
= Net income

CHAPTER 4: THE INCOME STATEMENT

discount if the company is having cash flow problems while simultaneously slowing cash going out of accounts payable. Conversely, profits can be increased by lowering or eliminating cash discounts.

Volume discounts often are called trade discounts. No discount might be offered on the first $20,000 in merchandise that a customer purchases. A trade discount of 2 percent can be offered for purchases between $20,000 and $50,000, and another discount becomes effective above $50,000.

Both the cash and trade examples vary, limited only by the needs and creativity of management to make sales and generate cash flow. Much is unaccountable when the original sale is made but adjusted retrospectively. This is another reason accrual accounting can only estimate profits but not determine cash on hand.

Cost of Goods Sold

Net Sales Calculation
Gross Sales
− Sales Returns
− Allowances
= Net Sales

COGS is expected to be the largest expense on the income statement. This represents the cost of the business's primary operations. Specific costs are included and excluded from COGS. Materials, labor, and direct overhead are counted, but advertising and administrative costs are not. Direct overhead varies with the amount of production occurring. Subtracting COGS from net sales gives the gross profit margin. Management watches this number closely because this represents the profit available to cover all other expenses. Dividing gross profits by net sales and multiplying by 100 gives the gross profit percentage. The Pretend Toys gross profit percentage is 38.3 percent: (355,000 ÷ 925,000) x 100.

If management needs to increase the gross profit, the product selling price can be increased, less expensive materials can be substituted, or labor costs can be reduced through automation or outsourcing. A service company performs the same calculation, but there will be less material and more labor costs associated with delivering the service.

COGS can be calculated easily using the current balance sheet and the balance sheet from the previous reporting period. Beginning inventory and purchases during the period are added together to determine what was available to sell during the period. The ending inventory is subtracted, leaving the amount actually sold. There are several ways to value inventory, but all are based on the cost of materials purchased plus labor expended.

Other Inventory Valuations

The way a business chooses to value inventory can have a material effect on profits and other ratios. The inventory valuation method each company uses will be included in the notes section of the financial statements.

FIFO and LIFO are frequently used inventory valuation methods, but others also are used. Average costing is accomplished by dividing the total manufacturing costs of all units in inventory by the number of units in inventory. Pretend Toys has 1,000 rocking horses, and it cost $10,000 to manufacture them; the average cost is $10 per rocking horse regardless if the cost of wood decreased or increased during the period. This method is best used by high-volume manufacturers with modest volatility in manufacturing costs.

Calculating COGS
Beginning Inventory
+ Purchases
= Goods available to sell
− Ending Inventory
= COGS

Specific costing is suitable to large-ticket items. A car dealership records the cost of each car purchased for inventory. When a particular car is sold, the specific purchase cost of the car is subtracted from inventory.

The lower-cost or market method is another method retailers use. It can defer income taxes into future years if the product's market price decreases.

Accurately costing inventory has a major effect on income and profits. Because the IRS is interested in collecting taxes on income, management is not free to change the inventory valuing process anytime. Changes require permission from the IRS, which is not easily granted. Any of the allowed methods will result in the same accumulative profit and taxes over time. However, frequently changing inventory methods can be used to lower profits and taxes from evening out over the years. The IRS strongly prefers companies select a method and use it year after year.

Operating Profit

After determining sales and COGS, the next step in the income statement is subtracting out selling, administrative, and depreciation costs to arrive at operating profits or EBIT. This number represents the costs associated with producing, marketing, and delivering the product to customers. It is the sum total of the company's expenses before taxes.

Both the gross and operating profits are of interest to investors as well as managers. Investors want to compare these numbers among companies they are considering for investment. By excluding interest and taxes, the comparison shows the efficiency of each company's operations. Operating profit is also useful to investors for evaluating management's ability to utilize the business's assets. Excluding interest expense, interest income, income taxes, and other non-operating transactions provides a clean profitability view of internal operations. Operating profits are frequently used in return-on-investment calculations.

Management has considerable leeway in affecting the operating profit. Often, internal operating profit reports are broken down by product line to reveal the profitability of each product. Focus can be placed on selling the most profitable products, while cost reduction efforts increase the profitability of less profitable products. Long-term profitability can be increased by encouraging volume sales that result in fewer transaction costs and lower freight costs. Over time, fixed costs can be reduced to improve operating profitability. Management can effect changes on almost anything above the operating profit line.

Similar to the balance sheet, companies select how much information to divulge on the income statement based on industry norms and specific needs. A company might include an expense line specific to fuel rather than to group it in COGS if transportation costs are a large portion of conducting business. Another company might separate labor and supplier costs if efforts are being made to reduce one or both of them.

Other, Interest, and Taxes

Other income and expense lines come after operating profit but before taxes. Other income can be interest on loans, sale of an asset, and other sources not associated with operations. Additional information about other income and expenses is in the notes.

Interest expense almost always has a separate line on the income statement because it is a financial obligation that cannot be avoided and is associated with the level of risk the company is taking.

Companies with ongoing or significant litigation may provide another line for these expenses. Alternatively, litigation might be captured in a single line labeled "other expenses," which can include obsolete inventory or financial losses resulting from closing a plant, along with other items.

Once the business's total income and expenses are accounted for, a summary of earnings before taxes comes immediately before taxes on the multi-step income statement. Net earnings are found once taxes are taken out. Shareholders are entitled to this as a result of all business transactions during

PRETEND TOYS INCOME STATEMENT FOR QUARTER ENDED SEPT. 30, 2007 (MULTIPLE STEP)	
Net Sales	$925,000
COGS	570,000
Gross Profit	355,000
Selling & administrative expenses	145,000
Depreciation expenses	17,750
Operating Profit (EBIT)	192,250
Interest expense	8,600
Earnings before taxes (EBT)	183,650
Taxes	64,278
Net earnings	$119,373
Common shares outstanding	150,000
Earnings per share	$0.80

the period. However, the company rarely distributes all the earnings to shareholders. Some or all is retained for growth and other needs.

Earnings (The Bottom Line)

Pretend Toys does not have any preferred stockholders, but if it did, the preferred stock dividend would be subtracted before calculating earnings per share for common stockholders. Dividends are not an expense but a distribution of earnings; therefore, preferred stock dividends come out after the bottom line is determined. Recall that preferred stockholders are guaranteed a dividend before common stockholders can be paid.

The earnings-per-share number, sometimes called the basic earnings per share, is important to investors. No matter how large a profit the company earns, individual investors benefit based on the earnings per share times the number of shares owned. In the case of Pretend Toys, a shareholder with 1,000 shares benefits 10 times more than the owner of 100 shares.

Often there is a second earnings-per-share line for diluted shares. Diluted common shares include the potential for additional shares to be included in the company's ownership at a future date. Sources of this potential ownership include convertible preferred shares, convertible bonds and other debt, stock options, and warrants.

Basic earnings per share always will be more than diluted earnings per share unless no convertible securities are outstanding. It is rare for large companies not to have convertible securities outstanding. Diluted earnings are a conservative or worst-case scenario because it is unlikely that all will be converted to shares. However, if the company does exceptionally well, an increased number of people holding these convertible securities will exchange them for an ownership position in the company.

Some companies include dividend per share following earnings per diluted share. Subtracting dividend per common share from earnings per common share reveals the retained earnings per common share.

Why Cash Accounting Is Not Used

The Christmas sales season makes a good example using Pretend Toys' quarterly income statement to reveal the importance of accrual accounting in keeping revenue and expenses grouped into the same period. Pretend Toys ramps up production during the late spring and summer to meet the Christmas toy demand. Half of the company's annual sales come from Christmas sales. However, most of the toys are manufactured between late spring and summer. Sales to retailers occur in August and September with shipping occurring in October and completed by early November. Most of the payments are received during October.

By reporting sales in the month they occur, accrual accounting groups the sales in the same period as the toys were manufactured, and the cost to manufacture is incurred. The result is a $177,500 operating profit. Looking at cash accounting for sales over the same period shows an operating loss of ($238,750) because payments are not received until the month after the accounting period ends. However, costs for materials, labor, and other expenses were paid during the accounting period.

Administrative and depreciation expenses also must be paid during the business quarter and before payments are received. EBIT under the accrual method is a profit of $136,813 and under the cash method is a loss of $279,438. The pattern of a profit for accrual accounting and loss for cash accounting continues as interest and taxes are subtracted from each side. The IRS does not care which accounting method is used; the accrual method pays $47,132 in taxes for the quarter. No taxes are due under the cash method, but they will be next quarter when the cash is received.

At the bottom line, the results are predictable. The $87,531 profit for the accrual method works out to $0.58 per share when divided by the outstanding common shares. More than half of the annual profit was earned during this period that cash accounting does not show.

The cash side shows a major loss for the quarter and negative earnings per share of $1.88 during the quarter that the company made more than half of its annual sales. This drives home the importance the role accrual accounting plays in being able to create meaningful financial statements.

Drawing Conclusions From Income Statements

Because income statement information is used in many different ratios and analyses, it is important to adjust for unusual items often found on income statements, especially statements of large companies. These are extraordinary and nonrecurring items that only affect the statement during one reporting period and are not expected to be repeated. One of the most frequently found is discontinued operations. Discontinued operations come from a management decision to close a plant and outsource production or completely cease operations. There will be many initial expenses the company must pay upfront, but it expects to more than recover these by reducing the cost of goods or must do this to discontinue a product that is no longer profitable. Another nonrecurring item results from selling or purchasing a subsidiary. Other examples include early repayment of long-term debt or terminating a pension plan. In all examples, the company does not expect the event to be repeated on future statements. These are brought to investors' attention so that adjustments can be made, enabling accurate comparisons between the current and previous or future statements.

When comparing years of data, readers should be sure that management does not slip recurring losses

PRETEND TOYS INCOME STATEMENT FOR QUARTER ENDED SEPT. 30, 2007		
	Accrual	Cash
Sales	$462,500	$46,250
COGS	285,000	285,000
Gross profit	177,500	(238,750)
Selling and administrative expenses	36,250	36,250
Depreciation expense	4,438	4,438
Operating Profit (EBIT)	136,813	(279,438)
Interest expense	2,150	2,150
Earnings before taxes (EBT)	134,663	(281,588)
Taxes	47,132	0
Net earnings	$87,531	(281,588)
Common shares outstanding	150,000	150,000
Earnings per share	$0.58	($1.88)

into the unusual events category. Claiming a foreign currency exchange loss is an unusual event. If a company does business in foreign currency, the loss or gain needs to be treated as ongoing business.

Tips for Reading Income Statements

- Subtract out or add back any unusual events before making comparisons, for both year-to-year comparisons of one company and for comparison with other companies.

- Convert dollar values to percentages to accurately compare companies. Spreadsheets are great for this task. For each company determine the net profit, gross profit, EBIT, and EBT.

- Analyze each company over multiple years (current profit / previous profit) x 100 = percentage change.

- Always read the notes and management discussion and analysis (MD&A). If you cannot understand it, do not invest.

- Pay attention to product lines in the MD&A. It is good to find highly profitable product lines growing in sales volume, but be concerned when low-profit product lines dominate sales.

- Yahoo Finance provides a good source of industry ratio averages for comparing individual companies against the entire industry: **http://biz.yahoo.com/ic/ind_index.html**.

Shortcomings of Income Statements

- Management can manipulate both revenue and expense reporting, which can affect the statement's accuracy.

- Revenues are not cash until the money is in the bank.

- Changes in inventory valuation methods can alter the numbers on an income statement dramatically.

- The income statement is an aggregate of financial transactions with little or no detail available for evaluation. The largest companies display tens of billions of dollars on each line. Significant discretion exists in how this is reported.

Income Statement — Balance Sheet Relationship

Recall the balance sheet is a snapshot in time of the company's results since it began, and the income statement describes what occurred for a specific period. The income statement results are added or subtracted to the accounts of the previous balance sheet to determine the company's financial position at the end of the current period, but the correlation is not direct.

As payments shown as sales revenue on the income statement are converted to cash, some will be kept as cash or equivalent, and some will be used to make payments on other accounts. This affects accounts payable on the liabilities side of the balance sheet. Some will be used as payment on forward accounts like insurance and leases, affecting the prepaid expenses on the asset side. Other cash receipts will be invested back into the company to purchase equipment and other assets. These show up as an increase in company assets on the balance sheet. Hopefully, some of the money will be shown one time on the balance sheet as dividends paid to shareholders and then be gone from the company's accounting system forever.

Business is dynamic and continues even when the accounts are closed for the accounting period. Some payments from sales shown on the income statement have been received and applied toward the balance sheet accounts, while some of the payments will be received in the next accounting period and be applied at that time. At best, while the income statement greatly affects the balance sheet, the relationship is indirect.

The most direct relationship exists with depreciation. The depreciation charged over the period on the income statement should equal the depreciation added to the accumulated depreciation on the balance sheet from the previous period. Depreciation shown on the income statement is for that specific period. What is shown on the balance sheet is accumulative until the asset is scrapped or sold.

Summary

The income statement is an estimate, particularly of revenues at the top and earnings at the bottom. Allowances, discounts, and nonpayment of accounts receivable all go toward lowering the final revenue and ultimately the final earnings. Assuming accurate accounting is performed, the expenses recognized by the accrual method are the most reliable figures on the statement. Still, there could be future adjustments to expenses for volume discounts or returns that the business receives from suppliers.

Income statements are presented in either single- or multiple-step form. The single-step statement can be converted to multiple-step, more useful to the reader, by rearranging the revenue and expense accounts and doing the math to obtain gross profit, operating profit, and earnings before taxes.

Of the five inventory methods to determine COGS, FIFO and LIFO are most often used. Though seldom done, it is possible to change methods. A change from LIFO to FIFO causes an immediate rise in earnings by lowering COGS. The first income statement this change appears on likely will show an increase in earnings. Remember, this is only an accounting change. There is no corresponding increase in revenues. The change uses cost data that are several years old and subtracts them from today's inflated revenue. If the accounting change is not caught in the notes, it will be discovered by reviewing several years of statements because this one-time dramatic earnings improvement cannot be repeated on a recurring basis.

Gross profit and operating profit are important because management has direct control of the operations that produce these numbers, which are best converted into percentages for comparison over multiple reporting periods. Steady improvement demonstrates good management practices, while erratic and declining changes show lack of management control.

There is a strong but indirect relationship between the income statement and balance sheet. Because both statements rely on accrual accounting, cash, the lifeblood of business, cannot be discerned.

CHAPTER 5

The Statement of Cash Flows and Statement of Shareholders' Equity

Despite the SEC's creation in 1934 to improve business's financial accountability to shareholders, not until 1987 did the statement of cash flows become required reporting (replacing the statement of changes in financial position). As critical as cash is to business, many private companies elect not to produce or distribute a statement of cash flows.

The concept of cash flow is simple. Positive cash flow occurs when more cash flows into the business than flows out. Therefore, negative cash flow is when more cash flows out than in. These depend on real transfers of cash, whether the format is electronic, check, or cash transactions. Here, the financial statements depart from accrual accounting, although cash flow has its own peculiarities, like positive cash flow resulting from taking out a loan and negative cash flow when loans are repaid. It is an examination of the corporate checkbook rather than profitability.

The Importance of Cash Flow

An exaggerated example illustrates the importance of cash flow. A business investment of $100,000 that loses 1 percent every year will still have $5 remaining after 1,000 years. This assumes that the 1 percent loss is on the capital remaining from the previous year. The first year's loss is $1,000. The loss in year 1,000 is only $0.05. Of course, the remaining value of assets in year 1,000 is a mere $5, probably the value of a pencil stub in inflated dollars. After 100 years of losses, the business still has $36,973 in assets. An important point is that losses are determined after all expenses are subtracted from revenues. The example shows that even a business with continuing losses can provide employment and other benefits for a long time if the cash keeps flowing. Although managers and employees can benefit from employment by a company with adequate cash flow that is losing money, investors will stay away. Companies without profits rarely pay dividends, and investments vaporize as the stock value drops.

The Sources of Cash Flow

The cash flow statement is divided into three sources of cash inflow and outflow: operating, investing, and financing. The income statement chapter points out operations as the most important business activity, which also applies here. Most cash flow should occur in the operations activity section. Below, "+" indicates cash flowing into the business, "−" indicates cash flowing out, and "0" indicates a non-cash transaction not affecting flow.

Cash Flow From Financing Activities

Cash flow from financing and investing cannot be overlooked. Financing activities involve transactions between the business and lenders and between the business and shareholders. Common transactions include:

+   Increases in long- or short-term debt

−   Reductions in long- or short-term debt

−   Paying dividends to shareholders

+   Selling treasury stock on the open market

−   Purchasing stock for stock repurchase programs

+   Selling preferred stocks or issuing bonds

0   Converting bonds or preferred stock into common shares

0   Converting long-term debt into short-term debt

The financing activities section can reveal if a company is in financial trouble. Watch for companies with limited profits and cash flow that are making early payments on long-term debt. This indicates a lender has called in a loan early based on information the reader probably lacks. Rarely is this good news. The business might be failing to maintain loan ratios specified in the covenants or have fallen behind in payments. More evidence of this might be found in the investing activities section if the company is forced to sell assets to pay off the debt early.

Exceptionally high positive cash flow from financing activities also can warn that a company is having trouble. Management taking out large loans that the notes identify as "working capital" it can indicate that cash flow is not adequate to sustain day-to-day operations. The reader should expect large loans to be taken out to finance expansion or growth opportunities that management willingly explains. Large companies like Ford Motors and several airlines have been financing operations with loans for several years — running up enormous debt that will need to be repaid before owners receive any benefits from the business. In reality, this should be just as visible on the income statement because the company will be operating at a loss rather than a profit. The cash flow statement gives the reader insight as to how much the company is borrowing, if this is in fact occurring.

Good news is found when large amounts of money come out of financing activities to pay shareholder dividends. This is especially encouraging if the income statement verifies the company is highly profitable. Paying dividends comes at the expense of financing growth, so if the business's strategy is growth, paying dividends might lead to growth by borrowing money. All remains fine as long as profits and cash flow support both.

Cash Flow From Investing Activities

Cash flow from investing generally covers assets the company uses for operations and investments. Common effects on cash flow are:

-   Cash payment for equipment, factories, or other assets

+   Receiving cash from selling equipment, factories, or other assets

0   Purchasing assets by issuing debt

-   Cash used to buy subsidiaries or stock of other companies

+   Cash received by selling subsidiaries or stock of other companies

-   Loaning money

It can be difficult to determine the meaning of major changes without a management explanation. When there are significant changes, the management discussion and analysis, as well as the notes, are expected to explain. A company should be replacing worn-out equipment and upgrading technology. Buying or building a factory easily costs millions or tens of millions of dollars. This might be daily business for companies that have billions of dollars in revenue, but for many companies, a new factory is an unusual event that needs communicating to investors.

The unexpected sale of a factory or equipment should alarm investors because it can relate directly back to the previous example of selling assets to pay off loans. The same applies to unexpectedly selling a subsidiary or stock in another company. However, there can be several positive reasons for selling these assets. Maybe management bought an ailing company at a bargain price with a plan to reinvigorate it and sell it at a premium. That simply would be executing management's plan.

Clearly, a significant change in cash flow from both investing and financing requires a management explanation to put it into perspective.

Cash Flow From Operating Activities

The cash flow statement operating section is where readers expect to see the most activity. Many experts contend the most important line from all four financial statements is positive cash flow from operations.

+ Selling products or services for cash

0 Selling products or services on credit

− Paying cash for inventory, labor, and supplies

0 Purchasing inventory and supplies on credit

+ Receiving dividends or interest from investments

+ Collection of accounts receivable

0 Recognize cost of goods sold

− Payment toward accounts payable

0 Accrue operating expenses

− Pay operating expenses

0 Accrue taxes

− Pay taxes

0 Accrue interest

− Pay interest

− Prepay expenses with cash

0 Write off prepaid expenses as they are realized

0 Write off depreciation and amortization as they are realized

SFAS 95 issued by the FASB requires interest payments and receipts be classified as operating expenses, not including payment of the principal portions of loans. Interest is considered an expense to benefit operations.

Direct or Indirect Cash Flow Calculation

Cash flow can be calculated directly or indirectly. The FASB prefers the direct method. However, more than 90 percent of public companies use the indirect method because it is less revealing about interest payments and interest receipts. The differences between the methods exist only in the important operating activities section of the statement.

The direct method determines net cash flow from operations by subtracting the sum of operating cash payments from the sum of operating cash receipts. The needed information can come directly from the accounting system or be calculated by adjusting asset and liability accounts from the balance statement. The main difference between direct and indirect is showing cash flow for interest payments and receipts using the direct method and only implying it with the indirect method.

The indirect method adjusts net income (from the income statement) by calculating changes in accounts from the previous period to the current period to determine operating activity cash flow. An increase to the receivable account is negative cash flow, while an increase in accounts payable is positive. Depreciation, amortization, and share-based compensation are added back in because they are non-cash transactions that did not require cash to be paid out. Deferred taxes also are added back because these have not yet been paid.

There is no direct accounting for interest received and paid because net earnings rather than cash from sales is used as the beginning point before changes in accounts

DIRECT METHOD
Cash Flow From Operations
+ Cash from sales
− Cash paid to suppliers
− Cash paid to employees
+ Interest received
− Interest paid
− Income tax paid
+ Other operating related cash received
− Other operating related cash paid
= Net cash flow from operating activities
Cash Flow From Investing
− Asset purchases
+ Asset sales
− Investments and acquisitions purchased
+ Investments and acquisitions sold
− Other investing cash paid
+ Other investing cash received
= Net cash flow from investing
Cash Flow From Financing
+ Cash from borrowing
− Loan payments (principal only)
− Stock repurchase program
+ Sales of stock
= Net cash flow from financing

INDIRECT METHOD
Cash Flow From Operations
Net earnings
+ Depreciation and amortization (non-cash)
+ Deferred taxes
+ Share-based compensation (non-cash)
+/− Change in accounts receivable
+/− Change in inventory
+/− Change in accounts payable, accrued, and other liabilities
+/− Change in other operating assets and liabilities
+/− Other
= Net cash flow from operations

are made with the indirect method. In accordance with SFAS 95, interest transactions must be summarized in the notes when using this method.

PRETEND TOYS COMBINED BALANCE SHEETS 2006 AND 2007					
Assets			Liabilities		
	2007	2006		2007	2006
Current Assets			Current Liabilities		
Cash	$120,000	$95,000	Accounts Payable, trade	$130,000	$99,500
Accounts Receivable	64,250	28,430	Accounts payable, other	1,000	3,750
Inventory	240,000	170,000	Accrued expenses	2,500	9,000
Prepaid Expenses	34,853	9,900	Short-term debt	1,000	4,000
Total Current Assets	459,103	303,330	Income tax payable	87,500	65,600
			Total current liabilities	222,000	181,850
Property, plant, and equipment			Long-term debt	90,000	95,500
Land, buildings, and equipment	270,000	255,000	Stockholders' equity		
Less accumulated depreciation	40,500	22,750	Capital stock	150,000	150,000
Net land, buildings, and equipment	229,500	232,250	Retained earnings	236,603	117,230
Other assets	10,000	9,000	Total stockholders' equity	386,603	267,230
Total assets	$698,603	$544,580	Total liabilities and stockholders' equity	$698,603	$544,580

Pretend Toys Statement of Cash Flows

The cash flow is a result of changes in the balance sheet accounts from one period to the next. Using the balance sheet from the beginning and end of the two periods, along with the income statement, reveals more detail about the statement of cash flow.

The balance sheet shows a cash increase from 2006 to 2007 of $25,000 ($120,000 – $95,000). Though not required, the actual change in cash often is shown at the bottom of the cash flow statement.

The income statement shows $925,000 in sales, but the

PRETEND TOYS INCOME STATEMENT FOR YEAR ENDED JUNE 30, 2007	
Sales	$925,000
COGS	570,000
Gross profit	355,000
Selling and administrative expenses	145,000
Depreciation expense	17,750
Operating Profit (EBIT)	192,250
Interest expense	8,600
Earnings before taxes (EBT)	183,650
Taxes	64,278
Net earnings	$119,373
Common shares outstanding	150,000
Earnings per share	$0.80

statement of cash flow shows only $819,180 received as cash, the difference being $105,820. The first place to look for the difference is in the inventory accounts and accounts receivable on the balance statement.

Ending accounts receivable	$ 64,250
Beginning accounts receivable	– $ 28,430
Change in accounts receivable	= $ 35,820
Change in inventory	+ $ 70,000
Difference in sales and cash	= $105,820

The calculation below uses the indirect method to find cash generated from sales. Recall the indirect method provides more information about the cash generated from operating activities. Use the indirect method in the operating section to find income taxes paid in cash. Beginning and ending taxes are found on the balance statement, while the

Sales	$925,000
+ Beginning accounts receivable	28,430
− Ending accounts receivable	64,250
+/− Change in inventory	70,000
= Cash from sales	$819,180

taxes owed for the period are found on the income statement. Simple addition and subtraction reveals taxes paid in cash is $42,378.

Beginning taxes payable	$65,600
+ Taxes for the period	$64,278
− Ending taxes payable	$87,500
= Taxes paid in cash	$42,378

Switching to the direct method reveals more detailed information. Payments to suppliers of $245,000 and $315,000 to employees, for a total of $560,000, can be extracted from the accounting system. Knowing the $570,000 for COGS shown in the income statement is for sold goods, the remaining $10,000 ($570,000 − $560,000) is a portion of accounts payable and accrued expenses.

The interest paid under operating activities is interest only on the debt the company is carrying. The principal payments for the debt are found in the financing section of the cash flow statement. The 2007 balance sheet shows $1,000 in current debt. The change in long-term debt is a decrease of $5,500 (95,500 − 90,000), which was paid early. Information about these principal debt amounts will be found in the finance section of the cash flow statement.

Examining the investing section shows $16,000 cash used to increase property, plant, and equipment from $255,000 to $270,000. There is also a $1,000 increase in "other" assets.

The financing section shows a $1,000 short-term loan was taken out. The entire 2006

Ending short-term debt	$1,000
− Beginning short-term debt	$4,000
− Early payment of long-term debt	$5,500
= Cash from financing	($8,500)

PRETEND TOYS CASH FLOW STATEMENT FOR YEAR ENDED JUNE 30, 2007	
Cash flow from operations	
Cash from sales	$819,180
Payments to suppliers	(245,000)
Payments to employees	(315,000)
Interest received	0
Interest paid	(6,050)
Income tax paid	(42,300)
Other operating cash received	0
Other operating cash paid	(161,330)
Net cash from operations	49,500
Cash flow from investing	
Asset purchases	(16,000)
Asset sales	0
Investments purchased	0
Investments sold	0
Net cash flow from investing	(16,000)
Cash flow from financing	
Cash from borrowing	1,000
Loan payment	(9,500)
Stock repurchase program	0
Sales of stock	0
Net cash flow from financing	(8,500)
Increase in cash	25,000
Cash balance June 30, 2006	95,000
Cash Balance June 30, 2007	$120,000

current debt of $4,000 was paid, and $5,500 of long-term debt was paid early. The resulting cash flow is a negative $8,500.

In sum, most of Pretend Toys' cash is generated from operations. Pretend Toys is profitable with adequate cash flow. Sales are increasing, and cash earnings are financing inventory growth to meet increased sales demand. Increases in property, plant, and equipment are financed with long-term debt, some of which is paid back early. Factory construction and equipment purchases are in place to enable growth. Occasional short-term debt can bridge gaps in cash flow, while management works to improve it. The asset growth increases shareholder equity, but the growth cost currently prevents the company from making dividend payments.

How Managers Improve Cash Flow

Managers have several techniques available to improve cash flow:

- Speed up the collection of accounts receivable by tightening credit policies, offering cash discounts, adding late charges to delinquent accounts, and pressuring delinquent accounts to pay (often the persistent company gets paid first).

- Choose between discounting prices to increase sales or increasing the selling price to improve the profit margin. The right choice will increase cash flow.

- Use factoring — selling accounts receivable at a discount to a finance company that collects the outstanding accounts.

- Slow down payables by taking full advantage of suppliers' credit offerings.

- Renegotiate loans to extend payment periods.

- Practice accurate inventory control that minimizes inventory on hand, thus reducing cash tied up in inventory.

- Accurately and carefully plan major expenditures, like factory expansions and deferring projects, with questionable paybacks.

- Convert debt to equity, bonds, and preferred stock convertible to common stock — lowering debt repayment expenses.

What to Learn From Cash Flow

- First, look at the bottom line to see if cash has increased or decreased, which can indicate the company's financial health.

- Determine how much money the company brought in versus reported as earnings.

- Look to see if cash receipts are changing in proportion to earnings over several reporting periods.

- Examine operating activities to learn if the company is running a healthy core operation that by far provides the majority of cash flow. A company with little or no cash generated from operations is probably in big trouble.

- Look at investing activities to be sure the company continues to invest in itself. New assets are necessary to replace the old and to grow the company.

- The financing activities can tell a lot about the company. Low operating cash flow along with significant borrowing or stock sales warns of a death spiral. A stock repurchase program often offers increases in price for stocks that remain outstanding.

- Compare cash flow with other companies in the same industry. A company with inferior cash flow will have difficulty meeting obligations during economic downturns.

- Review statements of cash flow because they offer less opportunity for management to manipulate the numbers than the income statement does.

Managing a Project With Cash Flow Projections

Detailed knowledge of future positive cash flows eases the budgeting for major projects. Often, the time when business is booming is also the time when cash runs short. Major contracts often require cash for upfront expenses that become handsome cash profits months later. This is a time when many private businesses look to banks for short-term loans. With some careful planning, the savvy businessperson accurately can forecast near-term cash flow to minimize the amount to be borrowed. This can even be a deal saver for a company close to exceeding its borrowing limit.

A small company landed three major projects that would take four months to complete, but they were staggered enough so all three completion dates would be met. Each contract called for a deposit the month it began and the balance to be paid at the end of the month it was completed. The manager knew that a bank loan was needed to cover expenses between

ORIGINAL LOAN CALCULATION	
Project 1	
Expense Month 1:	$13,000
Expense Month 2:	$2,000
Less Deposit	$5,000
Loan Amount	$10,000
Project 2	
Expense Month 2:	$17,000
Expense Month 3:	$5,500
Less Deposit:	$10,000
Loan Amount:	$12,500
Project 3	
Expense Month 3:	$32,500
Expense Month 4:	$5,000
Less Deposit:	$15,000
Loan Amount:	$22,500

when down payments were made and the final payment was received.

Expenses were estimated as part of the bidding process for the contracts. Total expenses for all three projects came to $75,000. The deposits totaled $30,000. After subtracting the difference, the manager concluded a loan for $45,000 was needed.

The manager observed that the loan requirements were spread out over four months and though a line of credit would be the best solution to reduce the amount of time the money was borrowed. Short-term loans can be expensive, and he wanted to keep as much of the profit as possible. Upon further thought, he realized that using cash flow from the beginning project to finance the second and third projects would reduce the amount he needed to borrow. He created a simple spreadsheet to forecast the cash flow from all three projects. The spreadsheet projects cash received and used to pay expenses for each project over the four months he knew there would be a cash shortage.

ORIGINAL LOAN TOTAL	
Loan 1:	$10,000
Loan 2:	$12,500
Loan 3:	$22,500
Loan Total:	$45,000

In the first month, a $5,000 deposit would offset partially the $13,000 in expenses and require an $8,000 loan to bridge the gap.

FORECASTING PROJECT CASH FLOWS		Month 1	Month 2	Month 3	Month 4
Project 1	Cash Receipts	$5,000	$20,000	$0	$0
	Cash Expenses	$13,000	$2,000	$0	$0
	Net Cash Flow	($8,000)	$18,000	$0	$0
Project 2	Cash Receipts	$0	$10,000	$20,000	$0
	Cash Expenses	$0	$17,000	$5,500	$0
	Net Cash Flow	$0	($7,000)	$14,500	$0
Project 3	Cash Receipts	$0	$0	$15,000	$35,000
	Cash Expenses	$0	$0	$32,500	$5,000
	Net Cash Flow	$0	$0	($17,500)	$30,000
Accumulated Cash		($8,000)	$3,000	$0	$30,000

He was pleased to learn that the $20,000 final payment from the first project plus the $10,000 deposit on the second project fully covered all the expenses in the second month and left $3,000 in accumulated cash to be used during month three.

In month three, he would receive the $20,000 final payment for the second project and the $15,000 deposit for the third project. This, along with the accumulated $3,000 from month two, would cover expenses in month three.

MONTH 3 AVAILABLE CASH	
Month 2 Surplus:	+ $3,000
Project 2 Final Payment:	+ $20,000
Project 3 Deposit:	+ $15,000
Subtotal	= $38,000
Project 2 Expenses	- $5,500
Project 3 Expenses	- $32,500
Cash on Hand	= $0.00

In month four, the third project would be paid in full for $35,000, and he would spend $5,000 for expenses, leaving $30,000 profit. The $30,000 would be used to fund expenses for future projects without another loan.

Through this simple cash flow calculation, the manager was able to reduce the loan amount from $45,000 to $8,000. The savings in interest charges is substantial: If the entire $45,000 had been borrowed over four months at a compounded interest rate of 11 percent, the interest charge would have been about $1,673. Through cash flow projection, the loan is reduced to $8,000 and repaid after one month. The interest charge drops down to about $28, a savings of $1,645 that becomes profit.

Statement of Shareholders' Equity

As business owners, shareholders are interested in their equity position. For stockholders in large corporations, the statement of shareholders' equity covers several accounts. However, smaller corporations can present changes in equity with just a few lines using the statement of retained earnings format.

Mega Corp. Shareholders' Equity

Presented first is the complicated large-corporation format. Begin with the first and last line of numbers in the chart on page 102. The first line provides the account balances from the previous period. In this example, the beginning balances are from year-end 2005. Each subsequent row of numbers shows changes that occurred in each account to arrive at the balances for year-end 2006.

Each row shows an activity affecting shareholders' equity, and each column represents the account affected. The first account is the number of shares outstanding or publicly owned. That column is the only one without dollar values. This is the number of shares outstanding. All the other columns are dollar values for each account.

At the end of 2005, Mega Corp. had one million shares outstanding. During the year, the company sold 3,000 shares that were exercised as executive bonuses, and 5,000 shares were sold as part of the employee stock ownership plan (ESOP). These 8,000 shares (3,000 + 5,000) became outstanding again and are eligible to collect dividends as well as vote at the annual stockholders' meeting.

MEGA CORP. STATEMENT OF SHAREHOLDERS' EQUITY					
	Common Shares Outstanding	Additional Paid in Capital	Treasury Stock	Retained Earnings	Comprehensive Gains
Balance Dec. 31, 2005	1,000,000	$10,000,000	($100,000)	$25,000,000	$2,900,000
Tax Benefit Related to Share Based Plans		35,000			35,000
Shares Paid Out (options)	3,000	25,000	75,000		100,000
ESOP Shares Paid Out	5,000	65,000	100,000		165,000
Treasury Shares Repurchased	(10,000)		(330,000)		(330,000)
Net Earnings				5,000,000	5,000,000
Cash Dividends Paid Out				(1,000,000)	(1,000,000)
Balance Dec. 31, 2006	998,000	$10,125,000	($255,000)	$29,000,000	$3,970,000

The board of directors authorized and the company purchased 10,000 shares on the open market as part of a stock repurchase program. These likely will be used in the future for distribution as stock options and sold through the ESOP. Based on what was sold and repurchased during the year, there were 998,000 shares outstanding at the end of 2006.

The treasury stock account is a contra account to the additional- paid-in-capital account. Because the additional-paid-in-capital account originally funded the treasury stock account, the two work in conjunction with each other. The treasury account records purchases and sales of the company's own stock. When the treasury stock is sold for more than what was paid to buy it, the difference is added to the additional-paid-in-capital account. As an example, the 3,000 shares paid out as stock options were sold for $100,000 but only cost $75,000 when purchased on the open market. The gain of $25,000 counts as additional paid in capital that adds to shareholders' equity.

The same is true for treasury shares sold through the ESOP. If the treasury account receives more than was paid for the stock, the balance is recorded as additional paid in capital.

In 2006, $165,000 worth of treasury shares were sold through the ESOP

ADDITIONAL PAID IN CAPITAL	
Option price total	$100,000
Treasury stock purchased total	- $ 75,000
Additional paid in capital	$ 25,000

($100,000 treasury account + $65,000 additional capital account). The ESOP also provides a tax benefit to the company. This resulted in a $35,000 tax benefit that also is counted as additional paid in capital.

While sales from the treasury account bring cash into the account, repurchase transactions cost the treasury account $330,000 to buy 10,000 shares on the open market.

The net earnings line comes directly from the bottom line of the income statement. Any dividends paid are subtracted from earnings to determine accumulative retained earnings at the end of 2006. Often a single line is used that shows only the retained earnings for the year.

The comprehensive gains column on the far right shows the accumulative affect from each transaction row. The bottom right comprehensive gains box is the total gain (or loss) in shareholder equity for the year. This number is specific to the period presented. It is not cumulative from past years. When all the stock activity, net earnings, and dividend activities are added and subtracted, total shareholders' equity increased by $3,970,000 for year-end 2006.

Pretend Toys Retained Earnings

Companies without the complications of treasury stocks, options, and ESOP can simplify this financial statement greatly by using the statement of retained earnings format.

Retained earnings from the previous period are taken from the balance sheet, and net earnings from the current income statement are added. Any dividends that are declared must be

PRETEND TOYS RETAINED EARNINGS YEAR ENDING JUNE 30, 2007	
Retained earnings June 30, 2006	$117,230
Net earnings June 30, 2007	119,373
Total	236,603
Dividends declared	0
Additional paid in capital	$ 25,000

subtracted out. What remains are the accumulated retained earnings. The period's retained earnings are easily determined by subtracting any dividends from the period's net earnings. Because Pretend Toys did not declare a dividend, the period's retained earnings are equal to net earnings of $119,373.

Retained Earnings Is Not Cash

A simple example demonstrates that retained earnings and cash are completely separate accounts within the business. This helps clarify why businesses keep some or all of the earnings rather than pay it out to shareholders as dividends.

Balance sheet changes make the best example because it contains cash, paid in capital, and retained earnings accounts. Although balance sheets typically are updated monthly, quarterly, and annually, they can be updated at any time. Here the balance sheet is updated after each business transaction. For simplicity, all transactions are made in cash without using credit accounts.

Step 1.

Assume an opening balance sheet with $1,000 of paid in capital.

Assets		Liabilities & Equity	
Cash	$1,000	Liabilities	$0
		Paid in Capital	$1,000
Total Assets	$1,000	Total Liabilities & Equity	$1,000

Step 2.

Purchasing inventory for $500 cash makes this change to the balance sheet.

Assets		Liabilities & Equity	
Cash	$500	Liabilities	$0
Inventory	$500	Paid in Capital	$1,000
Total Assets	$1,000	Total Liabilities & Equity	$1,000

Step 3.

The inventory is sold for $800 cash, which produces net earnings of $300 ($800 – $500). The $300 of net earnings becomes retained earnings.

Assets		Liabilities & Equity	
Cash	$1,300	Liabilities	$0
		Paid in Capital	$1,000
		Retained Earnings	$ 300
Total Assets	$1,000	Total Liabilities & Equity	$1,300

At this point, retained earnings appear to be the same as cash. The important point is to observe that cash and retained earnings are two separate accounts on opposite sides of the balance sheet. Although the $300 will remain in the retained earnings account, the $1,300 in cash is invested easily in other assets, still keeping both sides of the statement balanced.

Step 4.

Cash is used to purchase more inventory to be sold and invested in equipment the business needs to improve efficiency.

Assets		Liabilities & Equity	
Cash	$1,300	Liabilities	$0
Inventory	$ 600	Paid in Capital	$1,000
Equipment	$ 200	Retained Earnings	$ 300
Total Assets	$1,300	Total Liabilities & Equity	$1,300

The business could have made a decision to invest in advertising and inventory instead of inventory and equipment. The advertising would be recorded as an administrative expense. Regardless how the cash is invested on the asset side of the balance sheet, the retained earnings on the right side do not change. Although retained earnings and net earnings are repeatedly seen on the financial statements, they do not represent cash that the business can easily distribute to shareholders at any moment.

A well-run business constantly is using available cash for investments intended to create more earnings. This includes purchasing more inventory for sale, increasing factory capacity, adding new product lines, opening stores in new geographical locations, and many other opportunities that require investing cash generated from earnings. Businesses keep only enough cash on hand to meet near-term obligations or liabilities. The rest either is paid to shareholders as dividends or is reinvested with the intention of increasing earnings.

Summary

Businesses constantly seek to grow. Financing the growth has many different variations but generally involves either financing growth from earnings or borrowing and repaying the loan from earnings. Large growth plans often require companies to accumulate cash from earnings for one or more years. This can be accomplished by repeatedly investing retained earnings in other companies' stock until enough is available to complete the growth plan. The other companies' stock is sold on the open market to convert it back into cash. These activities are found in the investing activities of the statement of cash flows.

Some companies combine borrowing and retained earnings to finance growth. Borrowing is found in the financing section of the statement of cash flow, and the amount of retained earnings for the period is found on the statement of shareholders' equity or the statement of retained earnings. However, the interest paid for borrowing money is found in the operating activities section of the statement of cash flow.

Although not often done, established companies can sell stock shares on the open market to raise additional cash. The source of stock can be a new offering, stock previously authorized but not yet sold, or stock previously sold and repurchased as treasury stock. These transactions are found under financing activities on the statement of cash flow.

Other Uses of Cash

- Pay down debt
- Pay legal judgments and litigation costs
- Stock repurchase programs
- Mergers and acquisitions

Dividends

The board of directors authorizes every dividend payment to shareholders. Once the company pays out a dividend, the money is lost from the company forever. When public companies begin paying dividends, they are reluctant to discontinue paying them because shareholders begin depending on dividends as a return on their investment. This additional return on investment is quickly added to the price paid for the company's stock on the open market.

Rarely does a company pay the full earnings as a dividend. Even the largest conglomerates seek further growth and continue using a portion of retained earnings for this purpose while also paying dividends. As earnings continue to grow from business expansion, dividend payouts normally grow gradually also.

Even when paying a regular dividend, certain economic conditions can create a situation where a company accumulates large amounts of money that it cannot find appropriate places to invest. Long-term, it is not acceptable for a company to keep the earnings that shareholders are entitled to. This can lead to payment of a special one-time dividend. Microsoft found itself in this position in 2004. By 2003, Microsoft had amassed $49 billion in retained earnings. Plans for the money primarily included investing in emerging technologies to grow earnings. Microsoft also had several pending lawsuits centering on the monopolistic nature of its software. The lawsuits were settled without judgments, requiring payouts anywhere near the $49 billion in cash the company had retained. Microsoft was not able to find other appropriate investments for the retained earnings. In 2003, Microsoft began paying dividends for the first time but continued to hoard large amounts of money that needed to be invested or paid out to stockholders. In 2004, Microsoft finally declared a special dividend that distributed $32 billion to shareholders at rate of $3.00 per share. At the time, the regular dividend was $0.08 per share.

Dividend yields, earnings yield, total debt to total assets, and many other important ratios are revealed in the next chapter. Being able to read financial statements is only the beginning of digging out all the useful information they contain. Ratio analysis provides the ability to track one company over multiple financial periods and enables comparing two different companies with each other.

CHAPTER 6

Financial Ratio Analysis

Ratios create revealing relationships between two or more numbers from financial statements. Converting the numbers into percentages or ratios enables numbers from the company's financial statements to be analyzed for several purposes. The primary three purposes are better understanding the current reporting period performance, comparing current period performance with past performance (trend analysis), and comparing one company's performance with another's performance.

When comparing the results of different companies, it is important that they be in the same basic time frame when both companies were operating under similar economic conditions. Because companies have different financial years, it is not always possible to compare results from the exact same period. When comparing statements from slightly different periods, it is important to consider any economic impacts from the different periods. Businesses with peak sales during the Christmas season illustrate this importance. Comparing quarterly financial statements of one retailer with a financial first quarter ending in February with another that has a first quarter ending in May will not produce good results. The February first-quarter results capture Christmas sales, but the May first quarter results do not. The correct comparison is between the February first quarter and the fourth quarter of the previous year for the other company. Doing this captures the Christmas sales results of both companies.

Whenever possible, use annual financial statements that capture a full year of economic activity. Even if the companies have different financial years, the annual data capture the highs and the lows of the entire year.

Comparing companies in different industries is not appropriate because they operate under different conditions that affect the ratios. Even two companies in the same economic sector will have predictably different results during different economic conditions. Furniture stores and grocery stores are both in the retail sector. During an economic recession, sales for furniture stores will drop off significantly because purchases are discretionary while grocery store sales will remain relatively stable as consumers continue to purchase necessities. Profits from grocery stores are slim (0.01 percent industry average) but reliable, and profits for home furnishing stores are higher (4.90 percent industry average) but less reliable.

Yahoo Finance offers valuable industry information at **http://biz.yahoo .com/ic/ind_index.html.**

From there, choose the industry you are interested in analyzing and then find the "industry browser" link. This industry-specific Web page provides key ratio averages for the industry and top companies within the industry. Comparing company ratios with the industry's averages lets the business manager know how her business performed compared to the overall average. Comparisons to leading companies and competitors are also possible. The investor gains similar knowledge. Industry leaders can be easily identified and the purchase price of stocks assessed against earnings, profitability, and several other key ratios.

Categories of Ratios

Financial ratios are classified according to the information they provide. Commonly used classifications include Liquidity Ratios, Financial Leverage Ratios, Asset Turnover Ratios (also known as efficiency ratios), Profitability Ratios, and Stock Valuation Ratios.

Six Most Used Ratios

These six ratios include one important calculation from each of the five categories of ratios plus a second ratio from the profitability category. After all, the primary business of business is to make a profit. Besides profitability, two ratios seek to determine if the company is financially positioned to remain in business; one examines efficient use of assets, and another examines the stock price on the open market.

By themselves, these six ratios do not provide enough information to make decisions, but they do provide a beginning point to indicate if further analysis is warranted. Investors and managers have very different reactions to the same numbers. Investors finding these numbers unacceptable will decide the company is a bad investment and either look elsewhere, if seeking a new investment opportunity, or decide to sell their ownership if they already own shares. Alternatively, shareholders can dig deeper into the numbers to prepare hard questions about why they should continue ownership. The questions can be posed to their financial adviser or the company's board of directors at the annual shareholders' meeting.

Investors pleased with the first numbers will dig further into the ratios to learn the whole story and either continue stock ownership or seriously consider buying. The opposite should occur when a manager finds unacceptable numbers here. Rather than turn away, it is time to dig much deeper to learn the cause of unsatisfactory numbers and find a solution to the problem. Managers satisfied with the numbers should continuing working toward improving them.

Current Ratio

This ratio is used to determine a business's ability to meet near-term debt. It is of particular interest to lenders providing short-term credit. Lenders typically expect the ratio to be above 1.0. From the lenders' perspective, the higher the better. A value of 1.0 indicates the business has an amount of liquid assets available equal to current debt and can meet financial obligations during the next year.

> **Current Ratio = Current Assets / Current Liabilities**

Risk-adverse investors and conservative managers also desire the current ratio to be above 1.0. Aggressive investors believe a better return is achievable if more assets are invested rather than liquid. Inventory is included in current assets, which means the inventory must be sold to pay upcoming debt. For this reason, some financial statement readers prefer the quick ratio, which removes inventory from the equation. Paying current debt is critical to staying in business. There are several different ways it is measured. The quick ratio and cash ratio are found in the liquidity ratio section of this chapter. Both numbers are necessary to calculate the current ratios and are easily found on the balance sheet for the appropriate year.

The 2007 Pretend Toys balance sheet provides a current ratio of 458,353 / 221,250 = 2.1. For comparison purposes, the 2006 balance sheet current ratio is 303,330 / 181,850 = 1.7

A ratio of 2.1 in assets available to pay current liabilities shows that Pretend Toys is in a strong financial position and improving over 2006. One question that needs answering is why the company does not invest the assets or pay some to shareholders as dividends.

P/E Ratio

The price-to-earnings (P/E) ratio is used to assess if the cost to purchase the stock on the open market is acceptable to the amount of money the company is earning.

Current Stock Price / Earnings per Share = Price-to-Earnings Ratio

Earnings per share for the denominator of the equation come from the income statement. The current stock price does not appear on any of the financial statements. For publicly traded companies, the current stock price can be found in many different media. Most daily newspapers print closing stock prices from the previous day. The name of the stock exchange a specific stock trades on and the stock symbol need to be known to find the closing price in a newspaper. It is simpler to find the stock's price by looking it up on the Internet (**http://finance.yahoo.com/**). There is a symbol look-up button to find the stock symbol based on the company name and no need to know the stock exchange where it trades. Clicking on the symbol links to a page displaying the dollar value for the most recent stock trade. Several important ratios and other financial information about stock are shown, including the P/E ratio.

The current stock price for private companies must be provided directly from the company, which is much more difficult to obtain. An important piece of information to have along with the stock price is the time the company was last valued to establish the price and how it was determined.

Although not a public company, for calculation purposes, a fictitious stock price of $10 per share will be used. The 2007 P/E ratio is $10 stock price / $0.80 earnings per share = 12.5 P/E.

This tells the reader that other stock purchasers are willing to pay 12.5 times for each dollar the share earned. The stock price for public companies fluctuates during the trading day, and each change affects the P/E ratio. Tracking the P/E ratio over several weeks reveals what the overall market expects of future earnings. An increasing P/E ratio indicates buyers of the stock expect future earnings to increase. A decreasing P/E ratio indicates future earnings are expected to decrease. As no one can be sure about future earnings, this is just another indicator among the many available.

Acceptable P/E ratios depend very much on the industry being analyzed. Technology companies usually have high P/E ratios because they are expected to grow earnings rapidly, while utility companies tend to have stable earnings and lower P/E ratios.

Net Profit Margin

Often called the profit margin, this ratio is expressed as a percentage.

> **Profit Margin = Net Income / Revenue x 100**

Net income is again the bottom line on the income statement, and revenue is the top line from the same statement. All the expenses in between the top and the bottom lines determine the profitability of the company. Profit margin is the percentage from each dollar of sales that the company has available for retained earnings or to pay shareholders as a dividend.

Pretend Toys' 2007 profit margin is $119,373 / $925,000 x 100 = 12.9%.

Profit margins vary greatly from one industry to another, as well as from one company to another within the same industry. There are many causes for the variation. Some utility companies must comply with government oversight that caps the profit margin. Other companies have different financial structures where a high debt load adds considerable expense that must be paid from revenues. A company's pricing strategy for products largely impacts profits. Competition applies economic pressure that can keep prices low. Companies always are looking for a unique product that buyers are willing to pay a premium to purchase. Competition, financial structure, business expenses, and what buyers are willing to pay all affect the profit margin.

Profits also can be cyclical. A new and highly profitable product usually attracts other companies to imitate the product and eventually drives prices down. Products also go through a maturity cycle where they are highly profitable for a period but eventually have lower profitability as newer products come onto the market. Train transportation is an example of a long product cycle because it was highly profitable for decades when the world's richest men owned railroads. Eventually, people shifted to long-distance travel by cars and airplanes, which caused train transportation profitability to disappear. High technology often has a very short profitability cycle. Expect the new hot-selling gadget that enters the marketplace today to be replaced by a new, improved gadget next year.

Companies investing heavily in research and development of future products incur expenses that lower profits from products they sell today. Product mix, advertising, and internal control of expenses all have an effect on the profit margin. The profit margin is best viewed in context with other information about the company and what is expected to be the future profit margin. A company currently enjoying a high profit margin but expecting a significant increase in expenses often will see the price of stock decline based on future expenses. A company with a low profit margin about to introduce a new, profitable product will see stock price rise.

Debt-to-Equity Ratio

A measure of financial leverage, the formula for this ratio is:

Total Liabilities / Shareholder Equity = Debt to Equity Ratio

Both total liabilities and shareholder equity are found on the balance sheet. Pretend Toys' 2007 debt-to-equity ratio is $311,250 / $ 386,603 = 0.81.

This is an important part of a company's financial structure. The ratio tells readers how much debt the company is carrying per each dollar of shareholder equity. The Pretend Toys example shows that for every dollar of shareholder equity the company has $0.81 of debt. The theory behind this ratio is that by borrowing money the company will acquire resources that increase earnings beyond what can be accomplished with only the shareholders' investment. Two important considerations go into determining if management will successfully achieve this goal: First, how the borrowed money is invested determines how much earnings are increased. Second, no interest is paid for investors' money, but interest is paid on borrowed money. That means the resources purchased with borrowed money first must earn enough to pay the interest rate, and only what is earned above that amount adds value to the company. Success is achieved only when management decisions earn more money than it costs to borrow. Borrowing usually occurs over time. Ideally, a company will borrow when interest rates are low and refrain when rates are high. Long-term debt also can be tied to inflation with adjustable interest rates. Interest rate information is included in the notes of financial statements.

A ratio of exactly one means that shareholders equity is exactly equal to the amount borrowed. In theory, if the company goes out of business the lenders would be repaid everything and investors would receive nothing. In reality, assets would likely sell at fire sale prices, and the lenders would receive less than full value, while the investors still received nothing. A ratio higher than one divulges that a company has borrowed more money than investors have in equity. This can be rewarding to investors if properly used, but lenders often demand a high interest rate in return for the additional risk. A ratio below one shows less borrowed than shareholders have in equity. The result is a lower interest expense needing to be paid, allowing the company to retain more from sales. The ratio varies by industry and company but generally ranges between zero and two. A zero ratio shows no borrowing and a ratio of two shows twice as much borrowing compared to shareholders equity.

Return on Assets

Often called ROA, the formula for this ratio is:

$$\textbf{Net Income / Total Assets = ROA}$$

Net income comes from the bottom line of the income statement and total assets from the balance sheet. Pretends Toys' 2007 financial statements produce an ROA ratio of $119,373 / $697,853 = 0.17. Multiplying by 100 will express this as a percentage, the same as profit margin is expressed. For Pretend Toys, total assets returned 17 percent in earnings for the financial year ending in 2007.

This number tells readers how successful management is at converting resources into profits. Total assets comprise resources acquired with both investors and borrowed money. Using some complicated math, a proportional relationship with the debt-to-equity calculation shows how much of the ROA percentage comes from assets acquired from investors' funds and how much comes from borrowed funds.

The 0.81 debt-to-equity ratio tells readers that for every $1.81 of assets owned, $1 comes from investors and $0.81 comes from borrowing. The proportional relationship between ROA and debt to equity is:

$$\frac{1.81}{1} = \frac{0.17}{x}$$

Solving for x is accomplished by multiplying 0.17 on the right side by 1 on the left side and dividing by 1.81. The answer for x is 0.09 or 9 percent. In the proportional relationship, the 9 percent (x) is proportional to 1, which is the shareholders' portion of every $1.81 in assets. Therefore, 9 percent of the 17 percent ROA is generated from shareholder assets. Subtracting 17% − 9% = 8% shows 8 percent of the ROA was generated from borrowed money. This emphasizes that borrowed money is contributing almost as much to income as the shareholders' investments.

The higher the ROA, the better management is doing at earning a profit from resources. Two companies earning a profit of $100,000 but with different amounts of resources available have different ROAs. A company with $400,000 in assets has an ROA of 25 percent while a company with $600,000 in assets has an ROA of 16.6 percent.

Naturally, ROAs vary greatly from one industry to another. Consider the vast assets needed by an automobile manufacturer with factories all over the world. Contrast that with an Internet retailer that sells and ships products from a single warehouse to customers all over the world. If both have net income of $1 billion, the ROA for the Internet retailer will be much higher than that for the automobile manufacturer. Significantly different amounts of investment were required to earn the same profit.

Operating Margin

Also known as operating profit margin, the formula for operating margin is:

Operating Income / Net Sales = Operating Margin

The numbers for both the numerator and the denominator come from the income statement. Pretend Toys' 2007 operating margin is $192,250 / $925000 = 0.21.

Like the net profit margin, multiplying this by 100 and thinking of it as a percentage works best. This number shows the company's profitability from operations without considering interest and tax expenses. It is a measure of overall company efficiency. Leaving interest and taxes out of the equation makes this measure appropriate for measuring against other companies in the industry. A company with a higher operating margin is earning more profit than a company with a lower operating profit when non-operating expenses are removed from the equation.

These six ratios quickly pinpoint if a company is performing reasonably. Several more ratios provide additional insight to financial leverage, liquidity, efficiencies, profitability, and stock values.

Financial Leverage Ratios

It should be understood that businesses often use borrowed money for a variety of reasons. Several ratios compiled from the financial statements measure the different accounts involving debt. Previously explained debt to equity belongs in this group, along with the following.

Debt Ratio

Total Debt / Total Assets = Debt Ratio

Pretend Toys' 2007 debt ratio is $311,250 / $697,853 = 0.45. Its 2006 debt ratio is $277,350 / $544,580 = 0.51.

Also known as the debt-to-asset ratio, this number is similar to the debt-to-equity ratio except total assets are used in the denominator. Both numbers come from the balance sheet. Key to understanding the ratio is which side it rests on compared to the number one. Pretend Toys' debt ratio is less than one for both 2007 and 2006, showing that the company has more assets than debt. In fact, it has substantially more assets than debt, indicating conservative financial leverage that would be acceptable to many lenders if earnings are also at an acceptable level.

A debt ratio above one shows that the company has borrowed more than the total value of all assets. A portion of the loans would be unsecured, meaning that if the business assets are sold to repay debt, not only would the shareholders receive zero back from their investment, but unsecured lenders would lose at least a portion of the money loaned. A debt ratio of two means twice as much is borrowed compared to the value of assets.

Interest Coverage Ratio

Operating Profit / Interest Expense = Interest Coverage Ratio

Pretend Toys' 2007 interest coverage ratio is $192,250 / $8,600 = 22.35.

Both the numerator and the denominator are found on the income statement. This ratio determines how easily the company is able to keep up with the interest payments on borrowed money. A value below one says that the business is not able to meet interest payments from operations income and probably faces defaulting on loans. Any number above one is the number of times a company has earnings to pay interest. Pretend Toys has enough earnings to pay interest 22.35 times. Keep in mind that interest is tax deductible for a business, which is why operating profit is used in this equation rather than net earnings after taxes. Most financial analysts believe a business with a ratio below 1.5 to be in serious financial trouble.

Receivable Turns

> **1. (Beginning Receivables + Ending Receivables) / 2 = Average Receivables**
>
> **2. Sales / Average Receivables = Receivable-Turn Ratio**

Pretend Toys' 2007 receivable turns are:

1. $28,430 + $63,500 / 2 = $45,965

2. $925,000 / $ 45,965 = 20.12 receivable-turn ratio

This is a two-step formula. First, the average receivables is found by adding the receivables found at the beginning of the period to the receivables from the ending of the period and dividing by two. These numbers are found on two different balance sheets. Second, sales are divided by the average receivables.

Sales are the top line of the income statement. The resulting ratio tells how quickly the company is turning credit sales into cash that can be used

CHAPTER 6: FINANCIAL RATIO ANALYSIS

to make loan payments, meet other obligations, and pay dividends. On average, Pretend Toys' credit sales were paid 20.12 times during the year.

Dividing 365 days by this ratio converts it into average days of credit: 365 / 20.12 = 18.14 average days of credit. This means that on average, Pretend Toys' customers pay their accounts after 18.14 days. The importance is having cash available for other uses. The lower the average days of credit, the less money is tied up. Comparing average days from one period to another explains if receivable accounts are being managed properly or if the company has changed its credit policy. Companies write credit sales off as bad debt after either 60 or 90 days. When average days of credit approach these numbers, it indicates the company is having trouble collecting money.

Payable Turns

1. (Beginning Payables + Ending Payables) / 2 = Average Payables

2. COGS / Average Accounts Payable = Payable Turns

Pretend Toys' payable turns are:

1. $99,500 + $64250 / 2 = $81,875

2. $570,000 / $81,875 = 6.96

This is another two-part formula where an average of accounts payable is created from the beginning and ending balance sheets. To keep an apples-to-apples comparison, only the accounts payable–trade account is used in the denominator because the numerator is COGS. The accounts payable–other account is ignored. The ratio shows that Pretend Toys pays off its supplier credit accounts 6.96 times per year.

Dividing 365 days by the ratio reveals the average number of days it takes to pay bills. Pretend Toys averages 365 / 6.96 = 52.43 days to pay its bills.

The higher the number, the longer the company is holding onto cash with the ability to invest it elsewhere. At just over 52 days, Pretend Toys has the capability to maximize the use of the money. The down side is that failing to pay suppliers in a timely manner can alienate suppliers. Suppliers with choices of customers to conduct business with will show a preference for customers that pay faster. Also, Pretend Toys is failing to take advantage of any cash discounts that suppliers might offer. Cash discounts lower COGS to increase gross profit. Profits and cash are not the same thing. Management must perform a juggling act to maximize both.

Operating Cash Flow Ratio

Cash Flow From Operations / Current Liabilities = Operating Cash Flow Ratio

Pretend Toys' 2007 operating cash flow ratio is $49,500 / $221,250 = 0.22.

Cash flow from operations is found on the statement of cash flows, and current liabilities come from the balance sheet. This ratio shows if cash from operations will meet short-term obligations. The entire story is not told by itself because a company normally has additional money available to pay bills. Remember the current ratio used cash, cash equivalents, receivables, and inventory in a similar calculation. Important here is that an operating cash flow ratio with a value less than one says the company cannot pay current liabilities with the cash generated from operations. Other sources of cash are needed to pay current liabilities; these include cash savings, cash coming in from receivables, and selling existing inventory. A ratio below one says that, long-term, the company must reduce spending to a level that cash from operations can support.

Pretend Toys substantially increased cash and receivable. Once accounts payable are paid down with these funds, the ratio completely changes.

$120,000 (cash) + $64,250 (accounts receivable) = $184,250

$221,250 (current liabilities) - $184,250 = $37,750.

Recalculating the operating cash flow ratio using the revised current liabilities reveals that Pretend Toys is not in as bad of a cash flow situation as originally portrayed.

$49,500 / $37,750 = 1.31.

A ratio above one says there is adequate cash flow from operations to cover current liabilities.

Liquidity Ratios

Liquidity ratios take a closer look at the business's ability to generate cash to meet near-term obligations. Liquidity ratios continue to stress the difference between adequate cash flow and profitability. A quick glance at the income statement shows if a company is profitable or not, but recall those numbers can be manipulated by management; however, it is much harder for management to show cash where there is none. The current ratio described in the six most used ratios belongs to this category.

Quick Ratio

(Current Assets – Inventory) / Current Liabilities = Quick Ratio

Pretend Toys' 2007 quick ratio is $ 458,353 - $ 240,000 / $221,250 = 0.99.

Also known as the acid test, the quick ratio is a conservative variation of the current ratio to determine if a company is able to meet near-term liabilities. By removing inventory from the equation, it looks to see if bills can be paid from existing cash and accounts receivable. Any number below one tells the analyst that some inventory will need to be sold to pay current liabilities.

Receivables turns measured in days can be a factor here because it tells how long it takes after inventory is sold before the company expects to receive cash from the customer. A low quick ratio combined with a high number of days receiving payments from customers means the business will have trouble paying bills.

Pretend Toys' quick ratio of 0.99 says the company is close to meeting current obligations without selling more inventory but does not quite pass the acid test. The amount of inventory needing to be sold is easy to calculate. For Pretend Toys the amount of inventory that needs to be sold is $458,353 – $240,000 – $221,250 = ($2,897). Pretend Toys only needs to sell another $2,897 from inventory to meet all current liabilities.

Current Assets
- **Inventory**
- **Current Liabilities**
= **Inventory Sales to Meet Current Liabilities**

Cash Ratio

(Cash + Cash Equivalents)/ Current Liabilities = Cash Ratio

Pretend Toys' cash ratio is $120,000 / $221,250 = 0.54.

This ratio is more conservative than either the current ratio or the quick ratio measurements for determining a company's ability to pay liabilities because it excludes both inventory and accounts receivable. Cash equivalents are very liquid assets like stocks of another company that can be sold very quickly to raise cash. Cash ratios below one show that the company does not have enough cash and cash equivalents to meet current liabilities. Numbers above one say the company is in a strong financial position relative to current liabilities. A ratio of two indicates the company has twice the cash needed to meet obligations and management might instead choose to invest the cash or pay some out as a shareholder dividend.

Asset Turnover Ratios

If cash is the lifeblood of a business, assets are the body. How effective management is at converting assets into earnings is the primary reason for being in business. ROA is listed as one of the six most used ratios and belongs to this category. Creating the following ratios from financial statements further details how effectively management is running the company.

Return on Equity

Net Income / Shareholders Equity = Return on Equity

The 2007 return on equity for Pretend Toys is $ 119,373 / $386,603 = 0.31.

This ratio compares the company's earning to the amount invested by shareholders. For Pretend Toys, shareholder equity earned $0.31 for every dollar invested. Rapidly growing companies should see this number steadily increasing over the years. Mature and slow-growth companies will have little variation in this number. Since an important goal of business is to grow earnings, most investors seek a company that can steadily increase the return on equity.

Inventory Turnover

COGS / Inventory = Inventory Turnover

Pretend Toys' 2007 inventory turnover is $ 570,000 / $ 240,000 = 2.38.

The inventory turnover tells the reader how many times each year the equivalent of the company's entire inventory is sold. The importance of this number is that investors and managers do not want money tied up in inventory longer than needed. As long as sales are profitable, earnings will increase when more inventory can be sold.

The inventory turnover is converted to days of inventory when 365 days are divided by the inventory turnover ratio. The Pretend Toys' calculation for days of inventory on hand is 365 / 2.38 = 153.4 days. Theoretically, if Pretend Toys buys no more materials, it will take 153.4 days to convert existing materials into product and sell it.

Although all ratios vary by industry and company, this one can have the largest variation across industries. Recall that a manufacturer's inventory includes finished goods in the warehouse, work in process in the factory, and raw materials. Retailers' inventory is composed only of finished goods available for sale. Companies that primarily provide services usually have little or no inventory. Therefore, manufacturers are expected to have a lower turnover ratio than retailers, and service providers should have the highest turnover ratios.

Asset Turnover

Sales / Assets = Asset Turnover

Pretend Toys' 2007 asset turnover is $925,000 / $ 697,853 = 1.33.

This shows how efficiently assets are being used to generate sales revenue. The higher the number, the better. With assets in the denominator, both shareholders' equity and assets purchased with borrowed money are included in this ratio. Frequently low-profit-margin companies have higher asset turnover than high-profit-margin companies. The Pretend Toys example shows that, for every dollar of assets owned, $1.33 in sales is generated. This ratio is similar to ROA except sales revenue is the numerator here, and net income is the numerator in the ROA.

Profitability Ratios

Although considerable importance is placed on cash flow, the long-term profitability of a company is the most important measure. That is the reason for including two of the three profitability ratios in the six most used ratios (operating margin and net profit margin). Unprofitable businesses can survive for a long time when investors and lenders are willing to continue injecting cash. However, when the promise of profits disappears, so do the investors and lenders. This was a key cause of the Internet or dot-com bubble bursting in the early 2000s. That failed business model focused all efforts on rapid growth while ignoring the bottom line.

Gross Margin

Gross Profit / Sales = Gross Margin

Pretend Toys' gross margin for 2007 is $355,000 / $925,000 = 0.38.

Both numbers are found on the income statement. This ratio is the profit available when only the cost to produce or purchase products is considered. Pretend Toys made a profit of $0.38 for every dollar spent buying materials and manufacturing toys. This number is useful for comparing the operations efficiency of different businesses without considering the overhead, tax, and financing costs. If management reduces these costs, more profit becomes available to pass through to the bottom line. Also, if management is considering buying another company and restructuring overhead, this is a ratio to examine closely.

Indirectly it shows if a business is maintaining modern operations. Businesses that continually incorporate cost-reducing technology often have a higher gross margin. Those with outdated equipment and those that are heavily dependent on labor have a lower gross margin. The task for management is finding the right balance between the cost of upgrading technology and improving the gross margin.

Stock Valuation Ratios

Determining the value of stocks on the open market is a tricky task when the underlining requirement for a trade to occur is considered. For a trade to occur there must be a willing seller and a willing buyer. This implies that the seller believes the stock is valued at the right price to sell while the buyer believes it is the right price to buy.

Of course, there are many other underlying reasons that a trade occurs. Sellers may believe they have an opportunity to earn a better return elsewhere. The buyer and seller probably have different risk thresholds and different investing goals. Here, the many different ratios available to value stocks on the open market are presented. These ratios are also applicable to private companies if the financial data can be obtained.

The P/E ratio was included with the six most used ratios.

PEG Ratio

$$\frac{\text{P/E Ratio}}{\text{Annual EPS Growth}} = \text{Price to Earnings to Growth}$$

For the P/E ratio example, Pretend Toys' stock price was established at $10 per share, and the P/E was determined to be 12.5. This is the numerator for the equation. Determining the denominator takes more effort. The biggest challenge is estimating future growth of the earnings per share (EPS), clearly not an exact science. Estimating the future EPS is best left to professional analysts that specialize in specific industries and companies. It is known that Pretend Toys is working toward growing the company. To complete the calculation it is assumed the EPS growth rate will be 50 percent. The finished calculation becomes 12.5 / 50 = 0.25.

Because growth is critical to business and investing, knowledgeable analysts prefer the PEG ratio to the P/E ratio. The P/E relies only on historical data while the PEG anticipates the future. The PEG and several other ratios explained here are found on most Web sites that provide stock data on public companies. That is important because the expert analysis data have been incorporated, which significantly reduces the need for individuals to become experts on every company.

The number one is key to understanding what the PEG ratio discloses. A value less than one means the stock is undervalued based on projected earnings growth. A value over one occurs when the EPS is expected to decline. At 0.25, Pretend Toys is an excellent investment opportunity if management can achieve the projected 50 percent growth rate.

Generally accepted ranges for PEG are:

- **0.50 or less** — a buy opportunity if company management is likely to achieve growth
- **0.50 – 0.65** — worth considering buying
- **0.65 – 1.00** — There are probably better investment opportunities.
- **Over 1.00** — Consider selling if you already own it; future EPS is expected to decline.

Price / Sales Ratio

Share Price / Sales per Share = Price / Sales Ratio

Sales per share must be calculated for the denominator. Pretend Toys had $925,000 in sales and 150,000 shares or $925,000 / 150,000 = $6.17 in sales per share. Using the $10 share price, the ratio is $10 / $6.17 = 1.62.

The ratio shows how many dollars in sales the company has achieved compared to the stock price. This ratio ignores all expenses and varies significantly across industries. It has value in trend analysis for determining if sales per share are increasing and can be used to compare similar companies in the same industry.

Price-to-Book Ratio

Share Price / Book Value per Share = Price-to-Book Ratio

The book value per share is first calculated as:

$$\frac{\text{Total assets} - \text{intangible assets} - \text{liabilities}}{\text{shares}} = \text{book value per share}$$

Pretend Toys does not have intangible assets so the 2007 book value is:

$697,853 – $311,250 / 150,000 shares = $ 2.58 book value per share.

The price-to-book ratio is $10 / $2.58 = 3.88.

The lower the value, the better. Pretend Toys' ratio says the stock costs 3.88 times more per share than the value of company assets after all liabilities are paid. Generally, this ratio is preferred by value-orientated rather than growth-orientated investors. A lower value indicates the company might be undervalued by other investors if company management and the company's future are solid.

This ratio has more meaning to industries heavily dependent on tangible assets, like factories and vehicle fleets. Service industries have few assets to base the share price on. A low-asset but high-potential-earnings company is poorly represented by this ratio.

Another way to understand this ratio is if the company went out of business at these values, the investor could expect to receive $3.88 for every $10 invested after all liabilities are met.

Price-to–Cash Flow Ratio

> **Share Price / Cash Flow From Operations per Share = Price-to–Cash Flow Ratio**

The denominator first must be determined by dividing cash flow from operations by the number of shares. For Pretend Toys this is $49,500 / 150,000 shares = 0.33. Pretend Toys' $10 stock price is then divided by 0.33: $10 / 0.33 = 30.30.

This number shows that the stock costs $30.30 for each dollar of cash generated from operations. Many analysts prefer this ratio over P/E because of the ability for management to manipulate earnings. Recall that Pretend Toys has a P/E of 12.5, which is less than half of this ratio. This says that the company is showing more than twice as much in earnings than it is converting successfully to cash.

When comparing one company with another, the lower number is preferred because it shows the stock cost is lower compared to the cash the company is generating.

Dividend Yield

> **Dividend per Share / Price per Share = Dividend Yield**

Pretend Toys, like many young growing companies, does not pay a dividend. With a zero in the numerator, the ratio equals zero. More mature and well-established companies do pay a dividend. A company paying an annual dividend per share of $1 and having a stock price of $10 is paying a dividend yield of 10 percent ($1 / $10).

Investments in companies not paying a dividend anticipate growth will increase the share price. Companies not planning substantial growth pay earnings out as dividends. When two companies have equal growth, the company with a higher dividend yield is likely the better investment.

Earnings Yield

Earnings per Share / Share Price X 100 = Earnings Yield

Pretend Toys' 2007 earnings yield is $0.80 / $10 = 0.08 X 100 = 8%.

This is the annual earnings an investor acquires for each dollar invested in the company. It is the inverse of the P/E ratio. By expressing the value as a percentage, it becomes easier to determine what the earnings are for a given dollar investment. A $1,000 investment at 8 percent equals $80 of annual earnings.

What to Do With All the Numbers

Reading and analyzing the financial statements provides managers and investors with so much information that it can be overwhelming. Still, it is not enough information to make sound business and investment decisions. Steps can be taken to organize the information and use it in conjunction with the business strategy and other information that greatly simplifies decision-making.

Profits are essential to a business's long-term success, cash flow is critical to conducting daily business, and liabilities impact both profits and cash flow. Any analysis of a company needs to include some ratios that measure each of these segments. Once an investor determines a company poses an acceptable return on investment and meets his risk threshold, the investor needs stock valuation measures that determines if a stock is attractively priced.

Managers involved with a company having cash flow problems will focus heavily on the ratios that track cash flow. Those working to expand a

SAMPLE OF INDUSTRY RATIO AVERAGES

Industry Sector	Industry	Net Income	Current Ratio	Debt-to-Equity Ratio	Gross Profit	Return on Equity
Professional Services	Accounting	10.7%	1.4	1.5	90.2%	66.5%
Health Care	Hospitals & Residential Health Care	4.8%	1.4	1.5	88.0%	5.1%
Retail	Electronics & Appliance Stores	2.5%	1.8	1.2	35.1%	12.2%
Retail	Food & Beverage Stores	2.2%	1.2	1.9	24.4%	18.4%
Wholesale	Petroleum & Petroleum Products	1.3%	1.5	1.9	11.1%	7.8%
Construction	General Contracting	3.3%	1.4	1.7	14.7%	22.1%
Manufacturing	Pharmaceuticals & Medicines	14.4%	1.7	1.5	56.8%	22.8%
Manufacturing	Plastic Products	5.7%	1.6	1.5	32.2%	12.5%
Transportation	Air Transportation	5.7%	1.1	1.7	77.1%	22.4%
Financial	Savings Institutions	14.7%	0.6	16.5	94.6%	17.1%

Note: This information includes all U.S. corporations, both public and private. Private corporation data are compiled from federal income tax returns and dated because of the time required to compile them. These data should not be relied on for current research. They are provided only to demonstrate the different ratio ranges for a limited number of industries.

company want to see investments in assets growing while maintaining acceptable profit levels. A focus on improving profitability involves reducing liabilities and improving turnover of inventory, as well as accomplishing more with existing assets.

The next chapter looks at other information that is compatible with the ratio analysis and brings it all together for decision-making.

Investors can find almost all the ratios presented here on Web sites such as Yahoo Finance. Detailed company ratios are found by entering the company's symbol and clicking on the "key statistics" link. Comparable industry information is also available by going to **http://biz.yahoo .com/ic/ind_index.html**, clicking on the desired industry, and next clicking on the industry browser link. This information is primarily geared toward investors.

Managers needing industry ratios may need to compile it from several sources. Page 133 shows sample compiled data for a few select industries.

CASE STUDY: RATIO ANALYSIS AND HEALTH INDICATORS

Roger Bauer is founder and chief executive officer of SMB Consulting, Inc. Involved with small businesses since his early youth, Bauer obtained a bachelor of science in business administration from Sullivan University and embarked on a career helping small-business owners. Bauer has been featured in the *Louisville Business First* newspaper, and both he and SMB Consulting have been featured in the *Louisville Courier-Journal*.

His youth background is with a long-established family restaurant that was in business from 1870 to 1990 (120 years), which laid the foundation for an insatiable desire to learn about and improve businesses of all sizes.

Bauer has published numerous business articles on diverse subjects:

- Outselling Competition Before They Have Even Shown Up
- Helpful Hints Developing a Differentiation Strategy
- 5 Steps to Exceed Customer Expectations
- 6 Proven Steps to Prepare for the Complex Sale
- Increasing Your Company's Competitive Intelligence
- Gaining a Web Presence
- Many Others

He points out that small businesses without elaborate accounting systems or formal financial statements still can benefit from ratio analysis. From the most basic financial data a more detailed analysis can be developed. He guides readers to gain baseline insights about small-business statistics. A tool he uses and recommends is the Web site **http://bizstats.com/index.htm**, where small-business owners can benchmark their company financials against national averages. There are always exceptions to the averages; however, it is best to understand a valid exception and agree that it is desirable.

With his deep interest in ratio analysis, Bauer knows that a single set of numbers does not tell the whole story. Still, there needs to be a place to begin. He suggests for many small businesses it is with:

- Current Ratio
- Quick Ratio
- Inventory Turnover
- Sales to Inventory
- Collection Period
- Accounts Payable
- Industry-Specific Ratios

Just understanding the numbers does not help the business. SMB objectively conducts a full analysis to develop a strategic action plan. Each is unique to the

CASE STUDY: RATIO ANALYSIS AND HEALTH INDICATORS

business being analyzed. The plan focuses where the most benefit will be realized. It might be profiling the business's ideal customer and developing an effective marketing plan. It could be developing a customer loyalty program because a 1 percent improvement in customer satisfaction doubles profits in some industries. A differentiation strategy can be the right answer because there can be only one low-cost provider, and that company likely has the smallest profit margin.

Developing the strategic plan often involves gaining a better understanding of the competitive landscape. Competitor intelligence is invaluable for this purpose. It accomplishes two important objectives: One is to identify where the business is vulnerable to the competition. The other is identifying where the client business excels over the competition. The logical progression is a plan that reduces vulnerability and exploits advantages.

While each plan is customized to the business, frequent needs of small businesses include:

- Improve Upon Current Success
- Focused Direction for Action
- Cost Reductions That Enhance Profitability
- Appropriate Involvement by Senior Management
- Strategic Use of Technology
- Better Staff Training
- Quality People
- Effective Use of Consultants, VARs, Vendors, and CPAs
- Clearly Defined Vision That Employees Can Connect With and Are Motivated By

SMB conducted research and wrote a competitive intelligence report for a client in the highly competitive digital systems integration industry. The full report is 27 pages. Presented here is a high-level summary.

SMB Prepared Competitive Intelligence Report Summary

For each of the companies highlighted in this analysis, the following opportunities and threats apply:

SEGMENT OPPORTUNITIES	SEGMENT THREATS
• Expanding outsourcing to lower-cost markets (India, Mexico, etc.) • Leverage acquisitions to expand product offerings	• Competition (EDS, CSC, Accenture, IBM, HP, etc.) • Hardware becoming commoditized

CASE STUDY: RATIO ANALYSIS AND HEALTH INDICATORS

SEGMENT OPPORTUNITIES	SEGMENT THREATS
• Partner with smaller niche companies to penetrate additional markets	• Larger computer and/or software manufacturers shifting focus to services
• Expand commercial presence	• Convergence of Business Process Outsourcing and Infrastructure Outsourcing
• Expand further into outsourcing ($300B market with 8%–10% annual growth expected)	• Loss, or reduction, of business from existing clients
• Expanding electronic transaction business (47% of all transactions will be electronic by 2010)	• Deterioration of financial condition by existing client
• Further penetrate enterprise security market ($15B with 20% annual growth expected)	• Difficulties in executing acquisition strategy
• Unisys & EDS having problems with existing larger contracts — good opportunity for competition to penetrate some of their accounts	• Failure to manage operations or growth
	• Government clients — termination rights, audits, and investigations
• GM looking to go to multi-vendor strategy	• Pricing risks
	• Exercise of contract termination provisions and/or SLA penalties
• Government looking to renegotiate some of its larger IT contracts	• Loss of significant vendor relationship
• Better leverage intellectual capital to improve economies of scale	• Intellectual property infringement claims
	• Rapid technological changes
• Open Source/Linux offerings ($15B with 20% annual growth expected)	• Armed hostilities and terrorist attacks
	• Government budget fluctuations
• Microsoft Software Suite ($20B market with 10% annual growth expected)	• Disruption in utility or network services
	• Fluctuations in interest rates (Fortune 1000)
	• HP direct initiatives

It is evident that each company analyzed in this report has experienced the commoditization of hardware and technology with the lone exception of Unisys

CASE STUDY: RATIO ANALYSIS AND HEALTH INDICATORS

(which may explain one aspect of the company's recent struggles). The companies best equipped to handle this market in the future will accept this reality and adjust accordingly. It seems as though the successful companies have adopted a philosophy of discounting hardware rather heavily in order to gain pull-through services revenue as a result of the appreciating margins in the services sector. Prospective customers of these businesses often have the resources (specifically, easy access to the Internet) to accurately determine a provider's costs for the hardware they are purchasing and therefore measure a potential partner's mettle very early in the sales process. There is also more "shopping" of vendors even if there is a contract vehicle already in place for the goods and services desired.

SMB CONSULTING, INC.

4411 PEREGRINE PLACE

LOUISVILLE, KY 40241.

502-394-0460

info@smbconsultinginc.com

http://smbconsultinginc.com

CHAPTER 7

The Rest of the Financial Story

After reading the four financial statements and performing a ratio analysis, more information can be gleaned. The break-even analysis sheds light onto a business's profitability by relating the amount of sales necessary to cover overhead costs before a profit is generated. This analysis reveals actions to improve profitability and has several other applications where business managers can use it to improve profit decision-making.

Also explained in this chapter the notes that improve users' understanding of financial statements, along with management discussion and analysis (MD&A). MD&A explains what occurred within the business to create the financial results and provides management predictions. Financial statements are only a rear window to past performance. Forward-looking information forecasts financial performance and divulges business strategy. Readers use strategy information to assess management's ingenuity and probability of achieving the estimated financial performance. The reader also learns what information management provides that is best viewed cautiously.

Break-Even Analysis

The break-even analysis is an important tool in the investors' and managers' financial analysis toolbox. This tool is useful for predicting when an unprofitable but growing business will reach profitability, predicting when a business with declining sales will become unprofitable, finding ways to improve profitability, and forecasting the break-even point for a new business, a specific project, and new products.

The objective of a break-even analysis is to determine the level of sales that must be obtained to pay the fixed costs of the business. No matter how high the gross profit margin on sales, a certain volume of sales must be reached that covers all the fixed costs before a business begins making a profit.

The specific break-even analysis formula selected depends on if the overall business or a specific project is being analyzed. The basic equation is:

$$\frac{\text{Fixed Costs}}{\text{Gross Margin}} = \textbf{Break-Even Point in Sales Dollars}$$

The numbers to calculate the overall break-even point are on the income statement. Simple addition of line items from the income statement is needed to determine the fixed costs for the numerator. From the 2007 Pretend Toys income statement, the following fixed costs are added together:

Selling and administrative expenses	$145,000
Depreciation expense	$ 17,750
Interest expense	$ 8,600
Total Fixed Costs	$171,350

Recall that fixed costs are expenses not easily changed in the short term, including executive management salaries, mortgages, and loan payments. Special consideration must be given to taxes as a fixed cost. Income tax is not included in the basic break-even analysis because income tax is not paid until a profit is obtained. However, property taxes and sales tax would be included.

For the denominator, look back to the calculation for the gross margin (gross profit / sales). Pretend Toys' gross margin is 0.38 ($355,000 / 925,000). Recall that this is the ratio of each sales dollar available to pay all other expenses. The completed break-even calculation is $171,350 / 0.38 = $450,921. At the current levels of gross margin and fixed costs, Pretend Toys begins making a net profit only after sales reach $450,921.

The cost of running a business is not static. Changes in both fixed and variable costs will alter the result of the break-even analysis. If COGS rises due to increased material or labor costs, the gross margin will decrease, resulting in a higher break-even point. The break-even point will follow the direction fixed prices move long-term. Increasing fixed costs cause the break-even point to increase, and decreasing fixed prices lowers the break-even point. Almost always, there is some variation in both the fixed costs and the gross margin from one financial period to the next. Management's responsibility is to minimize the variation and ultimately increase profits by lowering the break-even point in any of three ways:

- Reducing fixed costs (eliminating salary positions, closing low-profit or unprofitable factories, reducing employee benefit costs, reducing distribution and marketing costs)
- Reducing variable costs (lowering labor costs through technology, negotiating lower supplier costs, substituting lower-cost materials, improving processes to increase output throughput at a lower cost)
- Increasing the sales prices of products

The best-managed companies combine all three methods in the pursuit of decreasing the break-even point and increasing profits. New businesses typically operate on a shoestring budget that results in low fixed costs. Careful budget control is also common when an established business expands into new markets or product lines. Businesses must be diligent about regularly conducting break-even analysis and find ways to improve profits.

Product Break-Even Points

Managers need to know the break-even point for a proposed new project or product before deciding to go ahead with it. Once that is determined, it can be compared with the sales forecast to ensure an acceptable profit is obtainable. Because these calculations depend on forecasted costs and sales, it is wise to have a safety margin between the break-even point and the total sales forecast. Determining the break-even point for a new or existing product uses the same formula. The only difference is existing products have historical data that improve the accuracy of the calculation, and new products rely on forecast data. The formula is very similar to the basic formula except it is calculated on a per-unit-of-product basis:

$$\frac{\text{Fixed Costs}}{\text{Sales Price Per Unit} - \text{Variable Price Per Unit}} = \text{Break-Even Point in Sales Dollars}$$

Finding the fixed costs of a product can be a challenge and certainly requires detailed information from inside the company. A company with multiple products assigns two sets of fixed costs to a specific product. First, a portion of corporate overhead will be assigned to each product. These vary by company but often include a portion of executive, administrative, insurance, and loan interest expenses shared across the entire company. There also can be a second set of fixed expenses specific to the product. A dedicated factory and equipment have the expenses directly attributed to the product along with any other fixed costs that apply only to it.

In the example of Pretend Toys, management is considering a new line of red wagons that will be manufactured on existing equipment in the same factory as other toys. Based on projected sales and planned production rates, it has been determined that 10 percent of the entire company's fixed costs are applicable to the red wagons. No additional fixed costs will be incurred. Finding fixed costs for this specific product only requires taking 10 percent of all fixed costs:

Selling and administrative expenses	$145,000
Depreciation expense	$ 17,750
Interest expense	$ 8,600
Total Fixed Costs	$171,350 X 10% = $17,135

The COGS or variable costs of labor, materials, and utilities is determined to be $15 per unit, and the sales prices will be $25 per unit. The break-even point is calculated at:

$$\frac{\$17,135}{\$25 - \$15} = 1,713.5 \text{ Units}$$

The break-even point in units can be converted to the break-even point in sales dollars by multiplying the break-even number of units by the sales price: 1,713.5 units x $25 sales price = $42,837.5 break-even point in sales dollars.

Forecasting Profits Using Break-Even Analysis

Calculations can be made to evaluate profitability based on different levels of sales. Once profitability is achieved, income tax comes into play and must be included in the equation.

All sales exceeding the break-even point are profit after subtracting COGS and income tax. Pretend Toys estimates sales of the red wagon at 28,000 during the next financial year. The effective corporate tax rate is 34 percent of profits. The other numbers needed are the product's profit per unit, which is the $10 ($25 – $15) in the denominator of the previous example, and the break-even point of 1,713.5 units. Forecasting the net profit for 28,000 units is determined with a simple four-step formula:

1. Total sales in units – break-even point in units = units sold at profit
2. Units sold at a profit x profit per unit = profit before taxes
3. Profit before taxes x tax rate = applicable taxes
4. Profit before taxes – applicable taxes = net profit

Pretend Toys' net profit from selling 28,000 units is calculated as:

1. 28,000 – 1,713.5 = 26,286.5 profitable units
2. 26,286.5 profitable units x $10 profit margin = $262,865 profit before taxes

3. $262,865 profit before taxes x 34% tax rate = $89,374 in taxes

4. $262,865 profit before taxes – $89,374 in taxes = $173,491 net profit

Project Break-Even Variation

There are two basic types of business projects that the break-even analysis can be applied toward. The first is very similar to the product break-even point except that which is deliverable to the customer is a service

$$\frac{\text{Fixed Costs}}{\text{Project Sales Price} - \text{Variable Cost of Project}} = \text{Break-Even Point in Dollars}$$

or result of the project. The only things that change are the words used to describe the project or service in the denominator, and the result is expressed in dollars instead of units. Interchanging the word *service* for the word *project* in the following example has the same effect.

The other type of project is internal to the business. Rather than sold to a customer, it is expected to improve a product's profitability. Both improvement project costs and improved product profitability must be included.

For example, Pretend Toys is considering substituting materials in the red wagon. Design changes and one-time changes to the manufacturing process are estimated at $35,000. The reduction in variable price per unit is expected to be $2 per unit, bringing COGS down to $13 per unit ($15 – $2). The break-even point for the cost of the project and the new variable price are calculated by adding the project cost to the numerator and using the new variable price in the denominator:

1. Fixed cost ($17,135) + Project cost ($35,000) = $52,135

2. Sales price ($25) – New variable price ($13) = $12

3. $52,135 / $12 = 4,344.6 break-even point in units

The break-even point has gone up substantially from the 1,713.5 units at the old variable price, revealing this project should not go forward.

Break-even analysis is a powerful tool in the business world. Several scenarios can be studied using the variations of the break-even analysis:

- Increased profits when the sales price is increased
- Additional profit generated by additional sales
- Increase to profits by reducing both variable and fixed costs
- Determining total profits from multiple products at different sales volumes (product mix)

The Rest of the Story

Once all the information is wrung out of the financial statements, there is still plenty to learn about a company from the notes, along with MD&A sections. Both of these sections are SEC requirements. They can be found in the 10-K filed with the SEC or as part of the company's annual report. The difference between the 10-K filing and the annual report is that the annual report contains a section commonly referred to as fluff.

The Fluff

The first pages of a company's annual report are fluff intended to reassure existing shareholders and bring potential investors into the fold. The fluff in the annual report begins with a letter to the shareholders from the chairman of the board or CEO. Consider this statement from the 2000 letter to Enron shareholders, the first year management is believed to have filed fraudulent financial statements:

> *Enron is increasing earnings per share and continuing our strong returns to shareholders. Recurring earnings per share have increased steadily since 1997 and were up 25 percent in 2000. The company's total return to shareholders was 89*

percent in 2000, compared with a negative 9 percent returned
by the S&P 500. The 10-year return to Enron shareholders was
1,415 percent compared with 383 percent for the S&P 500.

Enron is certainly a case of known fraud where the fluff was exaggerated and carried over into the SEC-filed financial statements. The point is that in this section of the annual report, management looks for special comparisons that place the company in the best light. Readers will not find a statement saying that the company's competitor's profits are 10 percent better than its own. However, astute financial statement readers will discover this by comparing financial results between competitors.

Next, in many annual reports come the staged glossy pictures and extracts of financial tables and graphs handpicked by management that highlight selected company achievements. Negative information almost always is saved for the small print of the notes and MD&A, which are monitored by the SEC.

Pro Forma Financial Statements

Similar to the fluff, many public companies make press releases of Pro Forma financial statements. Readers must clearly understand that these are not compliant with GAAP or SEC requirements and are not audited. The popularity of Pro Forma statements comes from the dot-com startup era when companies attempted to show they would be profitable except for certain expenses. Typically, businesses expand the definition of "extraordinary and nonrecurring" expenses beyond what GAAP and the SEC allow.

No standards similar to GAAP exist for Pro Forma statements, making it impossible to compare Pro Forma results of one company with those of another. Companies choosing to release Pro Forma results individually select what is included and excluded. The SEC has warned companies consistently that misleading investors with Pro Forma statements is considered fraud. One area of particular concern is the use of GAAP terminology, such as "net income," in Pro Forma statements. A 2006 academic study released by the *Journal of Business Ethics* found that in 2001, 10 percent of Standard & Poor's companies were releasing misleading Pro Forma statements. By 2003, of those companies continuing to publish Pro Forma statements, less than 1 percent were considered misleading. Although the accuracy of the data is improving, there is still no way to compare results between companies.

Management Discussion and Analysis

You can find a narrative explanation of a company's financial performance in a section of the quarterly or annual report entitled "Management's Discussion and Analysis of Financial Condition and Results of Operations." MD&A is management's opportunity to provide investors with its view of the financial performance and condition of the company. It is management's opportunity to tell investors what the financial statements do and do not show and includes important trends and risks that have shaped the past or are likely to shape the future.

The SEC rules governing MD&A require disclosure of trends, events, or uncertainties known to management that would have a material impact on reported financial information. The purpose of MD&A is to provide investors with information that management believes to be necessary to an understanding of its financial condition, changes in financial condition, and results of operations. It is intended to help investors see the company through the eyes of management and to provide context for the financial statements and information about the company's earnings and cash flows.

Restated Non-GAAP Financials

Many companies restate selected financial numbers in a non-GAAP format within the MD&A. Generally, the adjustments include or exclude revenue from events that management has deemed exceptional. These often include the one-time sale of a subsidiary business, discontinuing operations by shutting one or more factories, the effects of employee strikes, settlement of litigation, and income tax settlements with the IRS. Technically, management is correct that these are one-time occurrences and separate from ongoing primary operations. An astute financial statement reader only needs to review the non-GAAP restated financials for a couple previous years to learn how often the company has these types of exceptions. If the company has recurring settlements with the IRS, has a history of employee strikes, or regularly acquires and sells different business units, these events are not really exceptions to normal business. Each event may be unique, but it is predictable these types of events will continue to occur with a similar effect on the company's financial performance. Only the truly exceptional events should be disregarded when predicting future performance.

Forward-Looking Information

The forward-looking information section generally leads into the details of the MD&A. Forward-looking information is speculative, and actual results are almost certain to vary. What is often important in this section is a list of what management believes to be the largest risk factors the company faces: economic downturns or upturns, changes in political conditions, changes in regulatory conditions, pressures from competitors, success of research and development, success introducing new products and services, and retaining and attracting customers.

Companies conducting business on a global level face additional risks: unstable governments in the developing world, fluctuations in foreign exchange rates, changes in economic conditions in different global regions, and disruptions from foreign wars and terrorist activities.

Each industry and company faces unique risks and challenges. Manufacturers of consumer products face changing product preference, companies within the high-technology sector risk product obsolescence before development costs are recovered, and agriculture-based companies are at risk to weather conditions. The value to reading the forward-looking section is to learn about risks to the industry the company must overcome to obtain success.

Key Words and Phrases

Each MD&A is unique to the company that presents its financial statements. The discussion and analysis is a combination of explaining annual financial results and predicting future results. It can be time consuming but well worth the effort to begin with the MD&A from a few years ago. Look for key performance predictions made by management and track them through future MD&As to learn the results that were achieved eventually. Although this still does not predict future outcomes, it gives credibility to management's ability to understand the business and forecast results.

The SEC requires the MD&A section to be written in language the average investor can understand. Knowing whether a statement is based on facts or management opinion or is predicting the future is an important aspect when reading the MD&A. Certain words, phrases, and variations of these phrases help the reader decide how much to rely on the statement. The following list is certainly not exhaustive but provides a beginning for determining if a statement is opinion or forecast rather than a fact:

Additional considerations	Estimate	Management may
Anticipate	Eventually Far-term	Management views
Assume	Forecast	Monitoring
Discretionary	Future years	Near-term
Envision	Future outcomes	Outlook
Enter into	Long-term	Plan to

What Is in the Notes

While there is no set standard for the notes that accompany the financial statements, all cover specific information. The notes of large, complex companies will have a longer notes section than smaller companies. Very large companies like General Electric, Proctor & Gamble, Boeing, and 3M are composed of several different operating divisions that make them easier to manage. Typically, the notes break down the financial performance for each of the operating divisions. The SEC identifies some of the most important contents of the notes as:

- **Significant accounting policies and practices**—Companies are required to disclose the accounting policies that are most important to the portrayal of the company's financial condition and results. These often require management's most difficult, subjective, or complex judgments.

- **Income taxes** — The footnotes provide detailed information about the company's current and deferred income taxes. The information is broken down by level — federal, state, local, and/or foreign — and the main items affecting the company's effective tax rate are described.

- **Pension plans and other retirement programs** — The footnotes discuss the company's pension plans and other retirement or post-employment benefit programs. The notes contain specific information about the assets and costs of these programs and indicate whether, and by how much, the plans are over- or under-funded.

- **Stock options** — The notes also contain information about stock options granted to officers and employees, including the method of accounting for stock-based compensation and the effect of the method on reported results.

Earnings or revenue recognition is another note to look for. This is a primary way for management to manipulate sales and ultimately the bottom line of the income statement. Be wary of any changes to the way revenue is recognized, especially if the policy change appears more lenient in how it is reported. A conservative approach occurs when revenue is not recognized until the physical goods and title pass to the customer. This can be backed up further with provisions for discounts and returns.

Changes in accounting methods include how the statements would have read had the changes not been made. For instance, if a change in revenue recognition is made, there will be a statement of what revenue would have been if the accounting change had not been made.

Buying and selling other businesses is commonplace. In 2006, Boeing purchased one company for more than $1.78 billion and sold two major operations for $1.6 billion, along with several other smaller but similar transactions. Included in Procter & Gamble's 2006 annual report is the purchase of the Gillette Company for approximately $53.43 billion. The effects these transactions had on the financial statements are explained in the notes section. These transactions take many different forms, including using treasury shares to make purchases and borrowing to make cash purchases. Billions of dollars in assets and liabilities change hands as well. Explanations about how these transactions flowed on and off the financial sheets are found in the notes section.

The current portion of long-term debt is explained, along with the amounts of long-term debt coming due in future years. These tables provide both the interest rates and the principal amounts that must be repaid. The picture presented can foretell difficulties in coming years or if the company's obligations will be met easily with earnings from operations.

Details of how earnings per share, outstanding shares, and diluted shares are calculated will be explained in the notes. Included in this section is the number of preferred stocks and options that were converted into common shares, which lowers the value of previously outstanding common shares. Outstanding preferred stocks and options that are expected to be converted to common shares also are estimated. Executive compensation through stock awards are detailed, along with current information about stock repurchase programs that frequently are used to fund stock options and preferred stock conversions to common stock.

Look also in the notes for mention of pending litigation. In today's world, almost every major corporation has lawsuits on its hands. They come from every imaginable source: employees, dissatisfied customers, competitors, the IRS. Some lawsuits seek specific amounts that are included in the notes if management believes they are material in relation to the financial statements. In other cases, no specific amount is sought. Management also may provide an opinion about whether or not it believes the company will prevail in the lawsuit or if insufficient information is available to form an opinion. All this is important because management must retain earnings in anticipation of paying all judgments that the company loses.

Also important in the notes is the segment section, where information about company segments or divisions is found. Most large companies are divided into operating divisions based on strategic considerations. Some divisions are based on product type, others are geographic sales regions, and some may be customer types. Purchasing or selling other companies often leads to creating or eliminating an entire division within the company. Because large companies are required to present consolidated financial statements that net out any internal transactions, the contributions of each segment in the company to the financial statements is presented in the notes. At management's discretion, liabilities, assets, earnings, capital expenditures, and other financial information from each business segment is explained in the way it accumulates on the consolidated statements.

There is a wealth of information that cannot be ignored in the MD&A and financial notes sections. Professional analysts read these sections carefully and often use the information as a basis for questioning management about the accuracy of press releases and overly optimistic predictions of the company's future. This part of the financial statement combines management's explanation of past performance with its strategy for the future, the risks that exist, and the outcome it expects to achieve.

Monitoring the Financial Health of a Company

1. Understand the fundamentals of the business.

2. Monitor the past, present, and future of the company.

3. Read the 10-K and 10-Q reports when they are released and before management adds its spin to the financial reporting.

4. Maintain a spreadsheet of the company's historical data of the

financial ratios best suited for the industry and company.

5. Include on the spreadsheet industry averages and ratios of key competitors to benchmark the company against.

6. Never assume that an increase in earnings means good financial health; always take a long, hard look at the statement of cash flow.

7. Understand risks that threaten the business's success.

8. Understand the business strategy and how probable the long-term success is.

9. Consider worst-case along with best-case scenarios; the result likely will be in between.

10. Establish and adhere to sensible buy, sell, and hold criteria for investments.

Summary

Senior managers play many roles when leading a company. They must know the ins and outs of the financial statements, which in turn gives them insight into how financial performance can be improved. Properly executed, this maintains the company's attractiveness to investors and keeps Wall Street and lenders happy. Managers of private companies face the same challenges with the privilege of not publishing financial statements.

The constant need to present the business in the best light influences what management chooses to highlight through press releases, glossy photos, presentations at annual shareholder meetings, and other media. Through SEC oversight and required internal financial controls, the real story comes out in the financial statements, MD&A, and notes to the statements. With truly transparent financial statements, informed investors are able to understand the nuances of written reports, comprehend the financial numbers, and use ratio analysis to understand the accurate story about the company's performance.

Prepared with well-planned strategies, known risks, and a detailed historical

INDUSTRY AND KEY COMPETITOR HISTORICAL TRACKING CHART

	Industry Averages			Pretend Toys			Great Toys			Child's Play		
	2005	2006	2007	2005	2006	2007	2005	2006	2007	2005	2006	2007
Current Ratio	n/a	n/a	n/a	1.90	1.70	2.10	1.51	1.47	1.67	1.75	1.65	1.90
P/E	24.80	27.30	28.10	10.90	10.30	12.50	25.86	28.47	29.30	20.52	22.59	23.25
Profit Margin	8.00%	8.34%	8.60%	11.40%	6.87%	12.90%	14.50%	16.60%	18.68%	8.81%	8.63%	9.70%
Debt-to-Equity Ratio	0.53	0.52	0.47	0.94	1.04	0.81	0.74	0.76	0.75	0.46	0.40	0.33
Return on Equity	14.73	14.92	15.30	0.17	0.20	0.31	18.68	23.64	23.88	12.56	12.94	14.11
Dividend Yield	1.46	1.61	1.77	0.00	0.00	0.00	1.15	1.26	1.30	2.34	2.27	2.10
	Notes: Industry has wide variation between companies and is susceptible to economic conditions.			Notes: Well-positioned for substantial growth. Earnings continue to rise, and growth assets are being purchased. Capital structure changed to support the strategy			Notes: Largest capitalized company in the industry			Notes: Top analysts rate it buy or hold for past two quarters.		

Many variations to an analytical spreadsheet are possible. At a minimum, at least one ratio for liquidity, financial leverage, profitability, asset turns, and stock price valuation need to be included. Based on the industry and individual company, acceptable ranges for each ratio should be established. The example spreadsheet tracks only historical ratios. Another version can forecast ratios based on management's prediction of the future and track what is actually delivered.

analysis of the industry, company, and key competitors, investors and managers are better able to predict the company's financial future.

This example spreadsheet is not ideal for capturing needed data for every business seeking investors but does give the reader a way to begin the process. Once created, an analysis spreadsheet is updated easily when needed or after each period when 10-K and 10-Q reports are issued, at a minimum.

CASE STUDY: BUSINESS ANALYSIS

SMB Consulting offers a wide range of business consulting services, ranging from business concept to aiding the well-established business implement new technology or stay current on best practices. SMB's expertise comes from working across multiple industries and sharing the business knowledge gained without infringing on proprietary information. The company is experienced at:

- Revenue Development
- Market Research
- Marketing Programs
- Establishing a Web Presence
- New Product and Service Development
- Technology Selection Expertise
- Franchise Expansion
- Business Plan and Project Plan Development With Supporting Financials

Understanding Startup Costs

SMB Consulting employs a wide range of tools in the analysis, development, deployment, and monitoring of projects. Initial start costs are determined, and the recurring costs are projected carefully to develop the financial section of a detailed business plan. The business plan serves several purposes, not the least of which is to provide the new business owner with a roadmap that successfully guides him through the early months. A comprehensive business plan is almost always a requirement by lenders considering providing startup funding.

Shown is one of many spreadsheets SMB uses to begin establishing a financial baseline for a new business.

Project Management

Established businesses with unique projects can benefit from SMB's project

CASE STUDY: BUSINESS ANALYSIS

management and budgeting experience. One tool is the cash flow sensitivity analysis that uses various high and low cash flow estimates for validating that projects will be financially successful. In addition to feasibility studies, this tool is useful for identifying cost savings opportunities in existing operations.

Like the other tools, it is fully flexible. The example has the pessimistic and optimistic cash flow ranges set as a 5 percent variable from the expected cash flow. A simple change in the variable allows the entrepreneur to review multiple project outcomes. Analysis tools do not need to be complex to be useful.

Productivity Improvements

Productivity is an important business measure often overlooked by busy entrepreneurs. This simple ratio is derived by dividing revenues by equivalent full-time employees. It provides the business owner with a sense of what the average employee contributes financially to the business. A contribution level that is marginally above the profitability line can indicate there are too many employees or that new ways need to be found for improving what each employee contributes. Comparing revenues to the number of employees is especially important when deciding to hire additional employees.

Another important use of productivity measures helps determine if it is financially desirable to keep some functions in-house that are not part of the core operation. Just as substitutions can be made for materials, changes in the labor structure are possible. Maintaining staff for nonessential functions can draw down profits. SMB identifies these opportunities and facilitates transitioning the work to an outside source. Partnering with a business that specializes in a particular type of work often provides superior service at a lower cost.

Numbers certainly are not the only way to find improvement opportunities. Balanced scorecards, root cause analysis, brainstorming, and ideation sessions are other tools for transforming a good business into a great business.

Industry Comparisons

For the established business, improvement project identification often begins with a comparison to national averages for businesses in the same industry. Data are available from companies with similar revenues. Advertising, fleet costs, office expenses — any one of the categories shown might be identified as either too costly or under-funded.

Upon identification, an in-depth study is conducted to fully understand the abnormality and if a need to make changes exists. A project feasibility study is conducted to determine the likely financial benefit if changes are made. Once accepted, a detailed project plan and schedule are developed to implement the best practice.

CASE STUDY: BUSINESS ANALYSIS

SMB Consultants' and clients' business goals are always aligned toward improving the business and ultimately the bottom line.

SMB CONSULTING, INC.

4411 PEREGRINE PLACE,

LOUISVILLE, KY 40241

502-394-0460

info@smbconsultinginc.com

http://smbconsultinginc.com

CHAPTER 8

The SEC and Independent Audits

The SEC has a daunting public responsibility in the administration of security laws. Each year it receives, processes, and disseminates more than 500,000 financial statements. The Dow Jones Industrials is a selection of 30 publicly traded stocks representing a wide cross section of industries. A snapshot of these stocks shows accumulative annual revenue of $2.5 trillion and earnings of $255.5 billion. On an average day, 472 million stock shares of just these 30 companies change hands. The New York Stock Exchange sees more than one and a half trillion shares traded on an average day. The NASDAQ trades approximately two billion shares each day.

The SEC also oversees stock exchanges, security brokers, dealers, investment advisers, and mutual funds. Its primary objectives are promoting disclosure of market information, maintaining fair dealings, and protecting against fraud.

The SEC — A Short History

Laws governing the securities industry are based on seven acts of Congress:

1. Securities Act of 1933

2. Securities Exchange Act of 1934

3. Public Utility Holding Act of 1935

4. Trust Indenture Act of 1939

5. Investment Company Act of 1940

6. Investment Advisors Act of 1940

7. Sarbanes-Oxley Act of 2002

Securities Act of 1933

Often referred to as the "truth in securities" law, the Securities Act of 1933 has two basic objectives:

- Require that investors receive financial and other information concerning securities being offered for public sale

- Prohibit misrepresentations, deceit, and other fraud in the sale of securities

This information enables investors, not the government, to make informed judgments about whether to purchase a company's securities. While the SEC requires that the information provided be accurate, it does not guarantee it. Investors who purchase securities and suffer losses have important recovery rights if they can prove that there was incomplete or inaccurate disclosure of important information. In general the required registration information is:

- A description of the company's properties and business

- A description of the security to be offered for sale

- Information about company management

- Financial statements certified by independent accountants

- 1929 – Stock Market Crashes
- 1932 – U.S. Senate investigates causes of 1929 market crash
- 1933 – Federal securities laws drafted
- 1934 – SEC established
- 1934 – SEC Act amended allowing formation of National Association of Security Dealers
- 1942 – SEC adopts rule 10B-5, for decades a crucial weapon for fighting market fraud
- 1950 – SEC loses congressional support and staffing levels drop below ability to monitor financial statements
- 1961 – SEC investigates Res Scandal and expels securities and specialists from AMEX criminal convictions and prison time results

1964– Borak ruling allows individuals to sue corporations that violate security laws without seeking SEC intervention. Rule 10B-5 civil suits increase significantly

1968 – NASD begins transformation to NADAQ with electronic stock price quotations. Courts reinforce laws against insider trading

1975 – SEC rule 19B-3 significantly reduces brokerage transaction fees

1976 – Sunshine Act requires public SEC meetings

1978 – Exchanges required to make stock quotes continuously available to information sellers

1984 – Insider Trading Sanctions Act allows penalties three time the amount of gains or avoided losses

Securities Exchange Act of 1934

Congress created the Securities and Exchange Commission. The act gives the SEC broad authority over all aspects of the securities industry, including the power to register, regulate, and oversee brokerage firms, transfer agents, and clearing agencies, as well as the nation's securities self-regulatory organizations. The various stock exchanges are all self-regulated.

The act also identifies and prohibits certain types of conduct in the markets and provides the Commission with disciplinary powers over regulated entities and persons associated with them. The act empowers the SEC to require periodic reporting of information by companies with publicly traded securities.

The Securities Exchange Act also governs the disclosure of materials used to solicit shareholders' votes in annual or special meetings held for the election of directors and the approval of other corporate action. This information, contained in proxy materials, must be filed with the Commission in advance of any solicitation to ensure compliance with the disclosure rules. Solicitations, by management or shareholder groups, must disclose all the important facts concerning the issues on which holders are asked to vote.

Prevention of insider trading is a major

portion of the act. It broadly prohibits fraudulent activities in connection with the offer, purchase, or sale of securities. These provisions are the basis for many types of disciplinary actions, including actions against fraudulent insider trading. Insider trading is illegal when a person trades a security while in possession of material nonpublic information in violation of a duty to withhold the information or refrain from trading.

Public Utility Holding Act of 1935

Based on years of utility company scandals negatively affecting investors and consumers, Congress provided the SEC with the authority to bring rogue organizations into regulatory compliance. Based on the Energy Policy Act of 2005, this authority was transferred to Federal Energy Regulatory Commission.

Trust Indenture Act of 1939

This act applies to debt securities such as bonds, debentures, and notes that are offered for public sale. Even though such securities may be registered under the Securities Act, they may not be offered for sale to the public unless a formal agreement between the issuer of bonds and the bondholder, known as the trust indenture, conforms to the standards of this Act.

1990– Following Black Monday of Oct. 19, 1987, the Market Reform Act grants the ESC power to take emergency action to maintain and restore orderly markets

1984 – Insider Trading Sanctions Act allows penalties three times the amount of gains or avoided losses

1994 – NASDAQ anti-competition practices result in $27M SEC settlement and $1B in private settlement costs

1995 – Congress acts to prevent frivolous lawsuits that corporations are forced to settle because it costs less than going to trial

1996– All U.S. public corporations required to file financial statements electronically with EDGAR

- 1998– SEC adopts rules requiring corporate SEC filings use plain English
- 2000 – SEC adopts regulation requiring corporate financial disclosure to be simultaneous to analysis and the public
- 2001 – Enron scandal begins unraveling
- 2002– Arthur Andersen Accounting Firm convicted in conjunction with Enron scandal
- 2002– Sarbanes – Oxely Act results from numerous high-profile corporate financial scandals
  - Public company accounting oversight board established
  - New audit rules created
  - Audit committee of independent directors
  - Increased statutory limits to bring private lawsuits

Investment Company Act of 1940

This act regulates the organization of companies, including mutual funds, that engage primarily in investing, reinvesting, and trading in securities and whose own securities are offered to the investing public. The regulation is designed to minimize conflicts of interest that arise in these complex operations. The act requires these companies to disclose their financial condition and investment policies to investors when stock is initially sold and, subsequently, on a regular basis. The focus of this act is on disclosure to the investing public of information about the fund and its investment objectives, as well as on investment company structure and operations. Remember that the Act does not permit the SEC to directly supervise the investment decisions or activities of these companies or judge the merits of their investments.

Investment Advisors Act of 1940

This law regulates investment advisers. With certain exceptions, this act requires that firms or sole practitioners compensated for advising others about securities investments must register with the SEC and conform to regulations designed to protect investors. Since the act was amended in 1996, only advisers who have at least $25 million of assets under management or advise a registered investment company must register with the Commission.

Sarbanes-Oxley Act of 2002

This is the most contemporary Congressional act on corporate financial responsibility. It directly resulted from the scandals that rocked the corporate world at the beginning of the 21st century. On July 30, 2002, President Bush signed into law the Sarbanes-Oxley Act, which he characterized as "the most far reaching reforms of American business practices since the time of Franklin Delano Roosevelt." The act mandated reforms to enhance corporate responsibility, enhance financial disclosures, and combat corporate and accounting fraud and created the "Public Company Accounting Oversight Board," also known as the PCAOB, to oversee the activities of the auditing profession. These new regulations are detailed in the next chapter, in relation to the scandals that made it necessary.

The SEC has issued hundreds of rules and interpretations based on the congressional acts. Four divisions and 19 different offices are assigned responsibility for rule writing, interpretation, and enforcement.

Divisions of the SEC

The four divisions are Corporation Finance, Investment Management, Enforcement, and Market Regulation. The 19 offices are Administrative Services, Chief Accountant, Economic Analysis, EEO, Executive Director, Inspector General, International Affairs, General Counsel, Public Affairs, Risk Assessment, Financial Management, Human Resources, Information Technology, Freedom of Information and Privacy Act, Investor Education and Assistance, Compliance Inspections and Examinations, Legislative and Intergovernmental Affairs, Administrative Law Judges, and Office of the Secretary.

An overview of each division and offices relevant to investors and business owners adequately covers this government bureaucracy.

Division of Corporation Finance

The Division of Corporation Finance oversees corporate disclosure of important information to the investing public. Corporations are required to comply with regulations that must be made when stock is initially sold and then on a continuing and periodic basis. The division's staff routinely reviews the disclosure documents filed by companies. The staff also provides companies with assistance interpreting the Commission's rules and recommends to the Commission new rules for adoption.

The Division of Corporation Finance Reviews:

- Registration statements for newly offered securities

- Annual and quarterly filings (Forms 10-K and 10-Q)

- Proxy materials sent to shareholders before an annual meeting

- Annual reports to shareholders

- Documents concerning tender offers (a tender offer is an offer to buy a large number of shares of a corporation, usually at a premium above the current market price)

- Filings related to mergers and acquisitions

Corporation Finance provides administrative interpretations of the securities acts and recommends regulations. Working closely with the Office of the Chief Accountant, the division monitors the activities of the accounting profession, particularly the FASB, that result in the formulation of GAAP.

The division's staff provides guidance and counseling to registrants, prospective registrants, and the public to help them comply with the law. For example, a company might ask whether the offering of a particular security requires registration with the SEC. Corporation Finance would share its interpretation of the relevant securities regulations with the company and give it advice on compliance with the appropriate disclosure requirement.

The division uses no-action letters to issue guidance in a more formal manner. A company seeks a no-action letter from the staff of the SEC when it plans to enter uncharted legal territory in the securities industry. For example, if a company wants to try a new marketing or financial technique, it can ask the staff to write a letter indicating whether it would or would not recommend that the Commission take action against the company for engaging in its new practice.

Division of Investment Management

The Division of Investment Management oversees and regulates the $15 trillion investment management industry and administers the securities laws affecting investment companies (including mutual funds) and advisers. In applying the federal securities laws to this industry, the division works to improve disclosure and minimize risk for investors.

The Division:

- Interprets laws and regulations for the public and SEC inspection and enforcement staff

- Responds to no-action requests and requests for regulatory exemptions

- Reviews investment company and investment adviser filings

- Reviews enforcement matters involving investment companies and advisers, as well as develops new rules and amendments to adapt regulatory structures to new circumstances

Depending on their size, investment advisers have to register with either the SEC or the state securities agency where they have their principal place of business. For the most part, investment advisers who manage $25 million or more in client assets must register with the SEC. If they manage less than $25 million, they must register with the state securities agency in the state where they have their principal place of business.

Suggested questions for interviewing potential investment advisers and financial planners:

- What experience does the adviser have, especially with the specific circumstances of the client?

- Where were they were educated or trained? What is their recent employment history?

- What licenses do they hold? Are they registered with the SEC, a state, or the National Association of Securities Dealers (NASD)?

- What products and services do they offer?

- Can they only recommend a limited number of products or services to clients? If so, why?

- How are they paid for services? What is the usual hourly rate, flat fee, or commission?

- Have they ever been disciplined by any government regulator for unethical or improper conduct or been sued by a client who was not satisfied with services provided?

- Ask for a copy of both parts of their Form ADV.

How investment advisers and planners are paid:

- A percentage of the value of the assets they manage
- An hourly fee
- A fixed fee
- A commission on the securities sold
- Some combination of the above

Each compensation method has potential benefits and possible drawbacks, depending on your individual needs. Potential clients should ask the investment advisers to explain the differences before doing business with them and get several opinions before making a decision.

Division of Enforcement

This division investigates possible violations of securities laws, recommends Commission action when appropriate, either in a federal court or before an administrative law judge, and negotiates settlements on behalf of the Commission. While the SEC has civil enforcement authority only, it works closely with various criminal law enforcement agencies throughout the country to develop and bring criminal cases when the misconduct warrants more severe action.

The division obtains evidence of possible violations of the securities laws from many sources, including its own surveillance activities, other divisions of the SEC, the self-regulatory organizations and other securities industry sources, press reports, and investor complaints.

All SEC investigations are conducted privately. Facts are developed to the fullest extent possible through informal inquiry, interviewing witnesses, examining brokerage records, reviewing trading data, and other methods. Once the Commission issues a formal order of investigation, the division's staff may compel witnesses by subpoena to testify and produce books, records, and other relevant documents. Following an investigation, SEC staff presents its findings to the Commission for review. The Commission can authorize the staff to file a case in federal court or bring an administrative action. Individuals and companies charged sometimes choose to settle the case, while others contest the charges.

Division of Market Regulation

The Division of Market Regulation establishes and maintains standards for fair, orderly, and efficient markets. It does this primarily by regulating the major securities market participants: broker-dealer firms; self-regulatory organizations (SRO), which include the stock exchanges and the NASD, Municipal Securities Rulemaking Board, and clearing agencies (SROs that help facilitate trade settlement); transfer agents (parties that maintain records of stock and bond owners); and securities information processors.

The division also oversees the Securities Investor Protection Corporation (SIPC), which is a private, non-profit corporation that insures the securities and cash in the customer accounts of member brokerage firms against the failure of those firms. The SIPC insures investor accounts if the brokerage goes broke, not investor losses from market declines or fraud.

The Division of Market Regulation's responsibilities include carrying out the Commission's financial integrity program for broker-dealers, reviewing and approving proposed new rules and proposed changes to existing rules filed by the SROs, establishing rules and issuing interpretations on matters affecting the operation of the securities markets, and surveillance of the markets.

Office of Investor Education and Assistance

The Office of Investor Education and Assistance (OIEA) serves individual investors by ensuring their problems and concerns are known throughout the SEC and considered when the agency takes action. Tens of thousands of investors contact OIEA each year to ask questions on a range of securities-related topics or to complain about problems with their investments or financial professionals. OIEA's trained specialists and attorneys provide information, seek informal resolutions to complaints, and collect data on investor contacts to track trends in the securities industry and provide intelligence to other SEC offices and divisions.

OIEA also carries out the SEC's investor education program, which includes producing and distributing educational materials, participating in educational seminars and investor-oriented events, and partnering with federal agencies, state regulators, consumer groups, industry associations, and others on financial literacy initiatives. OIEA provides input on rulemaking and other policy issues that affect individual investors.

Office of Compliance Inspections and Examinations

The Office of Compliance Inspections and Examinations (OCIE) protects investors through administering the SEC's nationwide examination and inspection program. Examiners in Washington, D.C., and in the

Commission's 11 regional offices conduct examinations of the nation's registered entities, including self-regulatory organizations, broker-dealers, transfer agents, investment companies, and investment advisers. The purpose of examinations is to detect fraud and other violations of the securities laws, foster compliance with those laws, and help ensure the Commission is continually made aware of developments and areas of potential risk in the securities industry. The examination program plays a critical role in encouraging compliance within the industry, which in turn helps protect investors and the securities markets generally.

Office of General Counsel

The General Counsel is the chief legal officer of the Commission and heads the Office of the General Counsel (OGC). The office provides a variety of legal services to the Commission and staff and is divided into five groups: Appellate, General Litigation, Adjudication, Ethics, and Legal Policy. The office prepares all the Commission's appellate and friend-of-the-court briefs, litigates all non-enforcement matters on behalf of the agency, and assists in preparing Commission opinions on appeal from administrative law judges, stock exchanges, the NASD, and the Public Company Accounting Oversight Board. It also provides legal advice and counseling concerning federal securities laws, administrative laws, government ethics rules, and other laws that affect independent agencies.

Office of International Affairs

The Office of International Affairs (OIA) promotes investor protection and cross-border securities transactions by advancing international regulatory and enforcement cooperation, promoting the adoption of high regulatory standards worldwide, and formulating technical assistance programs to strengthen the regulatory infrastructure in global securities markets. OIA works with a global network of securities regulators and law enforcement authorities to facilitate cross-border regulatory compliance and ensure that international borders are not used to escape detection and prosecution of fraudulent securities activities. Using OIA staff's specialized knowledge of international markets and foreign laws and regulations, OIA provides the Commission and staff with advice and assistance in international enforcement and regulatory matters.

Office of Risk Assessment

The Office of Risk Assessment (ORA) is responsible for coordinating the SEC's risk management program. ORA was formed in 2004 to help the SEC anticipate, identify, and manage risks, focusing on early identification of new or resurgent forms of fraud and illegal or questionable activities. ORA focuses on risk issues across the corporate and financial sector, including issues relevant to corporate disclosure, market operation, sales practices, new product innovation, and many other activities of financial market participants. ORA groups responsibilities into three general categories:

1. Information analysis — A key component of ORA's activities is to analyze data on new industry trends and risks from a variety of sources, such as external experts, domestic and foreign agencies, industry and financial services, empirical data, and other market data.

2. Managing the agency's risk assessment process — ORA develops and maintains the overall process for risk assessment throughout the SEC, such as defining relevant risk frameworks and common risk language.

3. Serving as the agency's risk management resource — ORA serves as a resource for each division and office in their risk assessment efforts, working closely with them as they work to identify, prioritize, and mitigate risks.

Office of the Secretary

The Office of the Secretary schedules Commission meetings, administers the Commission's seriatim — the process by which the Commission takes collective action without convening a meeting of the Commissioners — and duty-officer process, and prepares and maintains records of Commission actions. The office reviews all SEC documents submitted to and approved by the Commission. These include rulemaking releases, SEC enforcement orders and litigation releases, SRO rulemaking notices and orders, and other actions taken by SEC staff pursuant to delegated authority. The office also provides advice to the Commission and the staff on questions of practice and procedure. In addition, it receives and tracks documents filed in administrative proceedings, requests for confidential treatment, and comment letters on rule proposals. The office is responsible for publishing official documents and releases of Commission actions in the Federal Register and the SEC Docket, and it posts them on the SEC Internet Web site, **www.sec.gov**. The office also monitors compliance with the Government in the Sunshine Act.

The other 13 offices making up the SEC are a combination of support internal to the SEC and offices that coordinate activities with other government agencies.

Third-Party Audits

Independent audits of public companies are governed by generally accepted auditing standards (GAAS). These are grouped into three categories:

- General Standards
- Standards of Fieldwork
- Standards of Reporting

The major requirements of an independent audit are to adequately plan the audit in advance, remain fully independent of the company, and obtain an adequate amount of reliable evidence to support findings and the opinion.

General Standards:

1. The audit is performed by a person having adequate technical

training and proficiency as an auditor.

2. In all matters relating to the assignment, independence in mental attitude is to be maintained by the auditor.

3. Due professional care is to be exercised in the performance of the audit and the preparation of the report.

Field Standards:

4. The work is adequately planned, and assistants are to be properly supervised.

5. A sufficient understanding of internal control is to be obtained to plan the audit and to determine the nature, timing, and extent of tests to be performed.

6. Sufficient competent evidence is to be obtained through inspection, observation, inquiries, and confirmation to afford reasonable basis for an opinion regarding the financial statement under audit.

Reporting Standards:

7. The report shall state whether the financial statements are presented in accordance with GAAP.

8. The report shall identify those circumstances in which such principles have not been observed consistently in the current period in relation to the preceding period.

9. Informative disclosures in the financial statements are to be regarded as reasonably adequate unless otherwise stated in the report.

10. The report shall contain either an expression of opinion regarding the financial statements, taken as a whole, or an assertion to the effect that an opinion cannot be expressed. When an overall opinion cannot be expressed, the reasons therefore should be stated. In all cases where an auditor's name is associated with financial statements, the report should

contain a clear indication of the character of the auditor's work, if any, and the degree of responsibility the auditor is taking.

Readers might have expected a much more extensive list of standards. In fact, the next tier down are statements on auditing standards (SAS) issued by the American Institute of Certified Public Accountants. The SAS is lengthy and codified. It details the implementation of GAAS and addresses many specific subjects.

The Audit Process

The audit process is composed of four primary stages or activities:

1. Audit Engagement Acceptance
2. Preliminary Planning
3. Evaluation of Internal Controls and Substantive Testing
4. Reporting

Audit Engagement Acceptance

Auditors must have a documented quality control process that defines how audit engagements are accepted. This is particularly important when the auditor has not previously been engaged by the company. Typically, the auditor begins by investigating the business's reputation in the industry and inquiring if the business has been audited and who conducted the audit. If there has been a previous audit, SAS 84 requires the new auditor to communicate with the previous auditor after receiving permission from the business for financial information to be divulged. The initial inquiry with the previous auditor typically involves:

- Fraud by the business, illegal acts, and any concerns about internal controls

- Management integrity

- The reason management may be seeking to engage a different auditor

- If any disagreements between the auditor and management were unresolved

After evaluating the information from the initial inquiry, the new auditor may ask further about:

- Reviewing the previous auditor's working papers

- If the business maintains adequate financial information to conduct an audit

- If accounting work is likely to be required before the audit

- The level of cooperation the business's management is likely to provide

Based on this evaluation the auditor determines to accept or reject the engagement.

Audit Planning

Highlighted in a previous chapter is the necessity for the auditor to have knowledge of the industry where the company conducts business. A letter from management is required for an audit that is similar to the letter described in Chapter 2 for compiled and reviewed financial statements. Critical sections of the letter outline external users of the audit and acknowledgement that management is responsible for the company financial statement, and the auditor provides only an opinion if the statements are fairly presented and GAAP compliant.

When the auditor has not been engaged by a specific company before, additional information must be reviewed before planning the audit. Primarily this involves gaining a thorough understanding of the industry and business conducted by the company. This includes interviewing key personnel, reviewing SAS specific to the industry, industry-specific accounting publications, and additional review of any previous audit paperwork if available. This information is used to determine the areas in which the business is most likely to be at risk.

The next step in planning is to determine and document the analytical procedures that will be used. These vary by industry and even for each audit. Typically included are comparisons of current-year balances and ratios with previous years, identifying relevant transactions and events to be tested, and determining the extensiveness of the test. The results of each event analyzed will be documented during the audit.

The documented analytical procedure is provided to management so the accounting staff can collect and organize the records necessary for the audit.

Evaluation of Internal Controls and Substantive Testing

The next step is the evaluation of the business's internal financial controls. The auditor studies and evaluates the controls to determine the accuracy of financial information provided and how well the business's financial assets are protected. Also assessed is the likeliness the controls are to result in a misstatement of financial condition. Based on the risk assessment the analytical procedures may need to be more stringent, or it might be found that less testing is needed than originally planned.

The substantive testing is the most time-consuming portion of the audit. Every significant transaction is examined for GAAP compliance and proper classification within accounting systems, and the results are summarized. Inventory also will be examined if it is relevant to the business's operations.

The testing results are reviewed in whole and individually to assess the accuracy of the financial system. The analytical procedures that were used are reviewed again based on the test results to ensure that additional testing is not required. Any misstatements found during testing are evaluated to determine if they are likely to materially affect the financial statements. The testing and review results are used to draw a final conclusion of the audit.

Reporting

Testing results and the final conclusion are reported to the audit committee or senior management of some private companies. If it is a public company, the auditor's opinion is released to shareholders and the general public. Auditors' opinions are worded carefully, and most follow a standard format. The unqualified opinion typically reads:

THE UNQUALIFIED OPINION

To the Stockholders (or Board of Directors)

Pretend Toys, Inc.

We have audited the balance sheet of Pretend Toys, Inc., as of June 30, 2007, and the related statements of income, retained earnings, and cash flows for the year then ended. These financial statements are the responsibilities of the Company's management. Our responsibility is to express an opinion on these financial statements based on our audit.

We conducted our audit in accordance with U.S. generally accepted auditing standards. Those standards require that we plan and perform the audit to obtain reasonable assurance about whether the financial statements are free of material misstatement. An audit includes examining, on a test basis, evidence supporting the amounts and disclosures in the financial statements. An audit also includes assessing the accounting principles used and significant estimates made by management, as well as evaluating the overall financial statement presentation. We believe that our audit provides reasonable basis for our opinion.

In our opinion, the financial statements referred to above present fairly, in all material respects, the financial position of Pretend Toys, Inc., at June 30, 2007, and the results of its operations and its cash flows for the year then ended, in conformity with U.S. generally accepted accounting principles.

Under a Magnifying Glass, CPAs

September 3, 2007

The Unqualified Opinion

Informally referred to as a "clean opinion," the unqualified opinion is what both management and investors want to see.

The first paragraph describes what was audited, along with the responsibilities of the auditor and management. The second paragraph describes, in general terms, how the audit was conducted and can include any limitations of the audit. It also includes a statement that the audit relied on GAAS. The third paragraph gives the auditor's opinion on the financial statements and whether they are in accordance with generally accepted accounting principles.

The Qualified Opinion

A qualified opinion will state that the financial statements are presented fairly with either one of two exceptions: Portions of the financial statements do not conform with GAAP, or the auditor was not able to examine or verify a portion of the statements. An example of this occurs when it is physically impossible for the auditor to verify inventory accuracy. In both situations, the auditor's letter is modified to reflect the qualified opinion and the cause of the qualification.

Other Opinions

An adverse opinion results when the auditor believes the financial statements materially misstate the financial condition of the company and do not conform to GAAP. A disclaimer of an opinion is issued when an opinion cannot be formed. Although rarely issued, conflicts of interests, lack of management cooperation in the audit, or the auditor's concern that the company will be able financially to continue operations can result in a disclaimer.

Auditor opinions and management letters clearly establish management's responsibility for the financial statements and that auditors only provide an independent opinion. For public companies, this responsibility rests primarily with an audit committee, which is composed of outside directors. The audit committee engages the auditor and ensures cooperation with the internal accounting department, CEO, and CFO. The final audit report is delivered back to the committee, and they disseminate it internally to the company and to the entire board of directors. The board of directors then releases it external of the company. Because private companies are not required to produce, audit, or distribute financial statements, there is no requirement for outside directors on the audit committee. Often the CEO and CFO also have the most authority on the board of directors and are part of the audit committee at private companies.

The Four Major Audit Houses

The U.S. Government Accounting Office estimates that 78 percent of U.S. public companies use one of the big four audit firms. Public companies choose these firms because they are well known and have the capability and capacity to perform complex audits. However, there are definitely limitations to having so few from which to select. None of the big four is an expert in every industry, further limiting the number a company can select.

Deloitte & Touche Tohmatsu

- 135,000 Employees
- 140 Countries
- $20.0 Billion in Revenues (2006)

Ernst & Young

- 114,000 Employees
- Over 700 Locations
- 140 Countries
- $18.4 Billion in Revenues (2006)

KPMG

- 113,000 Employees
- 148 Countries
- $16.9 Billion in Revenues (2006)

PricewaterhouseCooper

- 142,000 Employees
- 771 Locations
- 149 Countries
- $22.0 Billion in Revenues (2006)

Previously, it was the big five until Arthur Andersen LLP was convicted of obstruction of justice in June 2002 for its role in the Enron scandal. Although the U.S. Supreme Court overturned the conviction in June 2005, Arthur Andersen voluntarily had surrendered its license to practice as a CPA firm in 2002. The reduction to only four major auditing firms has affected the audit industry. Audit fees for the services of the remaining firms rose between 25 and 33 percent by 2004. More important to investors is the affect on government oversight. Experts in the field believe the auditors' fear of severe government sanctions is reduced greatly by the loss of Arthur Andersen. The previous threat of a full-year sanction from conducting audits likely would cripple the ability for public companies to obtain audits from the remaining three firms. Punitive financial penalties are more likely than being altogether sanctioned from conducting audits.

Audit Changes Resulting From Sarbanes-Oxley Act

The Sarbanes-Oxley act may be the biggest change in public company financial accountability since the SEC was created in 1934. The act is a direct result of the major business scandals in the late 1990s and early 2000s.

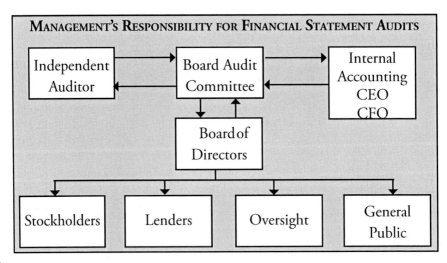

Section 201(c) of SOXA requires the SEC to adopt rules that further limit the non-audit services that an audit firm can provide to its audit clients. These limits are predicated on three basic principles, violations of which would impair the auditor's independence:

- An auditor cannot function in the role of management.
- An auditor cannot audit his or her own work.
- An auditor cannot serve in an advocacy role for his or her client.

The following categories of non-audit services are prohibited:

- Bookkeeping or other services affecting accounting records and financial statements
- Financial information systems design and implementation
- Appraisal or valuation services, fairness opinions, or contribution-in-kind reports
- Actuarial services involving amounts recorded in the financial statements and related accounts
- Internal audit services related to the internal accounting controls, financial systems, or financial statements
- Human resources — searching for or seeking out prospective candidates for managerial, executive, or director positions, acting as negotiator on the audit client's behalf
- Broker-dealer, investment adviser, or investment banking services
- Legal services — any service to the audit client that could be provided only by someone licensed to practice law
- Expert services — expert opinions or other services to an audit client for the purpose of advocating that audit client's interests in litigation or regulatory or administrative investigations

Other Effects of the Sarbanes-Oxley Act of 2002

- Created the Public Company Accounting Oversight Board to oversee auditors of public companies and further protect the interests of investors

  o Auditors of public companies will be inspected by the PCAOB at a minimum of every three years.

  o The PCAOB has authority to discipline both firms and individual accountants.

- Section 404 of the code requires companies to access their internal financial controls and auditors to determine their effectiveness on an ongoing basis.

- Requires at least one independent board member of the audit committee to be a financial expert.

- Created criminal liability for destroying records even if an investigation is not in progress

- Requires the CEO to personally certify the financial statements are accurate and accept personal criminal liability if they are proven incorrect

- Specifically prohibits the company from loaning money to executives

Small-Business Fraud

The lack of audits of small businesses greatly increases the opportunity for employee fraud to occur. This is especially true when the business owner turns over accounting responsibilities to an in-house accountant or bookkeeper. There are three general categories business fraud falls into:

1. Skimming cash money before it is recorded on the books. Most owners are aware of the potential for this and have controls in place to prevent employees from handling customer cash and easily pocketing a portion of it.

2. Embezzlement occurs after the money is entered onto the books and is a common form of small-business fraud. There are two typical embezzlement schemes. In both, an employee establishes a business bank account in his name. False invoices are written from the employee's fictitious company to the real business, and the bookkeeper writes a check to his own account to pay the invoice. Another scheme is for the employee to open a fictitious bank account with a name very similar to a major customer of the real business. A steady flow of checks from the customer allows occasional checks to be diverted unnoticed to the employee's fictitious business account from which he is able to withdraw the funds. Both schemes average about 18 months before they are uncovered or until the real business begins having cash flow problems.

3. The third type of employee fraud is pilfering inventory or business assets. This can range from the minor theft of office supplies to large losses of shop machinery. Retail stores lose more inventory to employees than shoplifters. The amount of pilfered inventory depends on the type of inventory. Computer hardware is resold easily by employees at flea markets, at tag sales, in classified ads, on eBay, and via several other hard-to-detect sources. Industrial inventories like raw manufacturing materials are not as susceptible to theft.

Regular audits would uncover fraud through testing of accounting systems, examination of internal controls, and inventory counts. Unfortunately, most small businesses only engage an audit when applying for a major loan, preparing for a merger, or performing other seldom-occurring events. Fortunately, there are steps the business owner can take to minimize the possibility of employee fraud occurring:

- Perform background checks on employees, especially those with access to cash and accounting systems.

- Perform mini tests of the accounting system on a monthly basis. Randomly select invoices that show being paid, and contact the recipient to verify the account is in good standing.

- Schedule regular reviews of the accounting books with those responsible for entries.

- Use pre-numbered invoices and require accounting of each one.

- Establish multiple budgets and require approval if they must be exceeded; review the budgets on a regular basis with the responsible employee.

- If practical, separate accounting responsibilities between two or more employees — one responsible for incoming payments and the other responsible for paying bills. Occasionally change the responsibility between the two.

- Establish a spending limit above which owner approval is required.

- Conduct regular inventory checks for both merchandise and company assets.

- Make all this visible to employees so they know that fraud easily will be detected.

CHAPTER 9

Contemporary Corporate Scandals

Corporate scandals have been around since the industrial revolution with railroad barons in the mid- and late 1800s, the Teapot Dome scandal of the early 1920s, and the stock market crash of 1929 that led to the creation of the SEC. The 1980s saw two major scandals. One was the junk bond market scandal that involved insider trading, for which Michael Milken served two years of a ten-year prison sentence. The other 1980s scandal was the savings and loan crisis that resulted from the deregulation of the industry. It is estimated to have cost about $150 billion, of which the U.S. government subsidized $125 billion. The most recent rash of corporate scandals began in the late 1990s and exploded into the general media in 2002. What these had in common is fraudulent financial statements used to disguise white-collar theft.

2002 – The Year of Financial Scandals

More than 25 major businesses had scandals written about in the general and business media during 2002. The most notable, and with far-reaching affects to shareholders and employees, were:

- Enron
- Arthur Andersen
- World Com / MCI
- Tyco
- Adelphia
- Global Crossing

Enron

Without a doubt, Enron is the biggest story of financial cheats from 2002 and by some estimates the biggest to ever have occurred. While the collapse of Enron came from GAAP and securities violations, it also came from greed and lack of ethics. These were at the center of the company's culture; had company culture been more ethical, the damage would have been found much sooner and been contained. In 1999, the board of directors voted to waive the company's ethics code so that off-balance sheet transactions could occur, and conflict of interest provisions were waived for some executives. The bosses at Enron also froze employee retirement accounts from being able to sell shares of Enron stock while simultaneously allowing executives to dump stock as the company tanked. Kenneth Lay was the founder of Enron and surrounded himself with senior managers complicit in the demise of the company.

Through many different accounting schemes, financial losses were hidden and profits inflated. In October 2001 Enron declared a $618 million quarterly loss and wrote off $1.2 billion in shareholder equity. In November 2001, Enron revised five years of financial statements filed with the SEC. Removed from the statements were $586 million in profits and added was $2.5 billion in debt. In December of the same year, Enron began laying off employees and declared bankruptcy. In January, the U.S. Justice Department began an investigation that eventually resulted in many plea agreements and convictions.

How They Did It

Several elaborate schemes were used to defraud the shareholders, employees, analysts, SEC, and others. The typical arrangement was to remove under-performing assets from the financial statements rather than record losses from these businesses. The sales of the assets were recorded as profits that did not come true. In fact, the assets often could not be sold because of the poor performance.

In a specific case, three energy-producing barges theoretically were sold to Merrill Lynch for $7 million, and Enron claimed a $12 million profit. In reality, Enron guaranteed to buy the barges back from Merrill Lynch six months later at a profit to Merrill Lynch.

Other scenarios involved several sham companies set up and owned by Enron executives that would purchase the under-performing Enron assets using money Enron loaned to the executives. Not only were serious conflicts of interest created, but also money was laundered and paid as bonuses for the unethical acts.

What Changed and Where the Company Is Today

What was once Enron Corporation is now Enron Creditors Corporation. By early 2007, over $11 billion of Enron's assets had been liquidated and proceeds distributed to creditors. On November 17, 2004, Enron's bankruptcy plan became effective, and all common and preferred stocks were cancelled. Stockholders were issued an interest in either the common stock trust or preferred stock trust based on the number of shares they previously owned. In the unlikely event that Enron's assets exceed creditors' claims, stockholders will receive a distribution from the trust funds.

The Players

Kenneth Lay founded Enron in 1985 when Houston Natural Gas and InterNorth merged. Lay was CEO from 1986 until early 2001 when Jeffrey Skilling assumed the CEO role, only to abruptly resign from the position seven months later. Lay resumed the role of CEO. In August 2000, Enron's stock price stood at an all-time high of $90. Lay assured the stock market that Enron shares would reach the $130 – $140 range, although he had insider knowledge that accounting fraud was making it more difficult to perpetuate the appearance of profits that did not exist. Lay is estimated to have sold more than $90 million worth of Enron stock he owned, while encouraging outsiders to buy more and requiring employees to hold what they owned. Lay concealed as much as $70 million of his sales from SEC disclosure by repaying loans he had taken out from Enron with the stock sales. Lay's sales to repay the loans did not have to be disclosed for four months.

By August 2001, Enron's stock price had dropped to $42, and by October it was at $15. On October 28, 2001, Lay's wife sold another $1.2 million of Enron shares 30 minutes before public disclosure was made that Enron had hidden millions in losses from the public. The price share immediately dropped below a dollar.

Kenneth Lay was indicted on seven counts of securities and wire fraud, conspiracy to commit securities fraud and wire fraud, and bank fraud. One charge was dropped. He was convicted in May 2006 of all charges and faced up to 175 years in prison. Lay died of a heart attack before being sentenced.

As CEO of Enron, Jeffrey Skilling adopted an accounting system known as mark-to-market and developed a business model that required the company to hold almost no assets. The mark-to-market accounting method counts future profits as if they exist today. The combination of no assets and counting future profits early made financial statements, especially a balance sheet, a big inconvenience. Skilling placed many schemes in motion to drive Enron's stock price higher. With insider information that Enron was a house of cards and soon to collapse, he unexpectedly resigned as CEO four months before Enron declared bankruptcy. Immediately after resigning, he sold approximately $63 million of Enron stock, in addition to the $132 million he received in salary the same year. Among many fraudulent endeavors in the energy market, Skilling is suspected of being instrumental in the western U.S. energy crisis of 2000 and 2001 when extreme energy costs were coupled with rolling blackouts across the West.

Jeffrey Skilling was charged with 35 criminal charges, including securities fraud, wire fraud, conspiracy to commit securities fraud, conspiracy to commit wire fraud, false statements to auditors, and insider trading. The same jury tried Skilling and Lay, and in May 2006, Skilling was found guilty on 19 counts. He was sentenced to 24 years and 4 months in prison. Skilling was ordered by the judge to report to prison in December 2006 pending the outcome of his appeal.

Andrew Fastow was the CFO of Enron and mastermind of the off-balance sheet transactions that perpetuated the sham profits. Fastow helped a group of Enron executives set up partnerships that conducted business with Enron, although a clear conflict of interest existed. Elements of Enron's business that were losing money were sold to the various partnerships owned by the executives. Along with hiding losses, he was able to inflate Enron's earnings by an estimated $1 billion over a 12-month period. Additionally, the arrangement was for the partnerships to have their investment returned and be guaranteed a profit from Enron, although they assumed ownership of unprofitable business entities. The profits were funneled to the executives in a variety of money-laundering schemes, including one in which Fastow used a family foundation set up as a charity. Fastow's profits from these partnerships are estimated at over $45 million. Rather than face a trial on 92 indictments, Fastow agreed to plead guilty to two charges of conspiracy to commit securities and wire fraud. He agreed to a ten-year prison term, to return more than $23 million of the money, and to testify against other Enron officers. In September 2006, a judge gave mercy to Fastow for cooperating with the prosecution and sentenced him to only six years in prison. His wife was charged with six felonies but pled guilty to a single charge of signing a false income tax return and was sentenced to one year.

Enron hired Ben Glisan, Jr., from Arthur Andersen, and he became one of the executive partners in Fastow's off-balance sheet scheme. His initial investment of $5,800 grew to about $1 million in a few weeks. When faced with 23 charges of conspiracy to commit securities and wire fraud, he pled guilty to a single charge and was sentenced to five years in prison.

Dave Delainey was the head of Enron Energy Services. He pled guilty to one count of insider trading and was sentenced to two and a half years in prison. He also must return almost $8 million.

Richard Causey, chief accounting officer, pled guilty to one count of securities fraud and was sentenced to five years. He also agreed to forfeit $1.25 million and received a $25,000 fine.

Michael Kopper, a key assistant to Fastow and instrumental in setting up off-balance sheet partnerships and giving kickbacks to Fastow, pled guilty to money laundering and was sentenced to three years and one month.

Timothy Despain, assistant treasurer, pled guilty to one charge of conspiracy to commit securities fraud and was sentenced to four years of probation.

Paula Rieker, director of investor relations and trustee for employee retirement plan, pled guilty to a charge of insider trading and was sentenced to two years of probation.

Mark Koenig, former director of investor relations, pled guilty to aiding and abetting securities fraud. He was sentenced to 18 months in prison and two years of probation and was fined $50,000.

Dan Boyle, former vice president of global finance, was found guilty of conspiracy to commit wire fraud and conspiracy to falsify books, records, and accounts. Also convicted of lying to a Congressional investigator, he was sentenced in May 2005 to three years and ten months in prison and ordered to pay $320,000 in fines.

Arthur Andersen

Once the ethical watchdog for other companies, Arthur Andersen made a fundamental change during the late 1980s and 1990s that eventually destroyed the firm. Greed was again at the center as Andersen fell from grace. In 1989, the firm was divided into two operating units. One was composed of accounting consultants and the other of auditors. Consulting was the more profitable line of business, and the consultants wanted to keep a larger share of the revenue they brought in. As a result, the auditors became more aggressive cross-selling consulting services. The independent judgment of auditors became clouded as consulting fees greatly exceeded auditing fees.

In the case of Waste Management Inc., the consulting fee was $17.8

million compared to the audit fee of $7.5 million between 1991 and 1997. When the SEC took a close look at the audits in 2002, it found that many discrepancies had been overlooked by the auditor. The SEC filed a lawsuit against six former Waste Management executives, claiming the consulting fees compromised the independence of the auditor. Andersen was forced to pay the shareholders $75 million.

In a previous audit of Sunbeam Inc., Andersen was forced to pay the shareholders $110 million when it was found that Sunbeam had been inflating revenues for several years. The Boston Market, Inc., case cost Andersen $10.3 million when the company declared bankruptcy shortly after its IPO. Andersen's defense was simply that the SEC had approved the accounting discrepancies when it reviewed Boston Market prior to the IPO. The Baptist Foundation of Arizona case cost Andersen $217 million for a botched audit. In 1998, an official policy was issued that required auditors to bring in twice as much revenue from consulting work as they did from audit work. The policy forced many auditors into areas of accounting that they were not familiar with.

At Enron, Arthur Andersen became almost fully integrated with the company, hiring Enron's entire internal accounting team, attending Enron company meetings, and helping establish business strategies.

On March 14, 2002, Arthur Andersen was charged with obstruction of justice. Among the allegations was that Andersen informed Enron the accounting troubles would be ongoing but allowed Enron to characterize them as non-recurring. Andersen took no action when informed by famed Enron whistle blower Sharron Watkins that the off-balance sheet transactions were likely illegal. Nor did Andersen take action when informed of the illegal accounting methods by its own Professional Standards Group. Andersen employees at the Houston office supporting Enron and other offices around the world were instructed to destroy all documents that involved Enron. This began on October 23, 2002, one day after the SEC informed Andersen that an investigation would occur. The destruction of paper and computer files continued until November 8, when Andersen was served officially with a subpoena for the documentation. The actual obstruction-of-justice charge stems from Andersen partners instructing employees to continue withholding documents on November 9 and 10. Andersen was convicted on the charge, but it eventually was overturned by the U.S. Supreme Court on the grounds that jury instructions were so broadly stated that Andersen could have been found guilty even if there was no intent to break the law. The government elected not to try the case again because Andersen became a defunct firm when its prominent clients abandoned it.

WorldCom / MCI

In August 2003, the SEC issued a record $750 million fine against MCI in response to $11 billion in accounting fraud. An employee's report of the fraud to the board of directors in June 2002 was ignored, and a shareholder lawsuit was thrown out for lack of evidence the same year. In March 2002, the SEC began an investigation that proved the fraud charges were valid.

WorldCom changed the company name to MCI to distance itself from the fraud. MCI is a conglomerate built from mergers of many smaller companies in the telecommunication industry. The accounting fraud began to unravel when it was found that MCI misclassified charges that it paid to access other company's lines as assets rather than expenses. These operating leases were counted as asset purchases of between $540 million and $797 million for five consecutive quarters. Other similar instances were discovered as the SEC investigation continued. Booking the expenses as assets allowed MCI to depreciate the expenses over time rather than in the correct accounting period. As a result, MCI's profits appeared to be much higher than they actually were. When all the accounting dust settled, MCI was forced to write off $79.8 billion of assets that did not exist, including $45 billion in good will from the many corporations that had been acquired.

In addition to the $750 million fine, the board of directors agreed to a $54 million settlement that included $18 million of their own money. A judge threw the settlement out, and litigation on the matter continues. Institutional investors obtained a $651 million settlement, but the largest investor settlement to date is for $6.1 billion on behalf of 830,000 individuals.

MCI paid $331 million to 16 states and the District of Columbia to settle tax evasion charges.

CEO Bernard Ebbers received a 25-year prison sentence for securities fraud. CFO Scott Sullivan was sentenced to five years. The accounting director was sentenced to one year, and an accounting executive was sentenced to five months' jail time with an additional year of house arrest.

MCI successfully emerged from the largest corporate Chapter 11 bankruptcy in April 2004 with a new board of directors and new executive management team.

In January 2006, Verizon and MCI merged after Qwest fought to acquire MCI. The combined revenue of Verizon and MCI for 2006 was $88.1 billion.

Tyco

The Tyco scandal centered on top managers and directors enriching themselves at the cost of shareholders. As a member of the board of directors, Frank Walsh accepted a $10 million fee when Tyco purchased CIT group. Another $10 million was donated to a charity where he was also the director. CEO Dennis Kozlowski, CFO Mark Swartz, and chief legal counsel Mark Belnick were accused of taking $170 million in loans not approved by the board of directors. Kozlowski and Swartz also sold $430 million worth of Tyco stock without notifying investors as required by the SEC.

Kozlowski also furnished his company-owned Manhattan apartment at the expense of shareholders. Tyco paid approximately $1 million for Kozlowski's wife's birthday party. Altogether it is estimated that Kozlowski and Swartz cost shareholders $600 million. Both were charged with corruption, conspiracy, grand larceny, and falsifying records. A mistrial was declared during their first trial, but both were found guilty in June 2005 of stealing more than $150 million.

Kozlowski and Swartz began serving eight-year-and-four-month prison terms in September 2005. Their combined fines and restitution amounted to $239 million.

Other than the loss of the money, Tyco did not face bankruptcy or other insurmountable challenges. Many changes were made in top management positions, and the company remains viable.

Adelphia

The Adelphia scandal was a family affair that rivaled the size and depth of the WorldCom scandal. The Rigas family founded Adelphia and grew it into the sixth largest cable entertainment company. The SEC settlement of $715 million fell just short of the record $750 million settlement with WorldCom.

The Rigas family used the off-balance sheet method of hiding fraud similar to Enron. The difference was that Adelphia made loans to the family for $2.3 billion. Another $252 million was used to pay family debt, and the family fraudulently acquired $430 million of company stock.

Billions more in liabilities were concealed from the balance sheets, and earnings were inflated. In total, it is estimated the scandal costs investors as much as $60 billion.

In 2005, the auditing firm of Deloitte & Touche LLP entered into a $50 million settlement with the SEC and a $211 million settlement with investors without admitting guilt.

In July 2002, the SEC filed multiple charges against the father, John Rigas, and his three sons, Timothy, Michael, and James. In June 2002, Adelphia filed for Chapter 11 bankruptcy and was taken off the NASDAQ stock exchange.

The family gave up control of 95 percent of its assets, which amounted to approximately $1.2 billion. John Rigas was sentenced to 15 years in prison, and Timothy was sentenced to 20 years. In early 2007, both remain free while appeals are pending. Both still face additional conspiracy and tax evasion charges.

The jury deadlocked in the trial of Michael Rigas, and he agreed to plead guilty to a single count of making a false entry into a financial record. He was spared a prison sentence in March 2006 when he was sentenced to ten months of home detention and two years of probation.

Adelphia did not survive bankruptcy. The company's assets were sold to Time Warner and Comcast for approximately $12.7 billion. Adelphia remains in bankruptcy court, pending the distribution to lenders of the cash received from the sale.

Global Crossing

Global Crossing is another telecommunication company that filed for bankruptcy in January 2002 when accounting irregularities were discovered. Global Crossing was the fourth largest bankruptcy in American history.

With Arthur Andersen as auditor, Global Crossing was found to be exaggerating earnings in order to meet Wall Street estimates. The company booked revenue from long-term contracts before it actually was earned. Another of the company's favorite tricks was booking capacity swaps with other companies as revenue when in fact no money exchanged hands. Excess Internet capacity in one region was swapped with another company that had capacity available in a region the company lacked capacity. These agreements were for 15 or 20 years, during which money might exchange hands if both companies remained in business.

Several companies were positioning themselves strategically during the late 1990s for rapid growth in broadband Internet. The Internet demand never developed to the levels anticipated, and there was too much supply on the market and not enough demand. Revenues began to fall rather than rise. Global Crossing made it appear as though revenues continued to grow by claiming revenues that would be received years later, if ever.

In April 2005, the SEC concluded its investigation by issuing a cease and desist order against Global Crossing. Full cooperation with the SEC was cited as a reason no monetary fines were issued.

Global Crossing sold more than 60 percent of its assets to reduce debt before emerging from bankruptcy in December 2003.

Other Scandals of 2002

AOL is said to have inflated revenues by $30 million just prior to merging with Time Warner. The extra revenue was actually advertisements it had sold for other companies. AOL claimed revenue for the cost of the advertisements, as well as its rightful fee for selling the advertisements.

During preparations for civil trial, it was further discovered that AOL had mislead investors about the true number of service subscribers it had. When the 2000 through 2002 financial statements were corrected, the total amount involved was approximately $500 million.

Although no one went to prison, the financial penalties were severe. In an agreement with the Department of Justice in December 2004, Time Warner agreed to pay a $60 million penalty and establish a $150 million fund to compensate shareholders. In March 2005, Time Warner settled a separate suit brought by the SEC for $300 million.

Several larger investors did not join the class action suits settled by the Department of Justice and SEC, and lawsuits remain pending. By August 2005, Time Warner announced it had established a $3 billion reserve fund to resolve the entire legal problem. The company's auditor, Ernst and Young, contributed an additional $100 million.

Bristol-Myers Squibb inflated revenues by $2.5 billion between 2000 and 2001 by forcing distributors to take inventory it had no hope of selling — a technique called channel stuffing. Bristol-Myers agreed to cover the distributors' carrying costs and guaranteed a return on their investment until the products could be sold. In March 2003, earnings for the period were reduced by $900 million.

Bristol-Myers Squibb settled one civil suit for $300 million in November 2004. Criminal prosecution of the company was deferred for two years as part of the settlement. In August 2004, the company settled with the SEC for $150 million. It also agreed to an independent adviser who will monitor the company's accounting practices.

CMS Energy executed buy and sell transactions for the same energy product on the same day with the same trade partner in what is known as "round trip" trades to artificially increase the volume of energy trades occurring. The desired result was to artificially propel CMS Energy into the top ranks of energy trading companies. Over $5 billion in fraudulent trades were executed. Additionally, CMS Energy artificially inflated revenues based on these trades by $5.2 billion. This is a case where the independent auditor forced the company to restate the fraudulent filings with the SEC. The auditor was Arthur Andersen.

In March 2004, CMS Energy reached an agreement with the SEC to cease and desist from further round-trip dealing. No fine was imposed directly against the company, but the controller responsible for making the accounting entries was fined $25,000 personally. The SEC also filed civil charges against the company's former CFO and the president of the subsidiary responsible for the trades. In January 2007, CMS Energy reached a preliminary settlement with shareholders for $200 million.

Dynegy engaged in the same type of round-rip trading as CSM Energy. Dynegy also used off-balance sheet transactions to portray loans of $300 million as operations cash flow. The SEC found this to be a major concern because cash flow was thought previously to be immune from cosmetic manipulation. This manipulation went further by not conforming to GAAP.

In September 2002, the SEC imposed a $3 million penalty. The SEC made it clear that the size of the penalty was reduced to prevent further financial injury to shareholders. Fraud charges were pursued against three Dynegy executives that resulted in prison terms ranging from 30 days to 26 years. Appeals are pending. Among other charges, the three executives were charged with failing to disclose pertinent information from independent auditor Arthur Andersen.

In April 2005, Dynegy settled with shareholders for $468 million.

El Paso Electric Company engaged in the same round-trip trading as CSM Energy and Dynegy. Before reaching settlement, the allegations included revenues inflated by more than $800 million from round-trip transactions, hiding more than $1 billion in liabilities using off-balance sheet accounting practices, and overstating its energy reserves by 40 percent.

In March 2007, a settlement with shareholders was reached for $285 million. El Paso also has settled, or still faces litigation, in the billions for manipulating energy markets that led to the 2000 – 2001 Western energy crisis.

2002 Was a Bad Year

Corporate fraud has been around a long time, but 2002 was particularly bad. Enron has become a notable hallmark as one of the all-time corporate scandals because of all the damage done. Several of the others would have been more noticeable during 2002 if Enron had not garnered the level of attention it did.

The $715 million fine against Adelphia would have established a new SEC record if the WorldCom fine of $750 million had not occurred the same year. Criminal sentences were changed noticeably during 2002. Previous white-collar crimes commonly had resulted in prison sentences of two years or less. The SEC and Department of Justice sent a clear message to corporate America when these cases finally worked their way through the legal system. The most scandalous executives likely will spend the rest of their lives in prison, and 20-year sentences became common.

The Sarbanes-Oxley Act created a watershed event in new financial statement reporting requirements not seen since the SEC was established in 1934. The additional transparency and higher level of senior management accountability will improve the reliability of the financial statements for years to come.

Securities Dealer Fraud

Fraud of investors is not limited to corporations and the managers who run them. The SEC also maintains oversight of stockbrokers and investment advisers. Fraud by securities dealers does not typically involve accounting fraud. Rather it is when investors are steered toward inappropriate investments.

- Churning — the unethical act of excessive trading in a client's account to increase the dealer's commissions or fees.

- Biased investment advise — when an adviser or broker has a preference for a specific company for reasons not disclosed to the client.

- Inadequate research — Advisers are obligated to perform due diligence before making investment recommendations.

- Mismanagement of an account — Unless the account is a mere order taker that executes trade, the financial adviser must act in the best interest of the client.

- Nondisclosure — In addition to not misrepresenting an investment, advisers and brokers have an obligation to make a full disclosure of all known negative information about an investment.

- Continued risk – Fraud can occur if advice is given to continue owning an investment when risk is apparent and opportunity for gain is unlikely.

- Conflict of interest — can occur when an adviser, broker, or firm that employs them has outside ties to a business and advises an investment, although it is not in the best interest of the investor.

- Lulling — occurs when an adviser repeatedly reassures an investor when losses are occurring with the hope that the investor will invest more money.

- Unlicensed salespersons and securities — Almost all securities and the people selling them must be registered with a state or the federal government. Scam artists blatantly violate these regulations to steal people's money.

The National Association of Securities Dealers (NASD) is a private-sector overseer of security representatives. With an annual budget of $500 million and a staff of more than 2,500, the NASD keeps tabs on more than 5,600 brokerage firms and 663,000 registered securities dealers.

CHAPTER 10

Investment Strategies

Stock ownership comes with risks but also the potential for better rewards than investors will find available with federally insured savings accounts. The financial statements dwell on risk associated with financial management of the company and other risks acknowledged in the management discussion and analysis. There are other external risks commonly associated with securities that investors need to know about.

With so much emphasis on the risks of investing in public companies, one might wonder why people take the chance. There are time-proven strategies to minimize risk while greatly improving the opportunity for investors to reap the financial rewards based on thorough research. Professionals in the investment world know that a diversified investment portfolio and adhering to a personal risk tolerance can be coupled with a known time horizon to manage each individual's risk exposure. What follows is an explanation of the backbone of risk management based on investment strategies.

Management Risk

This risk is what financial statements are about — risk within a single company. Besides management making a bad business decision or becoming embroiled in a scandal, the competition may come out with a better product or service. Other factors positively or negatively affecting a company's performance include compliance to government regulation, key suppliers or customers going bankrupt, and lackluster demand for an obsolete product. Labor disputes, product quality, market expansion decisions, and all operational decisions fall under the responsibility of management.

Sociopolitical Risk

Social and political events impact investment markets. Effects on markets following the terrorist attacks of 9/11 were some of strongest since the crash of 1929. Following 9/11, the New York Stock Exchange was closed for six days. When it opened, the Dow Jones Industrial Average fell 685 points or 7 percent the first day. The Dow Jones was down 14.3 percent after a week, and $1.2 trillion in shareholder value vaporized. Airlines faced long-term financial troubles, while the defense and security industries experienced high demand for new and existing products.

Whether real, predicted, or only perceived, wars, pandemics, and political elections affect the markets. Depending on the event, it can affect specific companies, industry sectors, national economies, or the global economy. Some are foreseeable, and others are not.

Country Risk

Today's conglomerate companies do business in many countries. General Electric has operations in over 100 countries, 3M has operations in over 60 countries and sells products in more than 200, while Procter & Gamble employs people in over 80 countries and sells products in 140.

Changes in government economic policies in these many countries can be to the benefit or chagrin of companies doing business there. China and India have encouraged outside business investment for many years and are expected to continue doing so. Over time, employees in these emerging economies will demand better working conditions, higher wages, and better benefits. Employee retirement plans can be changed, health coverage may be affected, or in extreme cases national labor strikes may occur.

Even more extreme is if a country nationalizes an entire industry after a company spends years developing the business. It suddenly can find its assets and future in the country gone. Conglomerates are knowledgeable about uncertain national conditions and have risk mitigation plans. Often, it is the smaller companies that are surprised and without a plan to deal with changing conditions within foreign countries.

Inflation Risk

Most investors easily recognize that inflation can erode savings. While aggressive investors run the risk of losing capital with high-risk investments, the overly conservative investor risks that savings will not keep pace with inflation. Bonds, bond funds, money market funds, and certificates of deposits are investments that most often run this risk.

Interest-Rate Risk

Associated with fixed-income investments in bonds is the risk that bond prices will fall during times that interest rates are rising. Certainly, the investor can continue holding the bond with every expectation that the capital investment will be repaid at maturity. However, the holder gives up a higher rate of return offered through other interest-based investments.

Credit Risk

Bonds and bond funds run the risk that the company issuing the bond cannot repay the debt when it comes due. Credit rating agencies such as Moody's and Standard & Poor's assign ratings to bonds and bond funds. The higher the rating, the lower the risk and the lower the interest rate paid. Low-rated companies issue junk bonds with high yields in exchange for the additional risk.

CASE STUDY: CONSERVATIVE RISK INVESTING

Dr. Geoffrey VanderPal is the most credentialed financial adviser in Nevada. In early 2006, he earned a doctorate degree in business administration and finance (with honors) from Nova Southeastern University while completing a dissertation researching various hedging strategies and risk/adjusted return analysis methods based on equity index investing.

He obtained his bachelor of science degree in business with majors in finance, marketing, and management from Columbia College and his master's of business administration from Webster University. Dr. VanderPal's extensive education and training includes CERTIFIED FINANCIAL PLANNER (TM) certificant*, Chartered Life Underwriter, Certified Fund Specialist, and Certified Treasury Professional and Registered Financial Consultant (TM) designations, requiring thousands of hours of studying and preparation culminating in extensive examinations. He completed the Certification in Financial Planning from the University of California at Berkeley.

Prior to establishing Elite Financial Planning Group of America, Inc., Dr. VanderPal spent ten years in several senior financial planning and investment advisory positions with Citibank/Citicorp Investment Services, Inc., and First Union Securities, Inc. At the age of 25, he created and later sold a mutual fund company founded on an innovative balanced portfolio methodology providing risk reduction to investors.

In 2005, Dr. VanderPal was named by the Consumer's Research Council of America as one of "America's Best Financial Planners." He is a frequent public lecturer on financial matters to community groups, civic organizations, and business organizations. He has been quoted or featured in *Millionaire* magazine, *Mutual Fund* magazine, *Chicago Tribune, Northwest Herald, Nevada Business Journal, Journal of Financial Planning,* and other publications, including television.

Dr. VanderPal is an adjunct professor at the University of Phoenix. He also serves as an arbitrator with the National Association of Securities Dealers and the New York Stock Exchange, as well as a past president of the Financial Planning Association of Southern Nevada in 2004 – 2005.

Without a doubt, Dr. Geoffrey VanderPal's insights about conservative risk management are grounded in the best knowledge and experience available. Dr. VanderPal also contributes a case study on moderate risk.

Dr. VanderPal demonstrates how reduced risk in conjunction with compound interest produces exceptional results without risking principal. A conservative investment can be expected to return 6 percent annually that will compound into $133,823 after five years without risking the $100,000 principal.

CASE STUDY: CONSERVATIVE RISK INVESTING

In contrast, a risky investment desiring to obtain a 13 percent annual return must risk the principal. The extra 7 percent is the reward for any number of unforeseen world or economic events that can cause a loss of principal. Two years of economic instability could reduce the principal investment by 30 percent or up to $70,000. Recovering the lost principal and equaling the conservative gain of $133.823 within five years requires the risky investment compound at 24.11 percent for the remaining three years.

Looked at another way, if the decreased investment of $70,000 earns only 10 percent, it takes 8.8 years of compounding to reach $133,823, the conservative investment made in five years. At the end of 8.8 years, the 6 percent principal secure investment is worth $166,990.

Risk Assessment Ratios

Among the array of analytical tools available to investors, Dr. VanderPal finds two exceptionally useful for risk evaluation.

The Beta Coefficient

The beta coefficient measures an investor's portfolio volatility compared to the broad market. This is a risk indicator of how an investment is expected to react during gains or losses in the market. If the market gains 1 percent, an investment with a beta of one compared to that market can be expected to gain 1 percent also. An investment with a beta of two is expected to gain 2 percent when the market gains 1 percent. The same applies to a loss in the general market. An investment with a beta of two expects to lose 2 percent when the overall market loses 1 percent.

Novice investors may think of investments with a beta coefficient above one as an improved probability of exceeding market gains. The truth is that is a risk calculation where conservative investors prefer maintaining a portfolio having a beta coefficient below one.

The Sharpe Ratio

The Sharpe ratio was developed by Nobel Laureate William Sharpe to measure risk-adjusted performance of a portfolio. The first step is determining what would be a risk-free rate of return for a portfolio. This is subtracted from the rate of return the portfolio is expected to provide. The remaining percentage is what the portfolio is earning for taking the risk. Dividing the number by the portfolio's standard deviation creates a ratio comparable with alternative portfolios. The higher the Sharpe ratio, the lower the risk per unit of return, resulting in a better risk-adjusted return.

Considerations for Conservative Investors

- Hybrid Certificates of Deposit (FDIC-insured investments in precious metals, commodities, and stock indexes)

CASE STUDY: CONSERVATIVE RISK INVESTING

- Exchange Traded Funds (using stop loss orders to lock in returns and secure principal)
- Index Annuities (protect principal while investing in stock and bond linked-indexes)
- Insured Mutual Funds (principal guarantees provided by brokerage firms and insurance companies)

Tips for Investors Reading Financial Statements

- Notes provide vital information about accounting changes that impact statements.
- A inventory management change from LIFO to FIFO can reduce COGS on the income statement resulting in an inflated operating income.
- The Annual Report gives insight if management ideology is more aggressive or leans toward conservative risk taking.

At the core of his capital preservation and conservative investment philosophy is something all investors need to think about: "It's not what you make but what you keep that counts."

GEOFFREY VANDERPAL

ELITE FINANCIAL PLANNING GROUP OF AMERICA, INC.

7251 WEST LAKE MEAD BLVD., STE. 300

LAS VEGAS, NV 89128

702-383-5092

702-562-4106 (Fax)

drvanderpal@gmail.com

http://protectedwealth.com

Diversification

Also called asset allocation or not putting all your eggs in the same basket, diversification is supported by academic research for reducing overall risk to investment portfolios. Diversification reduces the risk that one company will perform poorly or that an entire industry sector will under-perform. It also can help protect against sociopolitical risks and risks associated when investing internationally. A properly diversified portfolio considers the investor's time horizon and investing goals.

Strategically spreading the risk around greatly increases the odds that all investments will gain during good times, and losses will be restricted to a small portion of a portfolio during troubled times.

Global markets, free trade agreements, oil shortages, and countless other factors affect business. However, the effect is different on different industry sectors and individual companies. The idea behind a diversified portfolio is that a single negative economic event should have a minimal effect when a portfolio is diversified across many industries and businesses.

Deciding on a conservative, a moderate, or an aggressive investment risk tolerance combined with the investor's time horizon are the first steps in finding a proper diversification model.

Conservative investors will have a small percentage in stocks and a larger portion in bonds or the money market. Aggressive investors will take more risk with a high percentage in stocks. Naturally, the moderate risk taker is somewhere in between.

The tragedy of Enron is a strong example of why employees should not over-invest in the stock of their own company. An employee already depends on the company for a paycheck and pension, and it does not make good financial sense to invest further in the company when many other alternatives exist. This is even truer when an employee has stock options in the company she is employed with. Through the hyperbole of Kenneth Lay, Jeff Skilling, and the others who were pushing Enron stock, many employees elected to keep too much of their retirement accounts invested in the company

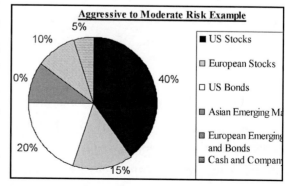

stock. Although much media attention highlighted employees losing both their job and retirement accounts, it did not have to be that way.

Enron employees talked about not being able to divest their holdings until age 50 and about a blackout period that prevented any changes in the allocation of retirement funds while the plan administrator was changed. In fact, only the company-matching contribution was required to remain invested in Enron stock until age 50. Employees could have divested two-thirds of their retirement accounts elsewhere. The situation with the blackout period was unfortunate, but the stock had fallen already from $80 to less than $15 when it occurred. As sad as it is for these Enron employees, they would have been much better off if they had diversified.

In the aftermath of Enron, Congress prohibited executives from being able to sell company stock during any blackout period. Congress also made it mandatory that employees are able to sell company stock they receive as matching funds. What Congress did not do is cap the percentage of retirement funds employees can invest in their employer's company stock. This remains the individual's responsibility.

Investment Time Frame

The length of time money can be invested without needing it for other purposes is an important consideration when making investing decisions. College educations, home purchases, and retirement commonly require access to investment funds. Investors should consider how far away they are from these life events when choosing investments.

The longer the investment period, the more volatility the investor can withstand. Over time, stocks in general rise and outpace inflation. This does not mean every stock will rise, but a diversified portfolio can be expected to rise. However, there are ample examples of periods when the stock market went through significant down turns. Investors with short time horizons run the risk of being forced to sell during a down turn. Those with enough time weigh portfolios more heavily in stocks than those who soon will need access to cash.

Conservative investors needing access to funds within one or two years typically keep funds in cash-equivalent investments. These include money markets and certificates of deposit. Conservative investors with more time often invest in suitable bonds.

Portfolios of moderate risk investors with at least five years invest in a combination of bonds and U.S. stocks. Aggressive to moderate investors with seven or more years might invest more heavily in stocks, along with diversifying into stocks of global companies and stocks of foreign companies.

Even once the appropriate mix of stocks and bonds is determined, there are many more decisions needed for a well-diversified portfolio. The chart captures the major industry sectors but is a very short list of the industries within each sector. Inside each industry are hundreds or thousands of individual companies. Some are large-cap companies with over $5 billion of capital invested, some are mid-cap with between $1 billion and $5 billion of capital, and some are small-cap with between $250 million and $1 billion. The dollar amounts vary depending on the expert consulted but are close enough for illustrative purposes.

Making individual choices between the thousands of investment opportunities can be a daunting task. Additionally, obtaining a properly diversified portfolio makes it necessary to invest in many companies in several sectors. Paying multiple brokerage commission fees reduces the returns earned on these multiple investments. It also makes for a small mountain of financial statements to analyze and keep track of. Many investors find mutual funds a preferred way to maintain a diversified portfolio.

Mutual Funds

A mutual fund operates much like a stock because the buy and sell price of the mutual fund shares varies depending on the fund's performance or net asset value (NAV), plus any fee the fund imposes at the time of the sale. Mutual funds use investors' money to buy stocks in various companies based on the funds stated criteria. Where an individual investor might own stock in one or two small-cap companies, by purchasing shares of a small-cap mutual fund the investor becomes much more diversified in small-cap companies through a single investment.

By purchasing ownership in separate mutual funds targeting large-, mid-, and small-cap companies and a foreign fund, an investor obtains hundreds or thousands of stock holdings for the cost and effort of a few transactions. Mutual funds combine the money of thousands of individual investors. Through cooperation between people that do not know each other, the mutual arrangement allows all fund owners to benefit through a jointly owned diverse portfolio. Investors do not

EXAMPLES OF INDUSTRIAL SECTORS

Basic Materials

Aluminum

Industrial Metals and Minerals

Oil and Gas

Synthetics

Consumer Goods

Appliances

Cleaning Products

Meat Products

Recreation Goods

Financial

Banks

Credit Services

Mortgage Investments

Real Estate Development

Health Care

Biotechnology

Drug Manufacturers

Medical Instruments

Specialized Health Care Services

Industrial Goods

Aerospace and Defense

Building Materials

Construction Machinery

Pollution and Treatment Controls

EXAMPLES OF INDUSTRIAL SECTORS

Services
Air Freight
Department Stores
Entertainment
Trucking

Technology
Communications
Data Storage
Scientific Instruments
Semiconductors

Utilities
Electric
Gas
Water

receive shares of the companies in which the mutual fund invests; rather they receive shares in the mutual fund with proportionate rights in the holdings of the mutual fund.

Like stocks, there are thousands of mutual funds to consider. Investment strategies vary greatly. Some funds invest in particular industry sectors, while others are based on indexes. An index fund strives to achieve performance similar to an index such as the S&P 500 or the Russell 1000. There are also asset allocation mutual fund models that seek maximum capital appreciation by timing the market. These mutual funds move back and forth between stocks, bonds, and money markets depending on market conditions.

Although mutual funds are a valuable tool for diversifying a portfolio, it is still important to understand the investment objectives of the particular mutual fund being considered.

Downside of Mutual Funds

For all the upsides of mutual funds there has to be a downside. Professional management costs eat into the gains before they can be passed on to investors. Mutual funds buy and sell stocks more frequently than an individual with a buy and hold philosophy. Whenever a stock held by the fund sells for a profit, a capital gain tax is incurred. Mutual funds pass these capital gains onto investors as a distribution, usually once a year. Investors pay taxes on the capital gain.

Sometimes this can cause confusion. An investor in a mutual fund might see the value of his investment decrease one year and still have to pay capital gains tax. An example would be if the mutual fund purchased stock in a company in 1999 for $15 and held it until 2005 when the stock was sold for $30. Capital gain is calculated by subtracting the purchase price from the selling price ($30 – $15), resulting in a gain of $15 for each share sold. The mutual fund buys and sells many stocks during the year. Some make a profit, while others are sold to limit the loss from a bad investment. At the end of the year, the fund subtracts total loses from total gains to determine the amount of capital gain that occurred. Net gains are distributed to investors.

An investor might buy into the fund only to see the NAV deteriorate shortly afterward. Although it is a declining investment, if the fund had a net capital gain, the new investor receives a taxable distribution.

Another scenario that can cause confusion is if distributions are reinvested automatically into the fund. The investor would not receive a check from the distribution but would receive the benefit of an increased investment in the fund. Although the investor receives no cash, capital gains tax is still due on the distribution.

There is relief for the investor holding the mutual fund in a 401(k), a traditional individual retirement account, or another tax-deferred account. Since these accounts are not taxable until retirement, the mutual fund distributions are tax-deferred.

Other professional management costs include accountants keeping track of everything, prospecting for new investors, and responding to questions coming from investors. Index-based funds strive to reduce these costs so that more earnings pass through to investors. An indexed mutual fund can be a great way to diversify a portfolio. One thing to do is understand the fee structure of any indexed mutual fund. The biggest difference between two funds simulating the same index should be the fees charged.

Value Versus Growth Investing

With an understanding about risk factors and diversification, the next investment decision hinges on one of two primary investment philosophies, value investing or growth investing. There are mutual funds that use these criteria along with the others mentioned.

Deciding the value a stock has is about future profits. Companies with profits headed down will see their stock price going the same direction. Of course, companies with improving profits are rewarded with rising stock prices. The basic question is how to value the future profits of a company.

Value investors look for stock where the current price does not reflect the real value of the company. Stocks that experience a bad but recoverable event or are in an industry temporarily out of favor can meet the criteria. These companies might have more value in their name, buildings, and other assets than the stock price reflects. Carefully chosen undervalued stocks see the stock price rise when the market recognizes the real value.

Growth investors seek profits primarily through exceptional capital growth rather than income from dividends. The objective is investing in a company that can grow earnings and revenue faster than the average company can. When the earnings growth is sustained, it translates into a high stock price. Peter Lynch is considered a guru of growth investing because of the performance of the Magellan Mutual Fund he managed from 1977 through 1990. Lynch averaged a 29 percent annual return over this period.

Value Investing

These are the boring and ugly stocks that no one is paying any attention to. This is Warren Buffet–style investing; he never bought into the Internet bubble that overestimated growth investing during the late 1990s. This is where reading and understanding a financial statement proves valuable. The basic idea is to find a company with real future earnings potential that has had a setback that will be overcome. The rest of the market undervalues the company's stock because they fail to see future earnings increasing. Often these companies hold the promise of strong dividend payments.

Value investors usually start by looking at the company's asset value. A company with a low price-to-book ratio can be an early indicator of an undervalued company with solid assets. One way that value investors look at assets is by determining book value (total assets – intangibles – liabilities) and capitalization (the total cost to purchase every share at the current market price). When book value and capitalization are approximately equal or book exceeds capitalization, other fundamentals are considered.

Intangibles are scrutinized closely, and actual value is added back in. Previous earnings history is examined for consistency and repeatability. Once these two items pan out, the reason for any slump in the stock price needs to be understood fully. Value investors look for logical reasons and management plans that can be trusted to correct the problem. When these elements come together, a value stock likely has been found. In the final analysis, a value investor establishes how much he thinks the company is worth, regardless of what it is valued at by the market. This is known as its intrinsic value.

Another common early indicator is the P/E ratio. Value investors are looking for a low price-to-earnings ratio. A high P/E indicates that future earnings already are built into the stock price, which is the opposite of what the value investor is looking for.

The PEG ratio is very much of interest to value hunters. The best value investors perform their own growth projections to create their own PEG ratio rather than to depend on market analysts. Where others see a PEG ratio above one, the value investor's projections would anticipate more growth and therefore a lower PEG.

Readers have learned that all the ratios and notes in the financial statement are important for understanding a company's fundamental financial situation. Value investors take a hard look at the current ratio and other leverage ratios to be sure the company is not over-burdened with debt that will hamper future financial performance.

Every value investor is looking for the right analytical tools to find the ideal undervalued stock that is about to begin increasing earnings and will be reflected quickly in a rising stock price. The value investor is not a speculative investor. Because the stocks one invests in are undervalued, there is little risk the price will decline. Theoretically, there is only an upside to stocks chosen by skilled value finders. The value investor then has the pleasant task of determining when the stock is valued correctly and deciding to sell. Of course, someone else has to be willing to buy at that price.

Growth Investing

The Internet bubble of the late 1990s is an example of a very strong growth-oriented market. At the height of the Internet bubble there was much talk about value investing being dead. When the bubble burst, growth investing fell out of favor. Like most everything in the stock market, value investing and growth investing go through cycles. Popularity in growth investing will return.

Technology always has been a leading choice for growth investors. In the 19th century, it was railroads, then came automobiles, pharmaceutical drugs, mainframe computers, personal computers along with software, and more recently the Internet.

Growth investing is about growing investment capital with a rising stock price rather than obtaining income from the investment. Investing in money markets, bonds, or dividend-paying stocks creates income. Growth investing is inherently more risky than other investment philosophies.

Growth company characteristics:

- Growing more than 20 percent per year
- The P/E ratio is close to the growth rate; a P/E ratio below the growth rate is better.
- Have a proven business model with room to expand into new markets.
- Have a healthy balance sheet and proven cash flow.
- Often in a little recognized industry with high growth potential
- Has a competitive advantage over others that might enter the market
- Usually does not pay a dividend so that earnings can be invested in growth

Common growth sectors are technology, health care, and consumer discretionary spending during good economic times. Technology continues to march forward and plays an important role in health care and often discretionary spending.

Health care has two dynamics pointing toward earnings growth that far exceeds inflation. First, the cost of health care continues to skyrocket on many fronts. New medical technology continues to be ever more expensive. People are living longer and availing themselves of long-term medical care. The baby boomers are now beginning to retire, which will increase drastically the number of people expecting quality of life as well as long-term medical care.

Consumer discretionary spending is definitely subject to volatility and cycles. When economic times are good, this sector prospers more than others do. People buy better cars, eat out more, go on more vacations, buy high-end products, and spend more. The demand side of the supply and demand equation eventually takes over, and prices for everything go up. An inflationary cycle begins, which further increases corporate earnings. History shows that, eventually, rising prices put pressure on discretionary spending. If a recession does not follow, the discretionary spending will at least become restricted, bringing earnings growth in the sector back in line with other sectors.

Emerging markets is another area where growth-oriented investors look. China, India, Brazil, and Russia dominate this category. Each has a competitive edge compared to mature business markets. In each case, the advantage is labor costs, raw materials, or rising intellectual capital. Usually, it is some combination of each. The governments of Brazil and Russia have not invested adequately in the infrastructures necessary to sustain rapid growth. China and India are the favored emerging markets based on government support. There lies the risk. Continued support by these governments is necessary for growth rates that reward aggressive investors. These governments lack experience at sustaining growth that must be considered carefully.

Fixed-Income Investing

Fixed-income investing is a strategy often followed after retirement but can be smart for any investor. Dependable high-yield dividend rates and bond interest rates are the primary objective rather than rapid capital growth. Naturally, the dividend yield ratio and bond interest rates are of particular interest for those pursuing an income-generating strategy.

There are two reasons this strategy is suitable for retirees. The income stream can supplement Social Security income, and a retirement pension comes with less risk to the capital investment than pursuing growth or value strategies. Companies with high dividend yields are often the most mature companies with a proven earnings record. They are paying high dividends because their growth plans are less ambitious than other companies' are. Ambitious growth and expansion increase the risk that goals will not be realized. On the other hand, companies not growing can be susceptible to a declining customer base. A combination of moderate growth and high dividends is appropriate for this strategy. Even a company commanding the lion's share of the global market needs to continue investing in new products and technology.

Dogs of the Dow

One successful income strategy is known as Dogs of the Dow. The Dow Jones Industrial Average is the most well-known stock index in the world. It is composed of some of the most successful companies with proven longevity. The strategy is quite simple. Pick the ten Dow Jones Industrial stocks with the highest current dividend yield and buy equal numbers of stock in each. Once a year, reevaluate the list. Sell any of the stocks that have fallen off the list and replace them with the stocks now on the list.

DOGS OF THE DOW			
Company	Stock Price	Current Dividend Yield	PEG
Altria Group	68.43	5.01	15.9
Pfizer Inc.	27.01	4.24	12.6
Citigroup Inc.	53.62	4.02	11.8
Verizon Communications Inc.	41.02	3.99	17.3
AT&T	39.6	3.62	14.5

DOGS OF THE DOW			
General Motors	29.31	3.34	8.8
General Electric	37.02	3.02	16.6
Merck and Co.	52.06	2.91	17.6
JP Morgan Chase & Co.	52.29	2.9	11.7
Du Pont De Nemours	50.49	2.87	15.9

The high dividend yield indicates that the price of the stock is probably down and the companies are out of favor (hence the word *dog*). If these were smaller and less established companies, that could be a concern. However, since these are stalwarts of the business world, there is less concern they are in serious trouble. Still, it is always wise to analyze the financials to be sure nothing serious has occurred.

The chart includes the PEG to demonstrate that, while these companies are not forecast for major earnings growth, moderate growth likely will continue.

Preferred Stocks

Preferred stocks are another option of the fixed-income strategy. With guaranteed income and less risk than common shares, they are a cross between corporate bonds and common stocks. Most have a fixed dividend close to the corporate bond rate, although there are a few preferred stocks with variable-rate dividends.

These also can provide some modest capital appreciation but not at the rate of common shares. The price a preferred stock buys or sells for moves more in tandem with a company's credit rating than with business events such as mergers or major contracts. Interest rates also have an effect on preferred stock values. As interest rates rise, the value of preferred stocks lowers because bank interest does not carry the risk of preferred stocks.

Preferred stocks are often convertible to common stock at the discretion of the investor. Many are also callable by the company that issued them. This means the company can buy the stock back and stop paying dividends at the company's discretion.

Learning about preferred stocks requires going beyond the traditional financial statements. There should be a preferred stock prospectus filed with the SEC as a 423B prospectus. Be sure to locate the correct prospectus. If there are multiple issues, they typically are identified as Series A, Series B, Series C, and so on.

A few things to look for:

- Are the dividends cumulative so that they are paid later if the company gets into trouble and suspends them?
- Has the board of directors ever suspended dividend payments?
- Are they callable; if so when, and how likely are they to be called?
- What is the conversion rate to common stock (often around one for one, which can be attractive if the common stock price rises)?

Preferred stocks are typically issued at $25 per share. The call date is of particular importance, especially if it is coming up soon. Almost all preferred stocks are redeemed for the $25 issuing price when they are called. When low interest rates have driven the stock exchange price up to $26 or $27 and the stock is callable within a couple of years, an investor would lose part of his capital at the $25 call rate without benefiting from several years of interest income.

DRIP

Dividend Reinvestment Plans (DRIP or DRP) are another option for the investor that does not actually need the income for living expenses.

These plans are run directly by the company. They allow investors to use dividends to buy additional company stock directly from the company. Although not appropriate for those needing the income, this investment option can be better than depositing dividends into a low-interest savings account or money market fund. These plans are a little like compounding compound interest.

There are many variables involved when calculating what a DRIP would be worth over a 20-year period, and all the variables are specific to the company selected. Dividend increases and the frequency of increases are important factors along with capital gain in the stock value. Stock splits also play a role because they lower the price of the stock, increasing the number of shares that can be accumulated. However, the role of stock splits is minimal because the dividend splits with the stock. Also, fractional share ownership is available through DRIPs.

An investor making a $10,000 initial investment in Johnson & Johnson in 1988 would have purchased 137 shares. Counting stock splits and all the dividends reinvested for 20 years, there would be 3,001 shares valued at $193,097 — an impressive return on investment at the cost of dividends.

Dividends reinvested are still dividends paid to the investor. Taxes need to be accounted for and reported on income tax returns. If the entire dividend is reinvested, the taxes will need to be paid from another income source.

There are several variations to these plans. Depending on company policy, they might:

- Be free, have a nominal fee for each purchase, or have a periodic fee

- Allow investors to begin by purchasing as little as one share

- Allow investors to add additional funds to the direct purchase program

- Sell shares at a discount compared to the open market

- Allow ownership of partial shares so that all funds remain invested all the time

- Some companies allow partial reinvestment of dividend and part paid directly to the investor

Those interested in DRIPs must contact the company's investor relations office to learn the details about a specific company's program. As with any investment strategy, finding a fundamentally sound company is the first step.

Allocation Balancing

The work is still not over once an investor determines a comfortable risk level, sets investing goals over time, develops an investing strategy, and purchases a diversified portfolio. At least once a year the portfolio needs to be revisited to make sure it remains balanced. Chances are that one section has done better or worse than others have during the year.

A good rule of thumb is that assets need to be reallocated when they become out of balance by 5 percent or more from the model being followed. This applies to individual stocks within the model as well. A diversified portfolio will have equity shares spread across several industries with different levels of performance during the year. Part of the gains made in the highly volatile technology sector may need to be sold and the proceeds used to purchase stock in a less volatile industry.

Take a $100,000 portfolio beginning the year with $40,000 in fixed income, $55,000 in equities, and $5,000 in cash. At the end of the year, the value has risen to $128,000, which is a good thing, but it might now be distributed $43,600 in fixed income, $79,050 in equities, and $5,350 in cash.

Only the cash portion remains within the 5 percent tolerance band of the allocation model. If this remains the correct allocation model, there are a few ways to rebalance. One way is to review the equities and sell off the lowest performers to purchase more of the best-performing

PORTFOLIO ALLOCATION MODEL
Capital Preservation
70% Fixed Income and 30% Equity
Income With Growth
60% Fixed Income and 40% Equity
Balanced
40% Fixed Income and 60% Equity
Growth
20% Fixed Income and 80% Equity
Aggressive Growth
0% Fixed Income and 100% Equity

fixed-income assets. Another way is to sell off the better-performing stocks and take the profit if there is a chance they might retreat. Move the funds into a more stable fixed income asset.

CHANGES IN ASSET ALLOCATION				
	Beginning	%	Ending	%
Fixed Income	$40,000	40.00%	$43,600	34.06%
Equities	$55,000	55.00%	$79,050	61.76%
Cash	$5,000	5.00%	$5,350	4.18%
Total	$100,000		$128,000	

A third way is to invest another $8,500 of new funds into bonds or another fixed-income vehicle. This would bring the total investment up to $136,500 and change the denominator in the calculation. The percentages come back within the 5 percent tolerance band. Certainly, it is a good idea to add to your investments on a regular basis, and during the annual allocation review is a good time to do so.

Tips to Keep Track of Investments

1. Read and understand all documents received from an adviser or broker. Make sure trade confirmations and account

statements are accurate.

2. All account transactions and statements should be sent directly to the investor, a trusted family member, or an accountant responsible for the investor's finances.

3. Keep notes of telephone calls and e-mails when communicating with a broker or an adviser. These can help reenact a transaction if questions come up later.

4. Immediately ask questions if confirmations and account statements are not received on a scheduled and regular basis.

5. If something appears to be out of the ordinary, ask questions of the adviser or broker immediately. If an unauthorized investment appears on the statement, contact the broker or adviser at once. Do not wait to see how well the investment performs.

6. Those that do not make investment transactions online should still access their account online. These accounts can be reviewed at any time, and trade confirmations are often provided in real time.

7. Do not make checks or other payments directly payable to brokers, advisers, or other individuals unless it is for a previously agreed-to fee. Investment funds should only be sent to the brokerage firm, a clearinghouse, or other financial institution.

Adding $8,500	
$52,100	38.17%
$79,050	57.91%
$5,350	3.92%
$136,500	

8. Conduct investment research independent of brokers and advisers. Read the SEC filings of companies before investing and review them while holding the investment.

9. Schedule periodic reviews of portfolios with brokers or advisers. Make sure the portfolio remains properly diversified and continues to meet investment objectives.

CASE STUDY: EXPERT ADVICE FOR MODERATE RISK INVESTING

As the most credentialed financial adviser in Nevada, Dr. Geoffrey VanderPal offers his expert advice to investors seeking higher rates of return on their capital assets with a well-thought-out risk management plan.

While there is no hard rule or line dividing the low-risk investor from the moderate-risk investor, Dr. VanderPal begins describing the distinction: "Conservative investors are those that are risk adverse and prefer not risking the investment principal. Moderate investors tend to place part of his or her portfolio in high-quality stocks and slightly lower credit-rated bonds, however still well within the investment grade territory." Drawing upon his extensive financial education, experience, and certifications, Dr. VanderPal explains the various investment risk factors to clients to ascertain the investment portfolio most appropriate for each client. A benchmark for the moderate risk investor begins with a composition of:

- 30 to 40 percent invested in the stock of large, capitalized, high-quality, corporations as the backbone of the portfolio
- A small percentage (15 to 30 percent) may be distributed among middle capitalized, small capitalized, and international corporations to provide strong asset allocation.
- 25 to 30 percent invested in high quality short- to medium-term bonds
- 10 to 20 percent maintained in interest-bearing cash equivalent accounts, such as certificates of deposit and money markets

Dr. VanderPal asserts that index-based mutual funds best serve many moderate risk investors because they provide the best diversification model. These also offer transaction fees and tax advantages that further shield the investor's principle and earnings. Obtaining proper asset allocation, while maintaining moderate risk, involves purchasing stocks in at least five sectors and industries with a maximum of 5 percent of assets invested in any single company.

Dr. VanderPal offers additional risk management advice for moderate risk investors:

- Stop loss orders on stocks and Exchange Traded Fund (ETF) securities can be used to lock in gains and reduce the investor's exposure to losses.
- ETFs offer the most efficient risk management method of investing internationally by focusing on a standardized international index or an index for a specific country, but care must be taken to avoid over-concentration of assets in a single country; proper global diversification reduces this risk.

CASE STUDY: EXPERT ADVICE FOR MODERATE RISK INVESTING

- What it all comes down to is that investment decisions need to be based on knowledge and facts, not greed and fear.

As an investing expert and independent financial adviser, Dr. VanderPal guides each client through his or her personal risk and volatility profile ensuring he or she understands the nuances of the many investment vehicles available. Investing goals are established based on the objective of safeguarding principal while carefully balancing risk with returns. Whichever level of risk is deemed appropriate, the most important step is engaging the investment process that can deliver long-term asset growth via investment returns compounded over time. Life's dreams are within reach for the knowledge-enriched investor. Developing a multi-stage investment horizon fortified with expert advice achieves financial dreams.

GEOFFREY VANDERPAL

ELITE FINANCIAL PLANNING GROUP OF AMERICA, INC.

7251 WEST LAKE MEAD BLVD., Ste. 300

LAS VEGAS, NV 89128

702-383-5092

702-562-4106 (Fax)

drvanderpal@gmail.com

http://protectedwealth.com

CHAPTER 11

Bringing Investors and Businesses Together

Aggressive investors wanting high rates of return and businesses looking for funding to rapidly expand operations have something in common — taking more risk in search of fortunes. Entrepreneurs have great ideas about how to create or, better yet, expand an existing company to earn money but need investment capital to make it happen. There may be a few readers who have made their fortune and now look for opportunities to help others do the same and, at the same time, earn an exceptional return for taking a risk at something they understand — building businesses.

Deciding When Outside Investors Are the Right Fit

The answer is not as obvious as it seems. Angel and venture capital is, by far, the most expensive funding businesses can obtain. An explanation of expected equity investment exchanged for the investment comes later, but it is substantial. Growing or getting started from other funding sources, or bootstrapping, is the best way to keep financial control of the business and may open more affordable borrowing options later.

Consider other funding sources first. If the business or owner has collateral, taking out a loan is a reasonable possibility; even at a very high interest rate, a loan is much less expensive than equity capital financing. Business owners may qualify for a Small Business Administration or U.S. Department of Agriculture guarantee, which makes loan applications more appealing to commercial lenders. Of course, loan payments must be made, and if the business fails, the lender becomes the owner of the collateral. Still, consider it carefully. In exchange for a few years or fewer of loan payments, all equity in the business remains with the entrepreneur.

Tips for Developing a Business Plan

Angel and venture capital is available in exchange for part ownership in the right business. When equity ownership of the business is traded for growth capital, owners learn that equity investors are not that different from other lenders. Answers to three basic questions are required:

1. How much money does the business need?
2. How will it be used?
3. How will the funding be repaid?

A solid, well-developed business plan with accurate financial projections is the language of business. A thorough business plan answers the questions both the owner and the investor should be asking. Business plans come in many formats, and some investors are specific about which to use. The business owner must make the plan interesting and realistic. Dull plans are not read and not funded; the same goes for unrealistic plans. In a bid to obtain funding at any cost, some owners request too little, which leaves the venture at great risk when the funding runs out before the venture achieves positive cash flow. Under-funding the project is a sure path to failure.

Typical mistakes made, by type of business plan writer, are:

- The Marketing Professional — hype and promise with little substance
- The Accountant — chock full of tables and dull

- The Engineer — graphs and tables with over-explanation of how things work and equally dull

An interesting and balanced plan focuses on defining the problem that will be solved with the new product or service, how customers will benefit, why customers will pay for the product or service, and how the product or service will be provided to customers.

Sophisticated investors never believe the financial projections; many immediately cut the number in half just as a beginning point for conversation. Nonetheless, financial projects must be provided. The underlying assumptions and rationale are at least as important as accurate numbers. The assumptions and projection rationale tell the potential investor that the owner has a realistic understanding of the target market. Detailed monthly projections of revenue, expenses, supplies, and asset purchases in an easy-to-update spreadsheet are expected by investors. Essentially, the projected financials are a monthly forecast of the balance sheet, income statement, and statement of cash flow.

Depending on the project size and complexity, business plans begin at about 20 pages in length and get bigger from there. But never confuse bulk with useful content. Show summaries in the business plan. Avoid needless detail. Multiple versions of a business plan are common. An internal plan with every operational detail is not necessarily the best version to show an investor. Important details and descriptive commentary may demonstrate the entrepreneur's mastery of the subject. The best place for this is as an attachment or appendix at the end of the plan. The reader can, at his or her discretion, go to the attachment or financial projections to get the detail.

Categorizing the Investment Need

The most likely source of equity funding depends on:

- Amount of funding needed

- Specific industry type being funded

- Growth stage of the business

- Geographical location

Funding Amount

A practical assumption is that an angel investor will put about $50,000 into an investment. Businesses needing $150,000 will need to find three angels to make the deal doable. If the project requires $3 million, that is 200 angels. It is not going to happen. Finding ten angels is difficult, and any more is nearly impossible. A reasonable conclusion is that angels can be found to fund up to $500,000 for the right project.

Venture capitalists, investment bankers, and other private equity sources shy away from small investments of around $2 million or less. It is about the same amount of due diligence and follow-up for a small deal as a large one. These investors, logically, want more for their effort and prefer larger investments. The $500,000 to $2,000,000 investment area is awkward.

Industry

Fortunately, angels are interested in all kinds of ventures, although the majority still go to the same industries favored by venture capitalists. Venture capitalists (VCs) are generally much more finicky. They only want to invest in the hot, new industries. In fairness, a good VC brings more than capital to a venture. Good VCs often have expertise and connections that will help propel the venture to its goals; therefore, they stick to what they know.

Generally, if the venture is in a mundane industry — anything other than medical/ health, IT, nanotechnology, environment, or the latest flavor — the most probable investors are angels, investment bankers, and other private equity sources.

Investment Stage

This criterion is critical. Despite the general description, "risk capitalist," professional investors do everything possible to minimize risk. Most often, they back away from early-stage deals. Stages translate roughly into:

- Seed — an idea or concept to visit an investor with. During the Dot-Com Craze of 1998 – 2000, VCs chased down people with ideas for Internet applications and gave them millions to develop their ideas; those days are long gone.

- Startup — The business is farther along with an organization and a fairly well defined plan on how to reach established goals.

- First Stage — The business is up and running with customers and is a going operation.

- Second Stage — The business needs capital to expand sales or obtain new, vital technology.

VCs prefer first- and second-stage deals. Their chief worries are abated. The venture has sales, costs, and a working business model. Seeds and startups come to them with ideas, but first- and second-stage companies are past the concept stage.

A more mature company appeals to lenders more than those still in the early stages of development. Mature companies have or should have fundable collateral and a creditworthy track record. Angels also have pulled back from seed and startup deals, but, generally, this is your target investor if you have an early-stage deal.

Geography

Angels generally do not like to invest in ventures more than a two-hour drive from where they live or work. To a lesser degree, VCs have a similar but expanded bias for deals in their area, but VCs are willing to make short flights for promising projects. Details about early operations come later, but, for now, understand investors will spend much time with owners in the early going — much easier to do if the investor and business are near each other.

Preparing the Proposal

The business plan is the centerpiece of the proposal. For obvious reasons, it needs to be written carefully. Some entrepreneurs hire someone to write their plan, which is not recommended by most experts. The business owner will present the plan and later defend it. It is more sensible for the owner to write the plan in his own language with the assistance of a professional business plan writer. Business plan software can help but also can result in a boiler plate appearance that lacks the ability to make a strong impression about the business and the owner.

Business plans must be neat, legible, and without spelling or grammar errors. Business plans should not give the impression they were put together hurriedly or the business owner is semiliterate. However, they do not necessarily need to be pretty or fancy. Investors care much more for content than form.

Preparation of a good business plan is a subject unto itself not addressed here. Instead, the following is a list of common misconceptions concerning business plans:

1. A Slick Business Plan Is Funded

A well-thought-out business plan is needed but not for the assumed reason. Sophisticated investors do not believe the optimistic financial numbers and wild claims seen in nearly all business plans because they never become reality. What investors want to see, from the business plan, is that the entrepreneur knows the business and can demonstrate how the investors' money will be used to build a high-growth, high-profit company. In fact, VCs and busy angels read few business plans and do so only after they have established an interest in the venture.

2. Top-Down Sales Forecast

The sales forecast starts with a large available market. The sales forecast is the new company taking a small percentage of the market and making a lot of money. This is the wrong approach. What this tells investors is the owner does not know the market and how to sell to it. The proper approach is to identify known customers willing to buy the product or service and how these customers can be persuaded to buy.

3. No Competition

The product or service is the greatest thing since sliced bread (which, incidentally, took over 12 years from introduction to gain initial market acceptance). No one else has anything like it. The new venture will have the market to itself or be so far ahead others cannot catch up. Intelligent investors know it does not take long for companies already serving the target market to come back with improved versions of what sells well.

4. Name Management Team

Entrepreneurs are nothing if not enterprising. They study venture funding and find they must have a qualified management team before investors will give them money. Unfortunately, the entrepreneur and his associates are all techies. They resort to Rent-a-CEO by finding a person who will lend his name to the business plan as CEO or board member.

This is an insult to a sophisticated investor's intelligence in implying they cannot quickly figure out the person is only along for the ride and had little or no input to the plan. A better approach is to go to the angel or early-stage VC with what you have. If it is a technical venture and the first hurdle is a working beta system, there is no reason to bring in a high-priced CEO early. Let the VC help pick the missing member of the management team. Experienced investors understand the initial management team often is lacking. They like filling in the pieces and, especially, having a known CEO in charge.

CASE STUDY: EXPERT ADVICE ON BUSINESS FUNDING

Tim Murray is president and owner of ManagementUplink.com. He shares his business knowledge and experiences with entrepreneurs desiring to take their business to the next level. Murray's previous business experience includes president of Coast Telecom Corporation and president of Urethane Systems, Inc.

He also served as vice president of Superior Continental Corporation and marketing manager of Communications Technology Corporation. His consulting experience includes work with contractors, retailers, manufacturers, distributors, service companies, and non-profit organizations.

He earned a master of business administration from UCLA, a master of science in applied mechanics from California Institute of Technology, and a bachelor of science in mechanical engineering from Rice University.

As an entrepreneur, he understands the challenges a business concept faces in becoming a reality and financially viable. Among Murray's proven business consulting services is an experience-based methodology to new business and business expansion funding.

Management Uplink's Different Approach

Having firsthand experience in investment banking, Murray cautions business owners from immediately seeking funding from very high-cost angel investors and venture capitalists. He would rather see the business owner retain the highest possible portion of financial interest in the company. Management Uplink supports the business owner in bootstrapping and seeking funding through commercial and guaranteed loans available from commercial lenders.

If internal funding is not practical, Murray works with companies all the way from venture funding to exit — venture sale or IPO. He works with entrepreneurs in a

CASE STUDY: EXPERT ADVICE ON BUSINESS FUNDING

unique way — becoming a partner rather than a contractor. The entrepreneur pays no front fees. Management Uplink takes compensation after the venture is funded successfully in a reasonable long-term retainer and company shares. His basic objectives are identical with the entrepreneur's — get the venture funded, operations managed professionally, and long-term share value optimized. Murray is a specialist in results-based management systems and applies this expertise to partner companies.

Management Uplink services include:

- Defining the venture, needed organization, and required funding
- Preparing business plan, financial forecast, and query letter
- Establishing a target list of prospective investors
- Contacting investors
- Assistance in presentations
- Assistance in negotiations
- Venture operations — core values, organization, plans, control, policies / procedures, and personnel evaluation / compensation
- Board of directors organization and service as a director or secretary / treasurer
- Consulting on exit plans — company sale or IPO.

MANAGEMENT UPLINK

16303 IMPERIAL VALLEY DRIVE / 1706

HOUSTON, TX 77060-3542

281-260-0513

tmurray@mgmt uplink.com

http://www.mgmt-uplink.com

Equity Investment Costs

Every would-be entrepreneur needs to memorize the golden rule of finance. It reads: He who has the gold makes the rules. The investor, not the entrepreneur, dictates equity shares and the form of investment. However, there are things entrepreneurs and business owners can do to help lead the investment in the direction best suiting them.

Angel and VC investment arrangements can take many different forms, but some are much more common than others. These aggressive investments span a spectrum — straight equity on one end and a straight loan on the other. On this basis, investment types can be categorized as follows.

Common Shares

As with pubic corporations, investing through common stock is the most common form of equity investment for VCs and angels. Also, it is the one into which the others usually evolve when the venture is successful. Common shareholders receive no assigned dividends and are paid last in the event the venture is liquidated. They bear the most risk. Management or owner shares are common shares. Owners and management get the opportunity for wealth only when and if company shares are sold. Many investors come in on the same basis. Common shares are ownership of the company.

Preferred Shares

As the name suggests, preferred shareholders get preference if the company is liquidated. Holders of preferred stock are in line before the common shareholders. As previously described, preferred shares often receive designated dividends (e.g., 6 percent annually paid quarterly). If these dividends cannot be paid, they accumulate and must be paid at a future date before common shareholders receive a dividend.

Loan

Sometimes investors actually come in as lenders, usually on more generous terms than are available from commercial lenders, particularly regarding collateral. As lenders, investors receive interest and maybe principal payments. Even if collateral is not pledged to their loan, they are in line ahead of common and preferred shareholders in the event of liquidation.

Warrants

Sometimes investors request and get warrants to purchase common shares at a set price. Warrants resemble the option grants that managers and employees can be awarded to improve performance. When the share price goes over the set price, the investor exercises the warrants and picks up an equity boost to his investment return. Warrants can be added to preferred shares and loan investments to make them more attractive to the investor.

Conversion

Preferred shares and loans can be converted into common shares. In fact, it is done often. The investor has the option to convert his or her preferred shares or loan anytime, but usually the option is exercised at exit, when the business is sold. That way, the investor has the advantages of the loan or preferred shares while in effect but can convert to common shares sold at a later date for more profit.

The investment may turn out to be a combination of these features. Remember, early-stage owners and those looking for aggressive investors to finance rapid growth need to be flexible with investors.

Angels

Angel investors provide most of the investment capital. The term originated with backers of Broadway productions. Angels are simply wealthy individuals who provide investment capital to businesses. They do it for a variety of reasons — to get a better return than the stock market affords, to keep their hand and interest in business, and to help a new generation of entrepreneurs.

Angels are plentiful and widespread. That is the good news. The bad news is they are not easy to find and approach. Angels mostly invest in ventures recommended to them by trusted associates — often other angels. The entrepreneur's objective is to obtain an introduction or recommendation. This is easy if the entrepreneur already knows an angel, which is seldom the situation. More often, an angel is a friend of a friend of a friend.

When it comes to finding an angel, entrepreneurs have to be shameless. They tell everyone they meet that they are looking for investment capital and why. They go farther by recruiting the management team, friends, family, and anyone willing to help do the same. In the age of the Internet, entrepreneurs create a mailing list of everyone the entire recruited network knows. A short e-mail is sent to a long list of prospective investors explaining what is wanted and what the business will do with it. Everyone on the list is asked to invest and to pass on the e-mail to someone else who may be interested.

Another technique is to let the angels find the entrepreneur. A publicist is hired to write a story about the entrepreneur and the venture. The publicist arranges to publish it in the local paper or trade magazine or arranges other appropriate coverage. The story always includes contact information.

In recent years, angels have come together in clubs with formal meetings and presentations by entrepreneurs. But unlike with VCs, entrepreneurs usually pay to play at the presentations. The angel clubs hire a secretary to screen and compile applications and use the fees they collect from entrepreneurs to pay the secretary's salary and for the expenses of the presentations. In many ways, presenting to an angel club is like going before VCs. Odds of being funded are very low, but entrepreneurs get a good evaluation of the venture and pointers on how to improve it.

The Internet provides funding sources, mostly angels and angel organizations. Entering words like "venture funding" into Google and Yahoo results in plenty of prospects. A word of caution: There are many "investor finders" often masquerading as "investment bankers" or "private equity" and making similar but untrue claims. It takes effort to separate the chaff from the wheat to find valid investors.

A common mistake in seeking funding is relying on a well-connected finder, usually one who requires front fees. Before going this route, the entrepreneur needs to consider how long before a finder (broker) wears out his or her welcome with the investors by bringing them less-than-fundable deals. Those with a fundable deal do not need a finder. If it is not a fundable deal, a finder will not be able to help.

Investors do not want to see large broker fees taken from the funds they invest in the venture. Investors want to see the money put to use in the company building markets, developing a product, and providing needed infrastructure.

Investors typically find deals through referrals from other investors and others they know. However, following the dot-com bust and resulting sag in the stock market, many former investment executives set up boutique investment banking firms and can steer deals to their friends still working with the venture capital companies and wealthy former clients. However, these investors are using the investment bankers to screen deals for them. If the investment banker recommends a project that does not have merit, the investment banker soon loses credibility with them. In the end, there are some finders that can put your deal in front of qualified investors, but be careful particularly with finders who want front fees.

HOW TO READ AND UNDERSTAND FINANCIAL STATEMENTS

Entrepreneurs come in every size, color, weight, national origin, personality, and gender. The common characteristic is optimism. The perpetually optimistic entrepreneur seeking investor funding must maintain the attitude of the boy who wanted a pony for Christmas. Instead of a pony he got a Christmas stocking filled with horse manure. His parents watched in amazement as he happily tore through the stocking. They asked why he was happy and he answered, "All this horse manure: There has to be a horse in there somewhere."

There are all kinds of angels — good, bad, evil, and even dumb. The wrong angel can make your life miserable. The wise entrepreneur learns all he can about the angel at the same time the angel is investigating the entrepreneur and venture. The two will need to work closely together for several years to achieve their common goal of growing the business.

Venture Capital

For all but a very few, funding from a venture capitalist is a pipe dream. VCs are extremely picky. They will look only at investments in particular industries, funding ranges, development stages, and geographic areas. Most see thousands of proposals in a year and maybe fund three or four. They are the most intelligent people on Earth. Most VCs have stellar backgrounds. They are top graduates from the top universities. They have led high-technology companies to the promised land. To get through the mass of applications, they quickly dump most. Entrepreneurs are given a quick exit when a proposal is submitted outside of the stated interest areas. VCs fund ventures brought to them as referrals but very few from unsolicited applications. The difficulty finding a worthy referral is the bad news.

The good news, if there is any, is VCs advertise what they seek in new investments. VCs and VC lists are found easily on the Internet and at any business library. Although thousands are listed, only a small subset will be interested in a particular venture. The list gets shorter if it is not one of the hot industries.

For many entrepreneurs the VC world really is a jungle, and full consideration needs to be given to alternative funding sources before going this route. VCs are professional investors. It is not a sideline for them but a business. VCs are very analytic. They can pick business plans apart and leave entrepreneurs wondering what they were thinking when they put it together. They see and reject thousands of business plans yearly and consequently are jaundiced.

Those fortunate enough to secure VC funding usually have an excellent relationship with the investor in the end. On the whole, VCs can bring knowledge, important contacts, and a seasoned perspective to the venture. Even though VC investment is unrealistic for all but a very few companies, VCs and their characteristics are included throughout this chapter. The entrepreneur is well served to treat all prospective investors as VCs — professional investors — and deal with them accordingly.

Friends, Family, and Fools (FFF)

FFF is a derogatory term VCs use for unsophisticated early investors. Parents, uncles, aunts, grandparents, and other family members want to help. It is natural for families to look out for one another. Also, friends can be a source of funding for similar reasons. These people have non-financial reasons to want to help the entrepreneur.

It may be the entrepreneur's only opportunity at funding when suitable angels cannot be found and VCs will not touch the venture. The eternally optimistic entrepreneur still knows the venture will work if funding can be found.

Funding experts strongly recommend not going for FFF funding. The odds are long even for the best-designed ventures. Despite intelligence and professionalism in funding, the typical VC only scores big on three of ten funded ventures. Half fail, and the others drift along without hitting their target numbers.

Professional angels spread their investments around on the same basis. That is the reason wealthy individuals do not usually sink more than $50,000 in a single venture. For FFF, the entrepreneur venture may be the only business investment they ever make. Overall, the odds of it hitting big are low. And the entrepreneur, in essence, is asking FFF to bet this one venture will bring big returns. Most times, it will not happen, and for the rest of their life, the entrepreneurs must face the FFF at family get-togethers, Thanksgiving, class reunions, and parties and explain again how the money was lost.

Another problem with FFF is they are unsophisticated. Even when a venture succeeds, it may need additional funding. Potential investors may take an interest in an experienced business owner but do not want to deal with unsophisticated investors. Bringing them onboard can poison the well when seeking future funding from professional investors.

The Professional Investment Process

Professional investors follow a standard process from the original contact through taking their profit and exiting the venture when goals are achieved. The sequence is:

1. Creating Interest in the Venture

2. Reviewing the Management Team

3. Negotiating the Investment Agreement

4. Starting Operations

5. Exiting the Business

Creating Interest in the Venture

Generating investment interest is similar to a full-court press in basketball. Entrepreneurs go for every possible funding source at full throttle as if it is their only hope at business success. This is done in parallel, not serially. When multiple sources of interest arise, sorting and prioritizing prospects is the entrepreneur's dream come true. But initially, it is pursuit of all prospects simultaneously.

The well-written and -constructed business plan, with well-developed financial projections, is an important tool. However, in the scheme of things, a good query letter and an elevator speech may be more important to success. The business plan and financial projection are not read until the prospect is interested. That is where the query letter and the elevator speech come in.

Query Letter

A query letter is not difficult to write. It is the executive summary of the business plan on steroids. It needs to be reviewed closely by the business owner and other respected individuals to get feedback and ideas for polishing it. The purpose of the query letter is to obtain enough interest to proceed with the investigation. The query letter is short and tightly written. One page is preferred but no more than two pages. Different versions of query letters may be needed for different prospects. Two investors with similar but slightly different venture criteria receive custom query letters emphasizing the venture's match to their criteria.

The first contact with prospective investors is through the query letter. Even when investors request a business plan first, the query letter becomes a cover letter attached to the plan. The query letter improves the chances of gaining the investor's attention before his eyes glaze over from reading hundreds of business plans.

For unsolicited funding proposals, e-mail is the simplest, easiest way to contact most prospects. To the few who refuse to work with the Internet, send faxes or snail mail. As soon as an interest is established, the move to personal contact through telephone calls and in-person meetings should be done quickly to maintain and enhance the interest.

Referrals are pursued through personal contact from the beginning whenever possible. The personal contact leads directly to the need for an elevator speech.

Elevator Speech

This somewhat humorous name comes from the idea that entrepreneurs want to get on an elevator with a captive investor on the first floor and be invited into his or her top-floor office to further discuss the venture. The mission is to get the VC interested in the deal before he or she gets off the elevator. This two- to five-minute speech needs to capture the listener's attention quickly.

This takes work and rehearsal. Like the query letter and the business plan, it varies with the audience. In most cases, entrepreneurs are speaking to intelligent laymen. The investor does not know the industry and business as well as the entrepreneur and definitely does not know the acronyms and buzz words. However, these people are intelligent, and it is important not to talk down to them but still come across with strong enthusiasm. The elevator speech conveys a fine blend of confidence and humility.

The elevator speech follows the basic concept of the business plan. What problem will the venture solve for customers willing to pay for it? Why is this the best solution? What resources are already in place (usually management)?

Presentation

The next step is an opportunity to make a full presentation. This is an expanded version of the elevator speech. Again, it is customized to the audience by carefully matching any known criteria. Entrepreneurs have more time to talk during a presentation but must be respectful of any time limitations. Rehearsing for the presentation includes making sure it ends on time and the most important information is presented. Comments should be sharp, pointed to the subject with a little but not a lot of humor. Many entrepreneurs have training in effective speaking that applies here.

Displays are used during the presentation. PowerPoint is a mixed blessing that should not be overused. Use charts, graphs, and visuals to illustrate important and complicated points. Graphics should be few in number, simple, and interesting.

Management

Entrepreneurs are familiar with the retail adage that lists the three major factors for success — location, location, location. VCs have a similar saying about new business proposals — management, management, management. VCs will take a first-rate management team with a second-rate business over a first-rate business and second-rate management team any day of the week. Having an experienced, proven management team is the single most critical factor for the success of new ventures. Several grading scales exist for evaluating management teams, and they go something like this:

> **A Team** — Experienced CEO in the same industry as the new venture with quality functional management in technology, marketing, finance, and other key positions. If the CEO

and, better yet, the management team have taken another startup or new company all the way to IPO or sale to a public company at a high multiple, put a star on the management team. Deals with A+ or A teams are usually funded.

B Team — This is an in-between team or experienced, proven management but in another industry or less successful management from the same industry.

C Team — This is, unfortunately, where many venture deals are. The management team is composed of bright individuals with a passion for the deal but no heavyweight experience. VCs walk away, but angels might be interested if they know and like the entrepreneur. Also, there is the situation where the entrepreneur engages the investor and gets help filling the management team holes.

Protection

No one wants to invest in a new technology or concept and watch it grow and become successful only to see the market taken away by predatory competitors. Unfortunately, patents are often useless — competitors violate the patent and then settle in court years later. It is a major reason why VCs and angels prefer high-tech, niche ventures rather than mundane ventures with built-in competition.

Skin in the Game

VCs want to see hard cash put into the deal by the founders rather than sweat equity. The reasoning is that the entrepreneur will take off when the going gets tough. This often occurs if entrepreneurs have not invested a significant amount of personal equity into the company before outside investors come in. Remember, experienced investors are jaundiced.

Negotiations

Negotiations are unique to each situation. Interested prospects will have concerns that must be addressed as discussions progress. The fortunate entrepreneur will have several prospective investors and more than one set of concerns to address. As much as anything, negotiations are about establishing a comfort level between entrepreneur and investor. It is the process of forming a partnership, in the sense of shared company equity, with the common goal of hitting target profits, cashing out, and becoming wealthy or wealthier.

VCs and angels will take all they can get in deals they fund. Early-stage investors, typically, look for returns of 20 times the amount invested or more in five years. Later-stage investors should, and usually do, take lesser returns. This can seem greedy. It probably is, but risk-capital investors have many failures. They have to see big, not modest or reasonable, returns on the ventures that succeed.

Due Diligence

No one buys a car without kicking the tires and looking under the hood. VCs and professional investors are not an exception. The investor will determine what, how, and when it will be done. But, generally, management background and experience will be vetted. If there is underlying technology, it will be reviewed carefully, as will assets if they are important to the venture. Much due diligence is testing the market. Always important is determining if target customers really will buy the product / service on the basis claimed in the plan. In total, due diligence takes up to three months. Professional investors are not hurried in their investigation.

Valuation

VCs have references and other methods of valuing a venture. It all boils down to what the entrepreneur brings, what investors bring to the deal, and equitably dividing the stock shares. Not surprisingly, investors' money counts much more than unfunded ideas. But there are other considerations besides the amount of money put up. Chief is the reluctance of most investors to manage the company. They require timely reports and the ability to influence and dictate strategy. However, they do not want to manage the company. They want the management team to manage. It is a reason most professional investors will not go for controlling shares unless there is a major imbalance in the inputs.

Bottom line, the shares and terms taken by the investor are negotiated. It improves the entrepreneur's position and frame of mind if he has more than one prospective funding source. That should be a primary objective in the funding process — getting two or more interested parties to the table at about the same time.

Starting Operations

The venture is funded and ready to start or expand operations.

A common misconception among first-time entrepreneurs is that investment funding will come up front, in total. What usually occurs is a conditional commitment is made by the investor to provide funding as needed and as earned by hitting agreed-upon milestone accomplishments. VCs frequently use a variation of an item called a "burn chart."

Burn Chart

Across the top of a burn chart, in linear time, are the company's short-term goals. It may be completion of a product beta test or opening a new distribution line or completion of a needed facility. These are all important milestones, which tell the investor the business is on track to hit targeted goals. Across the bottom, in the same time frame, is cash put into or burned by the venture. The burn chart captures the investor's two major concerns — what is invested and what the business is accomplishing.

Depending on the investor, management will be required to make weekly, maybe daily, reports. Management remains ahead of the game by maintaining open, honest communication with the investor. Every venture has unexpected developments, and most of these will be negative. Problems, as well as your accomplishments, need to be reported. Each problem should be accompanied with at least one credible solution. Experienced investors are not surprised when problems are encountered. What they want to see is that management is on top of the problems.

Results-Based Incentive Compensation

The management team must have strong commitment from the start. In exchange for delivering high performance, the management team should be compensated fairly. Incentive compensation is performance based. Management is rewarded directly for the contributions it makes to meeting and exceeding goals. A major mistake made by well-meaning CEOs is awarding stock to managers and key employees. Award options are earned by superior performance. Subpar performance results in no options. Excellent performance earns deserving managers more options.

Awarding options reflects on how the business should be managed — by the numbers. A good investor makes this a requirement. However, it should be done because it is the professional way to manage the company. Results-based incentive compensation is a fundamental part of a results-oriented management system.

Dealing With Multiple Investors

Ventures funded by a group of angels should establish a lead investor, a single person for management reporting. The lead investor communicates with the other investors. An example is a $500,000 investment with ten investors. If the CEO takes phone calls from and deals with ten investors, there will be no time to run the company. Establishing a lead investor may not be as difficult as it sounds. Typically, one or two lead investors bring the others into the venture. One is a logical leader. There still will be occasions when the CEO must communicate directly with all the investors to keep them at ease of mind.

Exit

The earlier excitement at startup operations was premature. When the venture obtains funding, the real story begins. The CEO must use the funds to build the company promised to the management team, the employees, and the investors. Once accomplished, the CEO has the problem he wanted all along — convert company stock into a saleable item.

The alternate exit strategies are standard:

- Sell the company to a private buyer.
- Sell the company to a public buyer.
- Establish a public market for company stock through an IPO.
- Continue running the company but disperse cash reserves and pay dividends.

All these options, except continuing to run it, are subject to external conditions. The market for IPOs runs in cycles, as do stock prices or more specifically price / earnings ratios. Shareholders want to cash out when stock prices are high, which is usually when IPOs are also popular.

Generally, the best option is a sale to a public company. In recent times, public company price-to-earnings ratios have run 20 times earnings or higher. This means the company sells at 20 times earnings without diluting its stock. For most ventures, this return will provide the payoff investors seek for their shares. If the business is in a humdrum industry with low P/E ratios, all hope is not lost. Some conglomerates of these companies pay high P/E ratios. Another option is finding a rollup where a group of private companies are combined and taken public.

Sale to a private company is much less attractive, as private companies generally pay much less than public companies — typically, five times earnings as opposed to 20 times for the public company. Besides, the public company may use its stock for purchase — basically trading its shares for yours with a delay when you can sell your shares in the acquiring company. Generally, this is better than a cash purchase. The IRS views the trade of stocks as tax neutral. You pay taxes when you sell the acquired stock. This presumes the acquired stock does not tank while you are holding it.

Generally, an IPO is viewed as a last resort. IPO markets are fickle. Some companies going strong, planning an IPO, find, when the time comes, the IPO market has fizzled, and they wasted a lot of time and money. Also, going through all the SEC requirements is a long and costly process. Reverse mergers are an option for taking a company public. The stock of the new business is traded for the stock of a defunct or shell company. It is a short cut, but reverse mergers have their own sets of problems.

These are good problems to have. Entrepreneurs only have them when they succeed. Exit you must. Investors must see a clear exit before they commit.

You Are the Angel

Bringing the chapter to its conclusion seems appropriate by describing the angel investor who comes forward to help others realize their dreams. Angels do not achieve this without a thorough understanding of financial statements and how successful businesses are managed. The number and the generosity of angel investors continue to grow. A recent report from the Center for Venture Research at the University of New Hampshire shows about 51,000 entrepreneurial ventures were funded in 2006 to the tune of $25.6 billion. Generous angels willingly give back and help others accomplish what they have. In return, they are able to keep a hand in new and exciting business ventures that offer well-above-average rates of return.

A first-time angel needs to set aside a designated amount of "mad money" available for investment. Divide the money into about ten different ventures to improve the probability that at least a few will be big winners. The professional investor develops a thorough and methodical process for evaluating proposals. It is doubtful angel investors will beat the VC average. Likely seven of ten investments will fail to deliver huge returns. It would be great to know ahead of time which seven those will be. Playing the averages and earning big returns from the winners keeps investors going, which in turn fuels growth, brings new products to market, and even opens new markets.

Angels have much to contribute to entrepreneurial businesses, and it is best done with a professional approach. Professional investors need to position themselves to see a large number of quality proposals rather than let only a few trickle through from direct referrals. A good way to do that is by joining an angel club. What the angel clubs do is rational. They advertise for proposals and screen proposals. They compare evaluations. It does not make each angel smarter, but the club does improve the screening processes. It is also a good resource when a pool of angels is needed to fund the rare but truly exciting new venture.

CHAPTER 12

Analysis of Starbucks' 2006 Annual Report

When Starbucks' financial year ended October 1, 2006, the company operated 7,102 stores and licensed another 5,338. Management's target had been to open 1,800 new stores during the year but actually opened an astonishing 2,199. Starbucks' total number of stores stood at 12,440 in 37 different countries. On average, six new stores opened every day. Starbucks is very much pursuing a growth strategy. Management's target is to open 2,400 new stores during 2007. Management believes the total market to be 40,000 worldwide stores with 20,000 in the United States and 20,000 international.

The company was capitalized at $28.2 billion with $7.8 billion in revenue for the year. The SEC-filed 10-K report states that Starbucks does not intend to pay dividends in the near future. All earnings will be retained as working capital and to repurchase outstanding stock shares approved in its stock repurchase program. During 2006, 14.5 million shares were repurchased, and up to another 21.5 million remain approved for repurchase.

Independent auditor Deloitte & Touche LLP issued an unqualified audit opinion for the financial statements and management's internal financial controls. The auditor noted accounting changes occurred during the year for the adoption of Statement of Financial Accounting Standards No. 123(R), "Share-Based Payment," and a change in accounting for conditional asset retirement obligations upon adoption of Financial Accounting Standards Board Interpretation No. 47 — "Accounting for Conditional Asset Retirement Obligations — an interpretation of FASB Statement 143."

A Look at the Top Ratios

STARBUCKS' 6 KEY RATIOS OVER 5 YEARS					
Ratio	2006	2005	2004	2003	2002
Current Ratio	0.79	0.99	1.76	1.52	1.58
P/E Ratio	45.66	39.23	45.68	39.67	39.08
Net Profit Margin	7.25%	7.76%	7.35%	6.58%	6.47%
Debt to Equity	0.99	0.68	0.37	0.34	0.33
Return on Assets	12.74%	14.07%	11.72%	9.83%	9.28%
Operating Margin	11.48%	12.25%	11.46%	10.42%	9.62%
* Share price based on average between high and low for the last quarter of the year / earnings per basic share.					

The key ratios confirm Starbucks' growth strategy. The current ratio reveals the company is becoming less liquid over time as more debt is taken on to open more stores each year. The P/E ratio has fluctuated within a reasonable range over the years but continues to keep future earnings built in. Net profit margin has risen steadily with a slight drop in 2006 when a record 2,199 stores where opened. New stores rarely perform as well as established stores. Also, they do not provide a full year of revenue, although they consume the company's revenue for construction, remodeling, employee training, and stocking inventory before the first revenue dollar is received. The MD&A predicts 2,400 new stores opening during 2007, which will continue to keep pressure on the profit margin.

Debt to equity has increased dramatically over the past two years as more debt is taken on to fund expansion. The MD&A explains that the company increased borrowing by $493 million during 2006. This was accomplished by increasing a credit line from $500 million to $1 billion during 2006. Starbucks has over $700 million in debt coming due next year, which explains the deteriorating current ratio. Including legally enforceable lease and purchase contracts, the company has $1.7 billion of debt due in the coming year. Long-term, this level of debt has the potential to slow Starbucks' rate of expansion when it reaches its credit limit.

The operating margin increased in a dependable manner from 2002 through 2005 before dropping back to 2004 levels during 2006. At first glance, this is a surprise because the MD&A states that revenues and per-sale transactions continue to increase. Clarification comes from the explanation of a change in accounting methods. In 2006, Starbucks began recognizing stock-based employee compensation as an expense — a move that FASB has been encouraging.

As a composite, the ratios show the company is achieving its growth strategy and likely will remain successful but must control borrowing.

Industry Averages

Starbucks is classified in the services sector under the industry heading of specialty eateries. This is a relatively small industry with total capitalization at $41.3 billion, of which Starbucks has $28.2 billion, or 68.3 percent, of the capital. Dominating the industry to this degree means that its own financial numbers heavily influence the averages.

STARBUCKS VERSUS INDUSTRY AVERAGES							
	P/E	ROE %	Div. Yield %	Debt to Equity	Price to Book	Net Profit Margin	Revenue Growth
Specialty Eateries	32.70	20.90%	1.20%	0.55	33.59	4.90%	13.50%
Starbucks	45.66	25.32%	0.00%	0.99	11.67	7.25%	20.00%
*Analysts predicted industry average growth rate per year beginning in 2005.							

By any reasonable standard, the P/E ratio is high and fully values future earnings. The number of stores Starbucks has opened each year supports this, and prospects are good it will continue to grow at the rate stated. With 12,440 stores and plans for 40,000, there is ample room for growth.

Return on equity is above industry average. Starbucks' number is skewing the industry ratio upward, which says others in the industry are probably below the industry average. There is no point in studying the dividend yield value since Starbucks does not plan to pay dividends anytime soon.

Debt to equity is high compared to the industry and has been climbing the last two years. This deserves additional attention, and other leverage ratios along with cash flow ratios will tell more of the story.

The price-to-book ratio is low by industry standards. This should be good news. Since the P/E ratio is high, a low price-to-book ratio indicates substantial physical assets supporting the stock price. Still, all outstanding stock is valued at 11.68 times the physical assets owned by the company. If Starbucks goes out of business because people no longer want to pay a premium price for coffee, there is no chance investors will recover their investment from the sale of assets, especially when debt is considered.

Of course, Starbucks' business plan is based on growth, so the fact that it significantly outpaces the industry is no surprise. The MD&A explains that stores open more than one year averaged a 7 percent sales increase during 2006. For the last five years, sales at stores open more than a year have increased revenues by at least 5 percent. In 2007, management expects this increase to be no less than 3 percent and no more than 7 percent.

The ratios are markedly better than the industry averages. Although management explains the high-debt ratio, it still warrants investigation.

Other Ratios

Preliminary and industry ratio analysis indicates further analysis of the stock value because P/E is high. It is a good idea to see how operations are performing during times of rapid growth. It is reasonable to examine changes over the years for these ratios:

- Payable Turns — Are suppliers being paid on time (leverage)?

- Operating Cash Flow—Measures both operational performance and ability to repay debt

- Inventory Turns — Is operational performance deteriorating at the cost of growth?

- Gross Margin — Are increasing profits coming from operations?

- Stock Price / Sales — Does revenue growth justify the high cost of the stock?

- Stock Price / Cash Flow — Does cash flow justify the stock price?

Starbucks' management shows consistency and general improvement in payable turns and inventory turns days. There is no sign that increasing debt is resulting in delayed payments to suppliers. Inventory management is acceptable considering the business model. Starbucks is not the traditional retailer that can turn inventory over quickly. Buying raw coffee beans for roasting at its own roasting plant is a manufacturing operation reflected by inventory taking slightly more than 70 days to turn over.

OTHER IMPORTANT RATIOS					
Ratio	2006	2005	2004	2003	2002
Payable Turns in Days	32.30	26.17	30.28	33.01	35.67
Operating Cash Flow	0.58	0.75	0.63	0.61	0.89
Inventory Turns in Days	73.05	76.53	70.17	74.25	71.15
Gross Margin	59.18%	59.10%	58.47%	58.63%	58.95%
*Stock Price / Sales	3.32	3.06	3.39	2.62	2.52
*Stock Price / Cash Flow	22.87	21.14	22.63	18.88	17.35
*Share price based on average between high and low for the last quarter of the year / earnings per basic share.					

Decreasing operating cash flow is a concern. Robust increases in revenue would be expected to translate into cash from operations increasing. A closer look at the ratio (cash from operations / current liabilities) is revealing. Once again, the increase in debt becomes obvious. Starbucks took on substantial debt during 2006, and operating cash flow will be needed to repay it — a clear reason why management continues to inform investors that dividends are not in the near future.

Gross margin shows flat to modest improvement. Indications are that management effectively is taking advantage of growth through economies of scale. As the company grows, it should be able to do more at less cost. Further improvement should occur with both gross and net profits improving in future years. All the management-related numbers are explainable and within reason based on the stated objectives of the company.

Stock price to sales has increased, making the stock more expensive for each dollar of sales generated. It is important to note that a stock split occurred in 2004. The effect is clearly seen in both stock price–based ratios. With more shares outstanding to spread sales and cash flow over, both ratios increased but remain relatively stable at the new values.

Overall, the numbers are very reasonable and even outstanding for a company experiencing Starbucks' rate of growth. Undoubtedly, this is a reason that Starbucks remains a favorite company for investors.

Starbucks Measures Up as a Growth Company

Chapter 10 pointed out the characteristics of a growth company as growing more than 20 percent per year, having a P/E ratio close to the growth rate (a P/E ratio below the growth rate is better), having a proven business model with room to expand into new markets, having a healthy balance sheet and proven cash flow, often being in a little-recognized industry with high growth potential, having a competitive advantage over others that might enter the market, and usually not paying a dividend so that earnings can be invested in growth.

Starbucks exhibits each of these with the exception of a P/E ratio close to the growth rate. The P/E ratio is actually more than twice the growth rate. Although the current investment strategy leans toward value investing,

Starbucks is bucking the trend with a proven growth strategy. The business model is well proven with room for growth. The balance sheet is in good shape. However, the recent large increase in debt should keep modest and conservative investors away from this company. The business model appears to have stretched as far as it can by primarily funding growth through earnings and is now on a new course through debt financing.

Although the Starbucks logo is extensively recognized, and the company clearly dominates the market, it still meets the definition of a little recognized industry because the total industry amounts to only $41.3 billion of capital. Its 68.3 percent dominance of the market gives it a competitive advantage over newcomers that might enter the market. Still, that does not mean it does not face substantial risks.

Risk Factors

Like any global corporation, Starbucks faces many risks that management acknowledges and plans for. Although it successfully sells coffee products at a premium price, the end product is still cost sensitive. A large increase in coffee prices or other costs must be either passed onto the customer or absorbed from the profit margin. Starbucks' best-of-breed branding strategy eliminates the possibility of substituting lower-cost materials.

Supplies

Starbucks negotiates the purchase of green coffee beans on an independent-contract basis rather than purchasing them on the commodity market. This is done to better control quality and to acquire the premium beans. As a result, Starbucks is subject to significant volatility in the marketplace. Whereas commodity buyers have many sources of beans, Starbucks is limited to specific suppliers and geographical regions that can provide the premium beans for its branded coffee. This leaves the company susceptible to weather, political, and economic conditions. Also, advocate groups work on behalf of growers to influence the price of beans through export quotas and restricted sales.

Starbucks' strategy to ensure an adequate supply of green beans is by using fixed-price and price-to-be-fixed contracts. Fixed-price contracts guarantee beans of a specific quality will be delivered over time at a known price. When commodity prices rise, fewer suppliers will enter into these agreements, and Starbucks must rely on the more volatile price-to-be-fixed contracts. These ensure quality beans will be supplied, but the price is determined after the contract is signed. The price is adjusted above a market index.

Starbucks is subject to volatility in commodity prices for dairy, paper, and plastic used in its products. Generally, Starbucks has one or more contracts in place for these materials, and management believes an adequate supply exists with some risk exposure to commodity costs for raw materials.

Competitors

Starbucks faces competition in almost every region that it operates. Often the competition is limited to independents or small regional chains for which Starbucks uses a "culture" strategy to maintain its competitive edge. While this strategy might work well against independents and small chains, there is a growing threat from fast food restaurants. McDonald's recently began testing the market with premium coffees at selected stores. Starbucks faces a financial heavyweight if McDonald's decides to compete aggressively. McDonald's' 2006 revenues were $21.6 billion, almost the entire capital value of Starbucks and convincingly more vigorous than Starbucks' $7.8 billion in annual revenues. Conceivably, McDonald's and other fast food heavyweights can financially out-market Starbucks in their most profitable markets and expand at a faster pace.

Starbucks also markets coffee beans and other consumer products through grocery stores, going up against well-established brands for customers more price-sensitive and less willing to make an extra trip to a Starbucks store. Other premium versions of coffees and teas are widely available through other specialty retail stores, as well as mail-order distributors.

Unions

Management generally believes it has a good relationship with employees. The company is viewed as progressive in the wages and benefits it provides to full- and part-time employees by food service–industry standards. Nonetheless, nine of Starbucks' Canadian stores have been unionized, and there is an active effort to unionize employees in the United States.

An employee vote to unionize a single store in Manhattan was scheduled in July 2004. The vote was never ratified, and the consensus is the union did not have enough employee support, even at this targeted store.

With more than 116,000 employees in retail stores, unions are likely to continue to work toward representation. Starbucks likely will continue to resist by maintaining positive employee relations through above-average wages and benefits.

Off-Balance Sheet Leases

During 2006, a few prominent financial media sources began questioning Starbucks' financial treatment of future operating leases. The financial notes show $3.9 billion in operating lease obligations, of which $2.4 billion is due within the next five years. The balance sheet only shows outstanding liabilities totaling $2.2 billion. Starbucks expenses the operating leases rather than capitalizing them, allowing the long-term obligations to be kept off the balance sheet (they are still accounted for in the notes).

Starbucks' response to this concern has been limited to a statement that it complies with GAAP. True, but the balance sheet probably does not reflect a substantial amount of debt at a time when it is becoming a concern.

Other Risks

As the world becomes smaller, concern that health pandemics could break out increases. Starbucks acknowledges that, as a public gathering place, it is likely to see a significant drop in customer traffic in the event one occurs. People likely will limit exposure to only necessary locations.

Management believes the market price of its stock reflects significant future growth and expansion of the business. This leads to the risk that the company will not obtain the predicted rate of growth. An abbreviated list of possible reasons the plan might not be achieved are:

- Less-than-predicted revenue growth from existing stores
- Inability to meet customer demand during peak sales periods
- Failing to open new stores at the planned rate for multiple reasons: lack of adequate real estate being available, generating inadequate cash flow to finance expansion, or inability to obtain favorable external financing conditions
- Future stores producing less revenue or drawing sales from existing stores in the near vicinity
- Failing to properly manage personnel and information systems during rapid expansion
- Economic factors decreasing discretionary spending
- Lack of product acceptance in new and untested markets
- Fluctuations of foreign exchange rates as it becomes more dependent on international sales
- Starbucks' expansion plans depend heavily on investing in developing and politically sensitive countries such as China

Every company faces risks, and Starbucks is no exception. In fact, companies with an ambitious growth strategy often face the biggest risks. This is certainly true of Starbucks as it expands internationally and domestically at an ever-increasing pace. What the company has going for itself and investors is a proven business model and strong brand name.

Legal Proceedings

Like any major corporation, Starbucks is subject to legal claims from any number of plaintiffs. The 2006 notes to the financial statements list three outstanding cases. Two national class-action suits challenge Starbucks' classification of store managers and assistant managers as exempt from overtime pay for work weeks exceeding 40 hours. Another is limited to California and challenges Starbucks for allowing shift supervisors to collect tips that the supervisors may not legally be entitled to.

The company believes a loss is unlikely in one case and has no stated opinion of the others' outcome. No estimates of costs are provided in any of the cases. However, Starbucks intends to defend itself vigorously in each case.

Additionally, the company acknowledges being party to other lawsuits resulting from normal business operations. It does not believe it faces any legal challenges that materially will affect its financial position or operations.

Market Segments

Until 2006, Starbucks separated operations into segments of the United States and International. A new segment called Global Consumer Products Group was added at the beginning of 2006. The company restated information from previous periods to reflect this change.

U.S. operations made up 83 percent of retail revenues, 57 percent of specialty revenues, and 79 percent of total net revenues. Sales in the United States are primarily through company-operated stores. International operations bring in 17 percent of retail revenues and 18 percent of specialty revenues and amount to 17 percent of total net revenues. International operations use a combination of company-operated stores and licensed stores. International operations remain in an early-development stage that requires a higher level of support in proportion to revenues than is required in the United States.

The company's Consumer Product Group represents 25 percent of total specialty revenues and 4 percent of total net revenues. The purpose of this segment is to market consumer products through distribution channels outside company operations. This is primarily selling coffee and ready-to-drink products through grocery stores and warehouse clubs.

From the segment information, it easily is discerned how dependent the company remains on U.S. sales. Assuming the Global Consumer Product Group is marketing primarily to U.S. grocery stores, the total revenue derived from U.S. sales is 83 percent (79% + 4%). Management's statement that international sales require extra support indicates this part of the expansion plan still carries high risk. It will take a few more years to know how successful it can become.

Strategies Other Than Growth

Starbucks' strategies reach beyond simply opening a coffeehouse on every street corner. At the center of customer satisfaction, Starbucks strives to create a culture of which customers wish to be part. This is created with carefully selected music that plays within the store and encouraging customers to linger over their coffee with a book or while online. It is a place where customers become friends and where friends come to meet.

A key element of this strategy occurred during the 1990s when Starbucks established a group dedicated to locating the best real estate locations and creating the right design for individual stores. Expansion was happening quickly then but nothing compared to today's rate of expansion. Having a mature real estate group in place certainly helped enable the current rate of growth.

Starbucks regularly renovates existing stores to meet changes in customers' life styles. The cultural aspect of Starbucks is to create a destination that customers want to come to as frequently as they go to work and home. It becomes an extension of their everyday world. The plan appears to be working, as more and more customers make it a daily routine to go out of their way for an expensive cup of java.

It was this extension into customers' everyday lives that led to decisions to sell branded products outside the store where Starbucks is not able to closely control the atmosphere. Starbucks coffee began appearing at airports, hotels, restaurants, and workplaces. Starbucks resisted this approach for a long time because of the lack of control over the experience. A firm decision was made not to franchise the business for this very reason. The expansion decision outside company stores involves carefully selecting licensees that have demonstrated an adherence to quality in line with Starbucks' policies.

Future Strategies

In 2004 Starbucks revealed that it intended to expand outside its core coffee operation. Having associated the coffee business with high-quality music that is differentiated from pop music resulted with the decision to acquire Hear Music in 1999. In 2004, Hear Music launched a satellite radio station. It has opened Hear Music Media Bars in five cities where customers can burn custom CDs by personally selecting tracks from the 15,000 CDs available. In March 2007, Paul McCartney became the first artist to sign with the label to release a new album. With this endeavor, Starbucks begins what could become a whole new industry carrying the unique Starbucks brand. Who knows what the entire Starbucks culture strategy will bring? The company may branch out as an Internet provider, a television channel, a moviemaker, and a full-service restaurant chain. Someday the Starbucks culture experience may become complete in all aspects of people's lives.

Strategic Changes Over Time

Developing and flawlessly executing strategies is a core competency at Starbucks. But it was not always that way. Chairman of the Board and former CEO Howard Shultz's early years with Starbucks lacked clear vision and strategy. Time was spent learning the details of coffee and the business. His vision to open Starbucks across the United States and Canada was turned down by the early owners, and there was no clear strategy linked to the vision. Shultz's early efforts were ideas for improvements but far from a honed strategy. A 1983 trip to Italy inspired the beginning strategy to differentiate from other coffee specialty stores by creating an American version of the Italian coffee bar. It began with a store named Il Giorale, where Shultz connected the brewed premium coffee strategy with higher customer expectations and the strategy to open a chain of stores. The need to attract venture capital required a fine-tuned business plan that documented the early strategy. The merger of Starbucks and Il Giorale refined the strategy in several ways. Shultz began clearly communicating the national strategy to employees. Other changes were creating early processes to involve employees more directly running the business, as well as a foundation for respect between management and employees. The business plan at this time had a goal of opening 125 stores in five years. Embedded in the plan were intentions for a strong brand name and corporate responsibility. These have remained at the foundation of the evolving business plan.

Several of the early stores had difficulties because needed elements of the strategy were missing. An early Chicago store is a good example that market knowledge was inadequate. Not locating inside a building lobby and tolerating high real estate costs resulted in one of the first stores being unprofitable. Similarly, choosing to compete directly with an already established competitor in San Francisco was a poorly chosen market before premium coffee had gained the appeal of a large customer base.

The national expansion effort was successful overall, and Shultz revised goals and objectives. The strategy to attract and retain employees that shared the company's attitude toward customers expanded. Over the years, employees acquired stock options that furthered their interest in seeing the company prosper. As a result, Starbucks easily outperforms similar companies in employee retention. It expanded employee retention with an alternative career path for employees not wishing to become managers. The Coffee Masters program provides in-depth training and study of the art of coffee making and furthering the interests of both the employee and the company. Coffee Masters can be recognized in the stores by their black apron.

The quality of the coffee was the beginning vision, and quality continues to be emphasized in the expanding product line. More quality focus is evidenced by not allowing independent franchises and refraining from selling coffee in supermarkets until there was packaging available to ensure freshness.

The early 1990s became a time of significant improvement to the strategy. The addition of the mission statement better communicated the company's purpose. Vertical integration occurred for better management of retail store locations and designs. The right management team to oversee the rapid expansion was in place. Partnerships to enter difficult but profitable markets became a strategy. The vision became "a Starbucks everywhere."

The early 2000s saw innovative use of technology through early adoption of Internet service in stores, the reloadable Starbucks card, and discontinuing catalog orders as no longer appropriate technology. The customer focus changed from being high-quality retail to a place customers want to be. The biggest change in strategy during these years was the expansion of branding and managing risk of quality through licensing. The Starbucks brand now appears in many places outside company-controlled stores. Starbucks' primary strategy continues to be expansion for financial growth, and management is making changes to enable this.

Strengths and Weaknesses

A strong brand name, strategic execution, and rapid expansion are clearly Starbucks' strengths. It has clear dominance of the market. Its strengths also have left it vulnerable because the business model is now well known and feasibly could be duplicated easily by a competitor with deep pockets.

With threats from giants such as McDonald's, the company must stay on its toes while continuing to execute the business plan. A good strategy would be to quickly saturate important world markets with the brand name before competitors can take root. It appears this is Starbucks' most current plan based on the announcement that China, India, and Russia are its targeted international markets.

Even with $7.8 billion in revenues and a history of being able to increase profits, cash is at the root of its weakness. In 2004, there were questions about what Starbucks would do with all the revenue flowing in. A few years later, in 2007, the operations cash flow is not adequate for planned expansion. The company has gone into significant debt to continue financing growth. It is the perfect mix for a growth company, a proven business model, substantial cash, and a very big market for sustained growth. Only time will tell if the company can carry the dream to the golden land.

Glossary

10-K Form: SEC form reporting audited annual financial results required from all publicly traded corporations.

10-Q Form: SEC form reporting unaudited quarterly financial results required from all publicly traded corporations.

Accounts Payable: Payables are claims that others have on the company for payment for goods or services rendered. Payables include credit purchases of raw materials, supplies, services, and similar items.

Accrual Accounting: Recognizes the impact of a transaction on the financial statements for the time periods when revenue and expenses occur. The intention of accrual accounting is to match revenue and expenses within a given period rather than when cash actually is exchanged.

Accrued Expenses or Accrued Liabilities: Are amounts owed for goods or services, whose benefits have been received but are to be paid in the future. Typical accrued expenses are payroll, payroll taxes, property taxes, rent, royalties, interest, and commissions. These are the opposite of prepaid expenses.

Additional Paid in Capital: See capital paid in excess of par value.

Adverse Audit Opinion: An opinion that is the opposite of an unqualified opinion; it is an opinion that the financial statements do not present fairly the financial position, results of operations, and cash flows of the company, in conformity with GAAP. An adverse opinion is inferior to a qualified one.

Annual Report: A document prepared by management to inform investors and potential investors about the company's past performance and future prospects. Typically, businesses use photographs and charts extensively to communicate the message. Management has wide discretion in the content, much broader than with 10-Q and 10-K filings with the SEC.

Assets: Any resource expected to provide a future economic benefit. Common examples are cash, accounts receivable, notes receivable, prepaid expenses, land, buildings, and equipment. They also can be anything that reduces future expenses.

Audit: The examination by an independent third party of the financial statements of a company or any other legal entity (including governments and individuals), resulting in the publication of an independent opinion on whether or not those financial statements are relevant, accurate, complete, and fairly presented. Audits of SEC-regulated businesses result in either an unqualified opinion or a qualified opinion. The primary objective of audits is to ensure that financial statements are fair, accurate, and free of material errors or omissions. Audits are performed by a firm of CPAs that examine the accounting system and financial statement for conformity with GAAP.

Authorized Stock Shares: The maximum number of stock shares the company is allowed to sell or issue. The original number is defined in the corporation's articles of incorporation. Typically, any increase must be approved by a vote of current shareholders. The number authorized is normally higher than the number outstanding to provide management with additional shares to sell to raise additional capital.

Average Shares Outstanding: This is the average number of common shares outstanding for the report period. The number of shares varies during the reporting year if there are distributions of stock to employees or executive bonus programs or if a stock repurchase program is occurring. Also see diluted stock shares.

Balance at Beginning of the Period: From the statement of cash flows, this is the cash balance at the start of the period. Subtracted from the balance at the end of the period gives the net increase or decrease in cash for the period.

Balance at the End of the Period: From the statement of cash flows, this is the cash balance at the end of the period. Subtracting the balance at the beginning of the period will give the net increase or decrease for the period.

Balance Sheet: One of the four major financial statements showing a company's financial position at a particular point in time. The elements of the balance sheet create the Balance Sheet Equation: Assets = Liabilities + Owners' Equity.

Board of Directors: The board of directors is responsible for the overall management of the company. The board of directors is elected by the shareholders to carry out the management of the company. A significant difference usually exists between the board of directors for privately held companies and those of publicly held companies. Publicly held companies have both outside directors and inside directors. Outside directors do not engage in daily management of the company but rather bring an unbiased outside viewpoint. Inside directors or executive directors are senior managers of the company that contribute knowledge of

daily operations. In contrast, the boards of directors of privately held companies are often the majority owners and engage in the daily functioning of the company. There may not be any outside directors overseeing a private company.

Capital: Sources of long-term financing that are available to businesses.

Capital Paid in Excess of Par Value: The amount of money a corporation receives when selling stock less the par value printed on the stock certificate.

Capital Surplus: See capital paid in excess of par value.

Cash Accounting: Recognizes the impact of a transaction on financial statements only when cash is actually received or distributed. Also see accrual accounting.

Common Stock: A security representing an equity share of ownership in a corporation entitling the owner to voting rights, a share in dividend payments, and capital appreciation based on a company's success. At liquidation, common stockholders are entitled to a portion of the company's assets only after bondholders, other debtors, and preferred stockholders have been paid what is owed to them. Common stockholders are considered the owners of the company.

Consolidated Financial Statements: Financial statements of a parent company and subsidiaries combined into an overall report as if they were a single company.

Cost of Goods Sold: Often abbreviated as COGS. This is the largest expense on the income statement. This category typically includes the cost of materials, labor, and direct overhead used to produce the finished product. The cost of goods sold is related to the company's inventory valuation method. Also see LIFO and FIFO.

CPA: Certified public accountant. In addition to a college accounting degree, a CPA must pass strenuous exams and abide by rigorous ethics codes. CPAs conduct independent audits following GAAP on financial statements to assure the user the information is presented fairly and accurately represents the condition of the company. Independent CPAs must not have any other business relationships with companies that they audit.

Current Maturities of Long-Term Debt: Long-term debt is debt owed beyond one year. Current maturities of long-term debt is the portion due within one year.

Deferred Income Taxes: Represents the differences between the company's tax accounting and financial reporting. Companies use one set of rules for calculating income and income tax liability and another set for financial statements. Most companies use straight-line depreciation for financial reporting and accelerated depreciation for tax purposes to lower the current year's tax liability. These taxes are not eliminated; rather they are deferred to future years. This account captures the difference between taxes paid under the accelerated depreciation method and straight-line depreciation.

Depreciation: An accounting method that reduces the value of equipment and property as it wears out. In this sense, property does not include land. Property is anything the business owns that has a value. Office equipment, delivery trucks, and manufacturing equipment, along with any buildings, are considered to lose value over time from wear and obsolesces. Depreciation reduces the value of the property over time. There are two common types of depreciation, straight-line and accelerated. The internal revenue provides tables that can be used to determine the percentage of depreciation that occurs each year. The straight-line method typically is used for financial statements. An equal percentage of the property value is reduced from the original purchase price each year using the straight-line method. For tax purposes the accelerated method is used. This method allows the property to be depreciated more in the early years, and less depreciation is allowed in later years. Depreciation is considered a business expense for tax purposes. Higher depreciation rates allow this non-cash expense to reduce profits and thereby reduce taxes that the business must pay. For this reason, it is common to find different depreciation values on a business's tax return than on the financial statements. Most but not everything owned by a business is depreciated. Land is not depreciated because it is assumed that land does not wear out. Most supplies like printing paper, pencils, and cleaners are not depreciated because they are rapidly consumed. Raw materials and product inventory are not depreciated because the company sells these for a profit.

Diluted Stock Shares: The full number of shares that would be outstanding if all possible sources were converted. These include convertible bonds, preferred stocks, and stock options. The word *diluted* implies that existing shareholders' percentage of company ownership will be reduced if conversions are made. Shareholders should consider carefully that share prices can decrease if enough additional shares enter the market. Earnings per share also will be affected, and dividends must be distributed among more shareholders.

Diluted Stock Shares EPS: Represents the effects on earnings per share if all convertible securities were converted to common stock or if all warrants or stock options were exercised. This includes bonds convertible to stocks and stock option grants that have not been exercised.

Dividends: The payment of all or a portion of earnings by the company to the shareholders. Dividends are paid on a per-share basis typically on a regular quarterly or annual schedule. However, dividends can be paid at any time the board of directors decides. Also see retained earnings.

Earnings Per Share: Abbreviated EPS. It is net income divided by the number of shares outstanding. It is the company's profit proportionately allocated to each outstanding share of common stock. The figure is calculated after paying taxes and after paying dividends to preferred shareholders, if any. Treasury stocks are not paid earnings.

Earnings: See profit.

EBIDA: Earnings before interest, income tax, depreciation, and amortization. An effective number for comparing operations between two or more companies because it eliminates financing and accounting variations between companies.

EBIT: Earnings before income tax, also know as operating profit or operating income. Cost of goods sold, administrative, and other operating expenses are subtracted

from net earnings to equal EBIT.

Employee Stock Ownership Plan: An ESOP is an IRS-qualified plan for employees that resembles a profit-sharing plan. Through company contributions, employees become partial owners in the business and theoretically deliver better performance from which both the company and the employees profit.

Equity: Also called shareholders' equity, owners' equity, or net worth. Equity is the amount left over when total liabilities are subtracted from total liabilities. The remaining amount is the net worth of the business to the owners.

Expenses: The Internal Revenue Service defines business expenses as an ordinary and necessary expense common and accepted within a given industry. Expenses typically are divided into two categories. Variable costs are those that change depending on the amount of product being manufactured or sold. Raw materials, labor costs, and electricity costs increase and decrease when production does the same. Rents, loan repayment, and property taxes are examples of fixed cost that cannot easily be changed in response to production rates. Businesses have a wide range of expenses that must be accounted for in the financial statements. Exact expenses vary by industry but include travel, advertising, maintenance, office supplies, legal costs, and insurance.

Extraordinary and Nonrecurring Events or Items: An extraordinary event or item that materially affects the company's finances. A nonrecurring event or item is not expected to be repeated. These must be explained fully in the financial notes and SEC filings. The consolidation of these items and events also must be reported as a separate line item on the income statement. These include, but are not limited to, restructuring costs, unusually large transactions not expected to recur, discontinued operations, unique transactions not commonly undertaken in normal business, and the effects of changes to accounting principles.

FASB: Financial Accounting Standards Board designated by the SEC in 1973 as responsible for defining accounting and reporting practices in the private sector. The FASB is wholly independent of any other business or professional organizations.

FIFO: First in, first out is an inventory accounting method. The company assumes that the inventory is sold in the chronological order in which it was purchased or manufactured. Inflation plays an important role because the inventory available for sale has the value established by materials and labor that is the farthest in the past compared to alternative inventory accounting systems. Also see LIFO and cost of goods sold. The accounting system used does not have anything to do with the order in which inventory actually is sold. However, once a method is chosen, it is generally not changed at a future time.

Financial Analyst: Employed within the investment industry to provide reports and buy or sell recommendations about certain companies. Normally, financial analysts specialize in a few companies or a specific industry. They are relied on for information by professional and individual investors when making decisions.

Financial Planner: An investment professional who helps individuals achieve their financial goals. Planners provide guidance in risk management, investments, tax planning, asset allocation, retirement planning, and estate planning.

Financing Activities: From the statement of cash flows, this includes issuing or repurchasing stock and bonds during the reporting period. Dividend payments are included in this section of the income statement.

Foreign Currency Translation Adjustment: Assets and liabilities of foreign subsidiaries are translated at the end of each accounting period at current exchange rates. The results of this fluctuating adjustment are accumulated through time in this account.

GAAP: Generally Accepted Accounting Principles are ultimately the responsibility of the SEC. However, the SEC has delegated the establishment of GAAP to the FASB. A CPA must state clearly in any audit, compilation of financial statements, or review of statement whether it is GAAP compliant or not. The objective of GAAP is to establish a level playing field for analysis of financial information by

decision-makers.

Goodwill: The difference between the book value of a company being acquired by another company and the higher price actually paid. An intangible asset gained by purchasing a business with an established customer base, well positioned in a market, for its outstanding geographical location, or other reasons not shown on the financial statements of the company being purchased.

Gross Profit: When cost of goods sold is deducted from revenues, gross profit is the result. Also known as gross income.

Income Statement: One of the four major financial statements, it presents how net revenue (money received from the sale of products and services before expenses are taken out, also known as the "top line") is transformed into net income (the result after all revenues and expenses have been accounted for, also known as the "bottom line"). The purpose of the income statement is to show managers and investors whether the company made or lost money during the period being reported.

Income Taxes Payable: Accrued income taxes to be paid within one year.

Institutional Funds: Large pools of investment money managed by professional investors. Union and corporate retirement accounts, insurance accounts, and other large sources of investment funds. Institutional funds employ professional investors full-time to manage the funds based on risk and return objectives.

Intangibles: Costs incurred or recorded previously, which could provide a future benefit to the company. Intangibles include goodwill, patents and copyrights, and non-complete agreements.

Investing Activities: From the statement of cash flows, these show payments for the acquisition of capital equipment or investments made during the period.

IPO: Initial Public Offering, A company's first sale of stock to the public. Securities offered in an IPO are often, but not always, those of young, small companies seeking outside equity capital and a public market for their stock. Investors purchasing stock in IPOs generally must be prepared to accept large risks for the possibility of large gains.

Liabilities: Are obligations the business has to other entities separate from the business. Money owed to suppliers and lenders are typical business liabilities. Liabilities are divided into short-term liabilities and long-term liabilities. Short-term liabilities are amounts owed within one year and often are called current liabilities. Long-term liabilities are anything that is not owed for at least a year. The five main subcategories of liabilities are accounts payable, accrued expenses, income tax payable, short-term notes payable, and long-term liabilities.

LIFO: Last in, first out is an inventory accounting method. The company assumes that the last item added to inventory is the first one sold. Inflation plays an important role because older inventory is valued at a cost in the past and probably does not reflect what it would cost to produce today. Also see FIFO and cost of goods sold.

Liquidity: A measure of an asset's ability to quickly be converted to cash without significantly discounting the value for the purpose of making the sale. A key measure is the willingness of multiple buyers to offer fair market value in a short time period.

Loans and Notes Payable: Amounts due within a year on loans or notes.

Long-Term Debt: Debt that must be paid in some time beyond 12 months into the future.

Managements Discussion and Analysis: The intention of the MD&A is to provide readers with information necessary to understand a company's financial condition, changes in financial condition, and results of operations. The MD&A requirements are intended to satisfy three principal objectives. First, provide a narrative explanation of a company's financial statements that enables investors to see the company through the eyes of management. Second, enhance the overall financial disclosure and provide the context within which financial information should be analyzed. Third, provide information about the quality of, and potential variability of, a company's earnings and cash flow so that investors can determine the likelihood that past performance is indicative of future performance.

Material Affect to Financial Statements: Concerns whether a transaction, omission, or error on financial statements is material to a reader's ability to draw relevant conclusions. It is often a subjective decision if something is important to the reader's ability to reach a proper conclusion. Multibillion-dollar companies present financial statements with values rounded to the nearest million dollars because showing smaller numbers is not considered material. A $100,000 error or omission on a multibillion-dollar statement is not likely to be material. However, the same error or omission for a $2 million company is material to the financial statements.

Net Income: The bottom line, the profit, or earnings. There are several interchangeable terms associated with this important number. This is the amount of money remaining when all expenses and taxes are subtracted from sales revenue.

Note Payable: A promise of future payment.

Note Receivable: A promise for future collection of cash.

Note Section of Financial Statements: The notes to financial statements identify the major accounting principles used in developing the amounts reported in the statements when alternative choices can be made from GAAP. The notes also provide details about major accounts and transactions, along with explaining extraordinary and nonrecurring events and items.

Operating Activities: From the statement of cash flows, the most important source of cash comes from operating activities as net income. Although depreciation and amortization are added back into this category, they do not contribute cash or create deductions. These are accounting transactions rather than cash transactions.

Operating Expenses: Vary greatly from one company to another and especially one industry to another depending on the expense involved with the company's sale of goods or services. Some companies choose to go into considerable detail about operating expenses, and others lump them together into administrative and general expenses. Generally, operating expenses in the purest sense include rent on land and buildings, salaries and wages paid, payroll taxes, property taxes, telephone, insurance, research and development, depreciation and amortization, and bad debts.

Operations: Are the primary activities of the business. For a bicycle manufacturer, operations include purchasing raw materials and components from suppliers and converting them into finished bicycles for sale to distributors. A manufacturer's operations take place in a factory. A retailer's primary activity is purchasing products and providing a way for consumers to purchase the products. Retailers' operations occur in retail stores and warehouses. Both types of companies engage in other activities, like investing profits and managing employee benefits, but these are not primary operations.

Other Current Assets: These are items the business will derive some benefit from within the next year, and include items such as prepaid insurance, prepaid income tax, and prepaid interest.

Outstanding Stock Shares: Stock shares that currently are held by investors. These include restricted shares held by corporate officers but do not include treasury shares. The number of outstanding shares is labeled "capital stock" on the balance sheet.

Par Value: The nominal dollar amount assigned to a security by the issuer. For an equity security, par value is usually a very small amount that bears no relationship to its market price, except for preferred stock, in which case par value is used to calculate dividend payments. Many states require that a par value be printed on the face of stock certificates, although in the real world there is no relationship to the actual value. Also see capital paid in excess of par value.

Pink Sheets: Companies with stock shares that trade through a daily publication published by the National Quotation Bureau. Companies trading stock shares through this system are not required to register with the SEC or provide audited financial statements. The symbol for these stocks is followed with .PK. Shares for these companies tend to be held by considerably fewer stockholders than those sold over stock exchanges. In comparison to stock exchanges, few transactions occur through these over-the-counter systems.

Preferred Stock: Some but not all companies issue preferred stock, which has important differences compared to common stock. Preferred shareholders are entitled to receive a fixed dividend before common holders. Preferred stockholders are also paid before common stockholders if the company is liquidated. Preferred stock often is non-voting.

Privately Held Companies: A company that does not have stocks traded on an open stock exchange. These companies often have a limited number of shareholders, and only those with more than 500 shareholders and over $10 million in assets are subject to SEC oversight. These also are known as closely held companies.

Process Income: See gross profit.

Profit: Any increase in shareholder equity resulting from an increase in assets received in exchange for the delivery of products or services to customers. Commonly referred to as the bottom line of the income statement. Under accrual accounting, revenue often is recognized at the time of a sale but before the customer actually pays for the product or services. Therefore, an income statement may show a company being profitable even though it has not received payment from customers. It is important not to confuse profits with cash.

Property, Plant, and Equipment: Also called fixed assets or abbreviated as PP&E, it includes land, buildings, equipment, and leasehold improvements. These assets are recorded at historical cost and then depreciated over the period they benefit the firm (land is not depreciated because it is assumed it does not wear out).

Publicly Traded Companies: A company that has issued securities (stocks and bonds) for sale to the public that now are traded openly on a stock exchange, such as the New York Stock Exchange, NASDAQ, or American Stock Exchange. All publicly traded companies are subject to SEC oversight.

Qualified Audit Opinion: A qualified opinion is generally inferior to an unqualified opinion. It means the auditor has qualified his opinion based on information not being available, a lack of adherence to GAAP, or an audit with limited scope. In the auditor's opinion, the financials are presented fairly except for a specifically stated section that could not be audited according to GAAP.

Ratio Analysis: Ratio analysis is the process of identifying certain numbers from financial statements, making a mathematical calculation with them, and evaluating the results.

Realized Revenue: Revenue recognized by accrual accounting but not yet received becomes realized revenue when cash is received.

Recognized Revenue: One of the four main principles of GAAP, recognizing revenue determines when it is entered on to the accounting books. Accrual accounting recognizes revenue when earned regardless if it has been paid or not. Cash accounting only recognizes revenue when it is paid.

Retained Earnings: The portion of net earnings kept by the company for investment rather than paid to shareholders as dividends. Shown on the owners' equity side of the balance sheet as an accumulative amount retained since incorporation. Also shown on statement of shareholders' equity as the amount of earnings retained for that specific period.

Revenue: Everything that a company receives in exchange for the delivery of products or services to customers. Often referred to as the top line of the income statement, it is all compensation received before expenses are deducted to determine if a profit has been made. Under accrual accounting, revenues are recognized at the time a sale is made but before the customer actually pays for the product or services. It is important not to confuse revenues with cash. Another word for revenue is *income*.

Sales: See revenues.

SEC: Securities and Exchange Commission established in 1934 by the U.S. government to protect investors; maintain fair, orderly, and efficient markets; and facilitate capital formation. The SEC was created as a result of the stock market crash of 1929.

Shareholders: Anyone who owns shares of a corporation that represent ownership of the corporation in proportion to shares owned and the number of shares issued. Shareholders are able to participate in some company activities, such as voting at shareholder meetings, receiving dividend payments, and electing the board of director. Through corporate ownership, the shareholders' liabilities are limited to their investment in stock.

Solvency: A measure of a business's ability to meet financial obligations. A company able to meet ongoing obligations is solvent. A company unable to pay bills and other financial obligations is insolvent and at risk of bankruptcy.

Statement of Cash Flows: One of the four major financial statements showing the changes in cash and cash equivalents available to a business during a specific period. The three sections of the statement are Operating Activities, Investing Activities, and Financing Activities.

Statement of Shareholders' Equity: One of the four major financial statements, it presents a summary of the changes that occurred in the entity's owners' equity during a specific period, typically for a quarter or a year. Increases to owners' equity arise from investments made by the owners (retained earnings) and from net income earned during the period. Decreases result from owner withdrawals (dividends) and from a net loss for the period. Net income or net losses come directly from the income statement, and investments are capital transactions between the business and its owners, so they do not affect the income statement.

Stock Exchange: A stock exchange is a private (not government-owned) organization where companies can raise capital through a variety of ways, including selling stock shares and issuing bonds. Individuals may buy these stocks and bonds and trade the same with other individuals. Companies whose stock trades on an exchange are deemed publicly traded companies. In the U.S., these companies must follow regulations established by the SEC and the stock exchange where they trade.

Stock Option Grants: Stock options are a form of equity compensation intended to improve management and/or employee performance. The right to purchase company stock is granted at a specific price (usually the current trading price). Managers and employees only benefit if the trading price of the stock increases. If the price increases, they are able to buy at the lower grant price and hold the stock for future gains or sell it at any time to reap the gain between the grant price and the selling price.

Stock Split: The dividing of a company's existing stock into multiple shares. In a 2-for-1 split, each stockholder receives an additional share for each share he or she holds. The holder of a single share would own two shares after this stock split. The mathematics of the split can be any ratio decided by the board of directors. It can be a 3-for-1 split, a 5-for-1 split, or any other variation. Typically, the market value of the shares is reduced in proportion to the split. A stock selling at $100 per share before the split likely will sell for $50 per share following a 2-for-1 split. A common reason for a stock split is if a company is doing well and the board of directors wants to keep the stock affordable for most investors. Berkshire Hathaway (managed by Warren Buffet) is an example of a stock that has never split. The cost to purchase a single share is over $100,000.

Subsidiary: A subsidiary is a separate corporation for tax and regulation purposes but controlled by another corporation known as a parent company. A parent company with 50 percent plus one share of ownership controls the subsidiary, although there are other share owners. When the parent company owns 100 percent of the shares, the subsidiary is owned wholly by the parent corporation.

Treasury Stock: Shares of company stock once sold by the company and later bought back on the open market. When a company owns treasury stock, it appears in the shareholder equity section of the balance sheet. The board of directors may authorize a stock repurchase program if they believe the stock is undervalued on the open market. Treasury stock does not have voting rights at shareholder meetings, and dividends are not paid. Repurchasing stock on the open market is intended to reduce the number of shares outstanding and thereby increase the value of the outstanding shares owned by

shareholders. However, the stock can be resold on the open market at any time to raise cash for the company.

Unqualified Audit Opinion: The highest of audit opinions, it says the auditor finds the financial statements are presented fairly based on GAAP and without a need to qualify the opinion.

Unrealized Gain on Securities Available for Sale: This represents price appreciation on financial assets (another company's stock) held by the company but not sold during the period.

Author Biography

Brian Kline

Brian Kline has been investing in a variety of stocks since the early 1980s when he made it a point to learn how to read financial statements. He also draws upon 25-plus years of business experience, including 12 years as a manager at a Dow Jones Industrial company (Boeing Aircraft Company). His investment holdings have included private businesses and public corporations. In the public corporation sector, the investments have been broad-based to include early Internet companies, high-tech companies, and the more mundane but reliable conglomerate companies. He also invests in mutual funds. Kline does not currently hold any investments in the businesses analyzed in this book. In addition to investing in corporate stocks and bonds, he has considerable investment experience in real estate.

Index

252-259, 262, 263, 265, 268

I

Improvement 35, 73, 86, 136, 144, 156, 257, 258, 267
Invest 11, 18, 69, 84, 98, 106, 108, 112, 122, 124, 200, 207-209, 211, 223, 230, 232, 238, 239, 246

L

Law 46, 160, 163-165, 168, 170, 181, 192
Liabilities 23, 32, 49, 51-53, 57, 58, 61, 67-69, 71, 72, 85, 92, 93, 106, 112, 115, 122-124, 130, 132, 134, 151, 152, 194, 198, 214, 257, 261
Loan 19, 45, 46, 50, 51, 53, 54, 57, 60, 68, 69, 87, 89, 95, 98-101, 106, 121, 140, 142, 183, 185, 227, 228, 236, 237
Loss 11, 17, 19, 49, 70, 73, 74, 82, 84, 87, 89, 103, 180, 186, 194, 205, 206, 212, 225, 263

M

Management 8, 10, 11, 13, 21, 23, 25, 27, 33, 34-36, 38, 41, 43-45, 47-52, 62, 65, 68, 77-79, 83, 84, 86, 89, 90, 96, 98, 116, 117, 123-127, 129, 130, 131, 139, 140, 142, 145-154, 156, 160, 161, 163, 166, 171, 174-178, 181, 193, 194, 199, 201, 202, 204-206, 211, 212, 214, 225, 233-236, 238, 244-250, 253, 256-260, 266-268

P

Performance 7, 9, 10, 11, 25, 26, 41, 49-51, 109, 139, 147-150, 152, 153, 173, 186, 201, 205, 210, 211, 213, 215, 222, 237, 249, 257
Profit 7, 17, 18, 20, 33, 40, 41, 43, 47, 57-59, 69-71, 73-84, 86, 89, 94, 97, 99-101, 111, 114, 115, 117, 118, 120, 122, 126, 127, 134, 136, 139, 140, 141, 143-145, 168, 186, 189, 212, 223, 233, 234, 237, 242, 254, 259

R

Ratio 7, 17, 46, 47, 57, 58, 84, 110-117, 119, 120-135, 139, 140, 153, 154, 156, 205, 206, 214, 215, 216, 217, 254-258
Report 13, 14, 22, 35, 45, 53, 54, 65, 73, 136, 137, 145-147, 151, 173, 178, 188, 192, 252, 253
Requirements 14, 15, 21, 27, 28, 32, 33, 36-38, 41, 45, 52, 74, 99, 145, 146, 172, 199, 251
Return 8, 17, 18, 25, 32, 38, 43, 47, 56, 62, 69, 76, 79, 107, 108, 112, 116, 125, 128, 132, 145, 146, 189, 197, 203-206, 213, 215, 221, 225, 227, 237, 238, 251, 252
Return on investment 17, 108, 132, 221
Revenue 7, 17, 23, 33, 56, 58-60, 73-76, 82, 84-86, 90, 114, 126, 138, 147, 150, 151, 159, 190-193, 195, 196, 213, 229, 253, 254, 257, 262, 264, 268

S

Shareholder 20, 26, 37, 39, 48, 60, 61, 71, 72, 81, 89, 96, 103, 115, 117, 124, 125, 153, 161, 186, 192, 202
Software 10, 50, 51, 52, 53, 108, 137, 216, 232
Stock 12, 14, 15, 17, 19-26, 36, 37, 39-41, 44, 46, 47, 49, 51, 64, 66, 69-71, 74, 81, 88, 90, 92, 93, 96-98, 101-103, 107, 108, 111-113, 115, 118, 128-132, 150, 151, 154, 159, 161, 163, 165, 168, 170, 185-188, 193, 194, 206, 207-216, 218-222, 225, 236, 238, 239, 248-251, 253, 255-258, 262, 267